The Naomi Story—The Book of Ruth

Biblical Performance Criticism Series

Orality, Memory, Translation, Rhetoric, Discourse, Drama

David Rhoads, Holly E. Hearon, and Kelly R. Iverson, Series Editors

The ancient societies of the Bible were overwhelmingly oral. People originally experienced the traditions now in the Bible as oral performances. Focusing on the ancient performance of biblical traditions enables us to shift academic work on the Bible from the mentality of a modern print culture to that of an oral/scribal culture. Conceived broadly, biblical performance criticism embraces many methods as means to reframe the biblical materials in the context of traditional oral cultures, construct scenarios of ancient performances, learn from contemporary performances of these materials, and reinterpret biblical writings accordingly. The result is a foundational paradigm shift that reconfigures traditional disciplines and employs fresh biblical methodologies such as theater studies, speech-act theory, and performance studies. The emerging research of many scholars in this field of study, the development of working groups in scholarly societies, and the appearance of conferences on orality and literacy make it timely to inaugurate this series. For further information on biblical performance criticism, go to www.biblicalperformancecriticism.org.

Books in the Series

Holly Hearon and Philip Ruge-Jones, editors
The Bible in Ancient and Modern Media

James Maxey
From Orality to Orality

Antoinette Clark Wire
The Case for Mark Composed in Performance

Robert D. Miller II, SFO
Oral Tradition in Ancient Israel

Pieter J. J. Botha
Orality and Literacy in Early Christianity

James A. Maxey and Ernst R. Wendland, editors
Translating Scripture for Sound and Performance

J. A. (Bobby) Loubser
Oral and Manuscript Culture in the Bible

Joanna Dewey
The Oral Ethos of the Early Church

Richard A. Horsley
Text and Tradition in Performance and Writing

Kelly R. Iverson, editor
From Text to Performance

Annette Weissenrieder & Robert B. Coote, editors
The Interface of Orality and Writing

Thomas E. Boomershine
The Messiah of Peace

The Naomi Story—The Book of Ruth

From Gender to Politics

Terry Giles

and

William J. Doan

CASCADE *Books* · Eugene, Oregon

THE NAOMI STORY—THE BOOK OF RUTH
From Gender to Politics

Biblical Performance Criticism Series 13

Cascade Books
An Imprint of Wipf and Stock Publishers
199 W. 8th Ave., Suite 3
Eugene, OR 97401

www.wipfandstock.com

PAPERBACK ISBN 13: 978-1-4982-0618-1
HARDCOVER ISBN 13: 978-1-4982-0620-4

Cataloguing-in-Publication data:

Giles, Terry.

The Naomi story—the book of Ruth : from gender to politics / Terry Giles and William J. Doan

x + 208 p. ; 23 cm. Includes bibliographical references and indexes.

(Biblical Performance Criticism Series 13)

ISBN: 978-1-4982-0618-1 (paperback) | ISBN: 978-1-4982-0620-4 (hardback)

1. Bible. Ruth—Criticism, interpretation, etc. 2. Bible. O.T.—Performance criticism. 3. Oral tradition. I. Doan, William J. II. Title. III. Series.

BS1315.52 G55 2016

Manufactured in the U.S.A.   01/28/2016

Contents

Acknowledgments

The authors would like to express their appreciation to Gannon University and, in particular, to the Department of Theology for a 2015–16 sabbatical granted to Terry Giles during which this project was brought to a completion.

We also would like to express our deep appreciation to our families, in whose honor these pages are dedicated.

Psalm 145:4 דור לדור ישבח מעשיך

Preface

> Having now shown that every book in the Bible, from Genesis to Judges, is without authenticity, I come to the book of Ruth, an idle, bungling story, foolishly told, nobody knows by whom, about a strolling country-girl creeping slyly to bed with her cousin Boaz. Pretty stuff indeed to be called the word of God! It is, however, one of the best books in the Bible . . .[1]
>
> —Thomas Paine

One of the best books in the Bible—Absolutely! But, an idle, bungling story, foolishly told—Most definitely not! The book of Ruth is an artistic, sometimes sly, and very captivating story that has enjoyed a long history of telling and retelling. It's the telling and retelling that this book is all about. Before a scribe first put the story to page, the Ruth story traveled aurally, generally presented for a female audience. It's that journey, before being written, that will occupy us in the pages that follow.

An argument can be made that Naomi should have lent her name to this story rather than Ruth. Naomi is the main character of the story.[2] Her's is the plight that seeks resolution. She is the initiator and planner of the activity driving the drama. Naomi is at center stage when the drama opens and when it comes to a close. This story is about Naomi. But, does it really matter? Does it matter if this small tale goes by the name of Ruth or Naomi? Yes. As the book of Ruth, the story emphasizes the personality of the Ruth character. It becomes a story of loyalty, kindness (חסד), and a loving devotion expressed in 1:16–17 that has made its way into countless wedding

1. Paine, *Age of Reason*, 110.
2. Saxegaard, "More Than Seven Sons," 273.

ceremonies. If, however, this short story is read as the story of Naomi, it becomes characterized very differently. As the story of Naomi, the story is about a woman caught in a tragic predicament, forced to rely upon her own wits to cleverly manipulate circumstances in order to secure a future for herself and her daughter. It is a search for a resolution to this predicament that propels the story's plot along its course. As the story of Naomi, the story is a search for security (1:9) and an ingenuous use of female power to influence male biased institutions for a desired outcome (4:17). Although based upon much of the same material, the Naomi Story is quite different than the book of Ruth. The Naomi Story is prior to and embedded in what has become the book of Ruth. In the process of scribal production, Naomi has been usurped by Ruth.

In the chapters that follow, we analyze the book of Ruth in an effort to recover the Naomi Story. We investigate and attempt to describe an oral substratum to the literary work. Having established a working "script," we ask questions about this oral composition: Who performed it and why? Who listened to and conveyed the oral tradition? Is it possible to place the tradition in a particular social context? Was it a favorite holiday or seasonal story? How and why did the oral story transform into a literary work? How did the story change when it was committed to writing? Did this change in medium effect a change in the social place of the story? Can the Naomi Story be reconstructed and retold?

During the course of our investigation, we've discovered that the book of Ruth began as a deceptively subversive story about Naomi, challenging some of the most basic ideological givens prominently conveyed in much of the biblical literature: a patrilineal economic system, the appropriateness of divine retribution, and the ethnic boundaries delineating "God's people." The Naomi Story in the book of Ruth is powerful. It is compelling in its seductive simplicity, yet amazingly complex in its artistry and rhetorical ambiguity. The Naomi Story repeatedly leads the listener to the edge of social propriety, holding up for examination some very basic social givens that offered false security for women in late eighth-century-BCE Judah. In the pages that follow, we will attempt to enter the world of the Naomi Story.

PART 1

1

The Naomi Story: An Oral Substrate

Oral Substrate

Commentators have struggled to describe the literary characteristics appropriate to the book of Ruth. Jack Sasson claims that Ruth is a "tale that hews closer to folklore patterns than most Biblical narratives."[1] Yet, at the same time the "fine prose quality" of the book is recognized.[2] But, not all agree that Ruth is prose.[3] Marjo Korpel is perhaps the most recent of a long line of commentators to suggest that Ruth is poetic in nature,[4] although according to Korpel, a "special kind of poetry."[5] All these descriptives, and more, used by commentators to characterize the book are true—but incomplete. The fact is, the book just doesn't fit. The difficulty encountered when attempting to describe the literary form of the book of Ruth is because the book sits astride the aural and the written. It is becoming clear that the story now rendered in the book of Ruth has a pre-history, with an identifiable oral substratum over which has been built a finely constructed novella.

1. Sasson, *Ruth,* 216.

2. Campbell, *Ruth*, 7.

3. A point also made by Black, "Ruth in the Dark," 20.

4. Korpel, "Unit Division in the Book of Ruth," 131–32. See also, Watson, *Classical Hebrew Poetry*; Nielsen, *Ruth*, 3.

5. Korpel, "Unit Division in the Book of Ruth," 138.

In delving into that pre-history, our first task is to define traces of that oral substratum (what we will now call the Naomi Story) in the book of Ruth. Others have sought for the same oral presence in literature from the ancient Near East with positive results. In constructing a case that points to the existence of an oral substrate to the book of Ruth, we will first consider characteristics that have been applied in search of an oral substrate to literature from ancient Egypt. Our next step will be to narrow our focus and look at characteristics that have been applied elsewhere in the Hebrew Bible. Finally, we will narrow even further and consider the semantic characteristics of the book of Ruth to see if remnants of orality can be observed.

Oral Substrate in Egyptian Prophetic Literature

Donald Redford has analyzed parts of the ancient Egyptian literary tradition and offers characteristics of its oral substrate that may have application to the Naomi Story and the book of Ruth. Redford suggests the following characteristics by which it can be shown that "oral composition has left numerous signs of its presence" in written texts.[6] Those characteristics will be introduced here and discussed in more detail later in this book in application to specific parts of the Naomi Story.

1. Dicitur—That is, an introductory phrase identifying an oral quote or reference (i.e., it is said).[7] If we applied this characteristic to the Hebrew Bible, it would perhaps most easily be seen in the often repeated formula found in the prophetic literature: "Thus says the LORD."[8] Of interest in the Naomi story is the use of both finite and infinitive forms of אמר (to say) as markers for direct, and less frequently, indirect speech. Galia Hatav contends that quotations introduced by לאמר (to say) signal that "the following record of communication may not be exact."[9] While quotations using a finite form of אמר (said) "signals that what follows is an exact quotation."[10] Finite forms of אמר occur 48 times while there are only 3 occurrences of לאמר in

---

6. Redford, "Scribe and Speaker," 206–14; see also Song, *In the Beginning Were Stories, Not Texts.*

7. Redford, "Scribe and Speaker," 206.

8. Miller, *Oral Tradition in Ancient Israel,* 73.

9. Hatav, "(Free) Direct Discourse in Biblical Hebrew," 7; see also Follingstad, *Deictic Viewpoint,* 475, 554. However, Miller, *The Representation of Speech,* 423.

10. Hatav, "(Free) Direct Discourse in Biblical Hebrew," 7.

Ruth (2:15; 4:4, 17).[11] All three occurrences of לאמר frame indirect quotations revealed by the narrator (2:15; 4:17) or a disclosure of inner thoughts (4:4) revealed by the speaker in direct speech. None of the occurrences frame or introduce dialogue.

2. Mnemonics—A second characteristic pointing to an oral substrate is the presence of catchwords, sequences, repetition of consonants, or other aural signals that are particularly effective when spoken and heard.[12] The book of Ruth preserves several series of catch words that have particular affect when presented orally. Some of these words have been especially troublesome when presented as a translation of a scribal work. That troublesomeness fades in oral presentation.

3. Oral Formula—a patterned distribution of accentuated syllables that, once again, has added force when received aurally.[13]

4. Wordplay—The strategic use of unusual or unexpected terms or grammatical forms that produce a mnemonic function or double entendre.[14]

5. Repetition and multiform embellishment that serves to expand or heighten tension in the delivery of the story.[15]

6. Structure—Oral stories are generally narrated without the personal involvement of the narrator in the story.[16] In the development of the story, the speaker employs:

---

11. This ratio, 16:1, is much higher than that appearing in other biblical narrative.

12. Redford, "Scribe and Speaker," 206–7. Ellen Davis also recognizes the aural character of ancient Israel's culture and notes the important role that verbal repetition plays in oral literature. Davis, "Beginning with Ruth," 14–15.

13. Redford, "Scribe and Speaker," 208–10.

14. Ibid., 211–13. Gary Rendsburg indicates a number of nonstandard grammatical constructions in the biblical text, such as gender neutralization and lack of congruence, which can be explained as traces of colloquial language. Rendsburg, *Diglossia in Ancient Hebrew,* 151–76. This reflection of a colloquial or oral substrate may be present in the incongruent use of masculine plural forms where the antecedent is feminine plural (1:8, 9, 11, 13, 19, 4:11). Timothy Lim considers unexpected masculine plural forms supporting evidence for a prevailing male voice in the Book of Ruth. Lim, "The Book of Ruth and Its Literary Voice," 273.

15. Redford, "Scribe and Speaker," 214.

16. Ibid., 214–15.

- Repetition of blocks of narrative material; the second version always padded out and longer than the first.[17]
- Subject fronting to mark the transition to a new topic
- Predictability in character
- Plot development through single linearity

As we will see, many of these characteristics (dicitur, wordplays, double entendre, repetition, plot structure, character development, mnemonics, invisible narrator, and, most of all, dialogue) have direct application to the Naomi Story. The fact that so many of the characteristics identified by Redford are applicable to the Naomi Story, doesn't prove the existence of the oral substrate to Ruth, but, at least, suggest the possibility.

Traces of Orality in the Hebrew Bible

Joining the search for orality, Robert Miller has also attempted to develop identifying characteristics of the oral, this time applied specifically to the literature of the Hebrew Bible.[18] Although Miller's objective is not like ours, seeking to reconstruct an extended oral substrate in a scribal composition, we find his taxonomy helpful in piecing together clues and characteristics for our reconstruction. Only those characteristics, identified by Miller, that have potential application to the Naomi Story are presented below.

1. *Repetition* is a primary characteristic that, Miller suggests, points to the presence of orality. Miller calls repetition a "sloppy competition between traditions in a given section of the Bible."[19] When multiple accounts appear "tumbling over each other" in near textual proximity, this could be "signs of orality."[20] But, and this advises caution, Miller contends the opposite can also be a sign of previous orality. Written accounts that lack what would seem to be appropriate and interesting, if not necessary, detail may evidence a written condensation of an oral composition (Gen 10:9; Num 12:22).[21] Related to this notion of repetition are parallel story lines that feature different primary characters.

---

17. Ibid., 214.

18. Miller, *Oral Tradition in Ancient Israel*, 68–78.

19. Ibid., 69–70.

20. Ibid., 70.

21. Ibid.

Miller, citing David Carr, points out the parallels between Moses and Jeroboam that "suggest the stream of tradition between the stories' origins and their writing."[22]

While we caution the overuse of repetition as a pointer to the presence of an oral substrate, it is noteworthy that both Redford and Miller observe the characteristic. Repetition has a very particular function in the Naomi Story. Repeating pieces of narrative, short and condensed descriptives, function as scene changers. For example, the Introduction to the performance ends in 1:6 with a statement indicating Naomi's return journey from Moab had begun. Act 1, scene one of the performance begins with a repetition of this action in verse 7, setting the stage for the dialogue to follow in 1:8–16. Likewise, 1:19a brings the preceding dialogue to a narrative conclusion while 1:19b repeats the action of 19a, but in a manner that introduces the dialogue to follow (1:19b–21). Similar repetitions can be seen:

1:22 Act 1 (scene 2) closing:	with the mention of barley harvest
2:2 Act 2 opens:	with gleaning of the harvest
2:23 Act 2 closes:	Ruth living with her mother-in-law
3:1 Act 3 opens:	repetition of Naomi, the "mother-, in-law instructing Ruth
3:18 Act 3 closes:	an encouragement to wait until we learn how the matter turns out. The man will not rest.
4:13 Act 4 opens:	Baoz took Ruth and she became his wife.

These repetitions bridge dialogue, helping to create a running narrative context for the character interaction.

2. Miller contends that oral literature tends to be replete with apparent grammatical problems like event heavy sentences, ambiguous references, inconsistent deictic orientation, and other illogical imperfections that betray a lack of textual editing.[23] Some of the grammatical problems resident in the book of Ruth resolve themselves in oral performance. But, we would be slow to label these "imperfections." In-

22. Ibid.
23. Ibid., 71.

stead, many of the grammatical problems in the book of Ruth become dramatic and poignant moments of performance when presented orally as the Naomi Story. These will be examined in more detail later in the book.

3. Stories that are the result of oral retelling tend to be humorous and have few characters,[24] since the actions of minor characters are eventually attributed to major ones. Certainly, the Naomi Story has few main characters: Naomi, Ruth, and Boaz. More, the characters generally appear in pairs, allowing the dialogue between the two characters to drive the action of any given scene. Dialogue dominates the Naomi Story in a way that highlights the interaction of two characters at a time. And, as we will investigate in chapter three, humor, often dry and unexpected, is liberally scattered throughout the story.

4. A characteristic Miller suggests as evidence for the presence of an oral substrate in scribal literature, with fascinating application to the Naomi Story, are *kennings*. A kenning is a verbal construction used to create visualization as part of a definition. For example, a bat becomes a tree-wolf; a squirrel is a tree-rat. There are several applications of this kenning idea in the Naomi Story. The first is in the names assigned to the characters of the story. Naomi's sons are strangely named and certainly evoke visualization. Naomi's own request for a name change (1:20) creates a way for the audience to visualize both her character, and her plight. In 1:19 the women of Bethlehem (House of Bread) ask "Is this Naomi" (Pleasant)? Has Pleasantness returned to the House of Bread? Visualization is created by the names, or labels, and particularly, in the renaming or change of name, given to characters in the story (particularly Naomi, Ruth, and God) as the plot progresses. Another application of the kenning concept may be found in the opening lines of the story. A grammatical peculiarity presents itself in 1:1, and following, concerning the oft translated *territory* of Moab. We will suggest (chapter three) that this peculiarity (literally: fields of Moab) is part of a word play carried by the storyteller throughout the Naomi Story.

---

24. Miller explains this in terms of character action, the actions of minor characters are eventually attributed to major ones. Miller, *Oral Tradition in Ancient Israel*, 72–73. In the Story of Naomi dialogue, not action, dominates character development. See also Oesterreicher, "Types of Orality in Text," 200; Russo, "Oral Theory," 16.

As with Redford's description of orality in Egyptian literature, the applicability of so many of Miller's identified characteristics of orality in the literature of the Hebrew Bible does not prove an oral Naomi Story standing behind the book of Ruth, but the parallels are growing. We now turn to an examination of the semantic structures found in the book of Ruth to see if the evidence for an oral substratum grows even further.

Semantic Structures Pointing to an Oral Substrate

Frank Polak has conducted extensive analysis on biblical narrative cycles and concludes: "Many tales, and even entire narrative cycles, are characterized by the *high number of clauses consisting of a predicate only, or of predicate with one single argument, the low number of clauses in hypotaxis, and the low number of expanded noun chains* . . . This style is characteristic of such narrative cycles as, e.g., the tales of the Patriarchs, of Samuel, Saul, and David, of Elijah and Elisha. In other words, *even though in their present form these cycles belong to written literature, they are based on a substrate of oral literature* [author's italics]."[25] Polak's conclusion is based upon a detailed analysis of linguistic styles evident in selected portions of the biblical text, charting the results, and proposing discourse typologies apparent in the material.[26] Polak identifies intricate sentence constructions (long intricate clauses), long noun groups, and subordinated clauses as characteristic of a written style while oral narrative, or written narrative stemming from an oral substrate (oral derived literature) tends toward "short, simple clauses in parataxis."[27] Polak has profiled his analysis using the following categories:

ELC—Explicit Lexicalized sentence Constituents: This category refers to the complexity of the sentence, noting the presence of "subject, object, or indication of place, time, manner, reasons or goal."[28] The number of

---

25. Polak, "The Style of the Dialogue in Biblical Prose Narrative," 62–63. See also Rendsburg, *Diglossia in Ancient Hebrew,* 151–76.

26. Polak, "Language Variation, Discourse Typology," 301–38. See also Polak, "The Oral and the Written," 59–105; Polak, "Orality: Biblical Hebrew," 930–37. Critiques of Polak are offered by Niditch, "Epic and History in the Hebrew Bible," 90–92; and Young et al., *Linguistic Dating of Biblical Texts,* 83.

27. Polak, "Style Is More Than the Person," 39. See also the analysis conducted in Polak, "The Book of Samuel and the Deuteronomist," 34–73. Polak, "Oral Substratum, Language Usage, and Thematic Flow in the Abraham–Jacob Narrative," 217–38.

28. Polak, "Language Variation, Discourse Typology," 305.

constituents occurring is presented in three groups: 0–1 constituents; 2+ constituents; 3+ constituents (present in a complex structure).

Mean Noun Group: "Nouns with attribute, including construct state, or in junction with additional nouns."[29]

Hypotaxis: Clause subordination including "relative clauses, infinitive clauses, participial clauses and clauses introduced by a conjunction."[30]

Complex Hypotaxis: The presence of clauses dependent upon subordinate clauses.[31]

According to the profile, and in general terms, the presence of "extensive elaborate clauses, the long noun groups, and the high number of subordinate clauses" tends to reflect a scribal medium whereas a low occurrence of these elements is more characteristic of a lean brisk style associated with an "oral substratum or to close contact with oral literature, and also to strong and many-faceted interactions with performances by oral poets and narrators."[32]

Polack provides the following analysis of sentence construction in Ruth.[33]

Text/Class	Number Clauses	0–1 ELC	2+ ELC	Hypotaxis	Mean Noun Group	Complex Hypotaxis	3+ ELC
Ruth 1:3–22	97	49.45	30.93	19.59	26.80	7.22	4.12
Ruth 2	129	50.39	27.91	21.71	23.26	5.43	3.11
Ruth 3	95	57.89	18.95	23.16	18.42	11.58	3.16
Ruth 4	90	38.89	33.33	27.78	35.00	12.22	8.89

29. Polak, "Style is More Than the Person," 41.

30. Polak, "Language Variation, Discourse Typology," 306.

31. Ibid., 306.

32. Ibid., 316–17. See also Polak, "Orality: Biblical Hebrew," 934.

33. Frank Polak, private communication, Oct 14, 2013. Polak has also constructed an analytical chart for Jonah displaying similarities to Ruth. Polak, "Language Variation, Discourse Typology, and the Sociocultural Background of Biblical Narrative," 327.

Text/Class	Number Clauses	0–1 ELC	2+ ELC	All Hypotaxis	Noun Pairs	Complex Hypotaxis	3+ ELC
Jonah 1:1–16	84	52.38	32.14	15.48	24.40	7.14	3.57
Jonah 3	43	46.51	37.21	16.28	44.19	9.30	6.98
Jonah 4	51	27.45	41.18	31.37	30.39	15.69	11.76

From his data, Polak concludes a major scribal revision in chapter four and a less extensive revision of chapter three. The distribution and complexity of sentence construction, in addition to the distribution of לקח and הלך, leads Polak to conclude a mid to late eighth century for the literary revision of Ruth 1–3 and an exilic literary revision of Ruth 4.[34] In all cases "the text of Ruth harkens back to an oral substrate, but might be a few generations removed from the oral performance."[35]

The measurable differences in syntax evident in the book of Ruth provide the best evidence leading to the conclusion that the book of Ruth is the product of several stages of scribal editing of a pre-existing oral story. The difficulty that we observed, at the beginning of this chapter, among commentators struggling to characterize Ruth, is, at least in part, because Ruth is multi-layered. Polak isn't the only, or the first, analyst to speculate the existence of an oral substrate to the book of Ruth. G. S. Glanzman proposed a three stage development for the book of Ruth, including a first oral stage involving an old poetic tale.[36] Edward Campell suggested that "a good if speculative case can be made that stories such as Ruth, and many of the others to which we have compared it, were transmitted orally for a period of time."[37] Campbell was also sensitive to the changes that may arise during the performance (perhaps singing) of the story: "Therefore while each performance was something new, a new creation, it was the same story."[38] It's this performed story—the Naomi Story that we will attempt to bring back to life.

Robert Miller intended the characteristics of orality[39] as markers of a probability of "orally derived bits in the Hebrew Bible."[40] Combined with the analysis of Polak and Redford, it seems quite certain that the present book of Ruth contains within it all the characteristics of a pre-existing

34. Others have noted the differences between chapter four and chapters one through three and have concluded chapter four fairly unimportant. Rauber, "The Book of Ruth," 175.

35. Polak, private communication Oct. 14, 2013.

36. Glanzman, "The Origin and Date of the Book of Ruth," 201–7.

37. Campbell, *Ruth,* 19; see also Wolfe, *Ruth, Esther, Song of Songs, and Judith,* 8.

38. Campbell, *Ruth,* 19. Susan Niditch is not convinced by either Campbell or a major source for Campbell: Lord, *The Singer of Tales.* Niditch, "Legends of the Wise and Heroines," 455–56.

39. Miller, *Oral Tradition in Ancient Israel,* 70–73. See also Pretzler, "Pausanias and Oral Tradition," 246.

40. Miller, *Oral Tradition in Ancient Israel,* 78.

oral substrate: a Naomi Story. The identification of an oral substrate is a statement about modality, and the identification of an oral modality ushers the analyst into a set of analytic constructs different than those applied to scribal literature. The telling of the Naomi Story constituted a performance that has, in the book of Ruth, left clues and remnants.

2

The Naomi Story: A Female Performance Tradition

The Naomi Story served the needs of a specific part of ancient Israelite society. The project, or dilemma driving the story toward a resolution; the point of view by which the story is told; the manner in which the characters of the story are developed; and the role those characters play in the story, all point toward the conclusion that the Naomi Story was told by women for women. The Naomi Story was part of the female performance tradition of ancient Israel.

Does Gender Matter?

So what? Does gender matter? Does the gender of the storyteller (and the audience) really matter? Does it matter if we posit a female storyteller?[1] In short—yes—very much so! And on several different levels. Although rooted in the imagination of an author, literature comes to exist independently of its author. A book, or text of any type, comes to have a life of its own, stretching, sometimes threatening to sever, its connections back to the author. Performance cannot. Oral literature, performance, can only occur when it becomes embodied by an actor/performer and so is much more dependent upon the characteristics of the actor/performer than a written text is on its author. The Naomi Story was performed as oral literature and that performance would appear very differently when told by a female storyteller or performer than

1. See Bauckham, *Is the Bible Male?*

if told by a male performer or storyteller. Performance is an event that occurs when a story is embodied by an actor or actors. The characteristics of the actors help define the performance. This is doubly true for the Naomi Story, which is a story with gender at its very center. The story is not just about women—it is about relationships between women.[2] The manner in which gender is embodied by the actors performing the story will impact how that story is understood by an audience. More, gender played a role as the Naomi Story became the book of Ruth. As the Naomi Story became the book of Ruth, it moved from a predominately female social context, to one dominated by the male scribe and his culture. The literary redaction of the performed story changed the gender of the story.

A Word of Caution: What Does Gender Mean?

Characteristics by which we form a personal identification are often cast in the appearance of objective reality, fixed and unchanging. In actuality, gender, age, ethnicity, and the like are culturally "framed" or determined, given specific meaning by the cultural norms that surround us.[3] Each of these characteristics is given a particular significance by the cultural connections they make in a specific time and place. Yitzak Feder has written; "As many modern studies of identity have argued, the differences that make a difference are not 'givens' determined by objective reality; rather, they are dependent on priorities determined by cultural discourse. . ."[4] And, as Feder reminds us, culturally informed "self-image is constantly reconstructed,"[5] dynamic, and changing over time. So the question is: even though gender is an important identifier in our culture (although changing in its signification)—was it important for the performance of the Naomi Story? What exactly did it mean for the story to be told in a female culture and later

2. Beverly Bow notes that the Naomi–Ruth relationship is one of the few in the Hebrew Bible that actually works out well for the women involved. Bow, "Sisterhood?," 213. The unusual positive outcome, even though also serving male interests, may suggest a female setting for the telling of the Story.

3. And the construction of a collective identity through the Naomi Story's characters seems to be a primary concern of the storyteller. For a discussion of collective identity see, Friedmand and McAdam, "Collective Identity and Activism," 156–58.

4. Feder, "The Aniconic Tradition," 252; see also, Barth, *Ethnic Groups and Boundaries*.

5. Feder, "The Aniconic Tradition," 253.

appropriated by a male culture? Clues as to how gender was significant in the Naomi Story need to be drawn from the story itself.[6]

Female Performer

Since performance, even dramatic reading or telling, involves not only the voice but body of the performer, everything about the physical presence, including the gender of the creator / performer of the Naomi Story are important factors in determining the manner in which the Story is presented.[7] The possibility,[8] perhaps even likelihood, that Ruth (or the Naomi Story) is an example of a short story genre "stemming from a woman's culture"[9] and told by Israelite women[10] is highly significant when investigating the manner in which the elements of the story (including: project, dialogue, plot, a search for security, and the dramatic use of desire,[11] sexuality, ambiguity,

6. Ibid., 253.

7. Thiem, "No Gendered Bodies without Queer Desires," 469.

8. Goitein, "Women as Creators of Biblical Genres," 4; Campbell, *Ruth*, 21–23. Bledstein, "Female Companionships," 116–33. LaCocque agrees that the book of Ruth had a "female author." LaCocque, *Ruth*, xvii.

9. Van Dijk-Hemmes, "Ruth: A Product of Women's Culture?," 135. Elsewhere, Brenner and van Dijk-Hemmes describe a voice present in the text and describe that voice as F (feminine/female) or M (masculine/male). Brenner and F. van Dijk-Hemmes, "Traces of Women's Texts in the Hebrew Bible," 7–8, 27. In that same publication, van Dijk-Hemmes speculates, "If this suggestion be accepted [the "guild" of professional storytellers], then it is quite possible that the Ruth and Naomi story belonged to the repertory of a professional storyteller, a woman old and wise like one of the heroines of the story, Naomi" (107). See also Brenner, "Naomi and Ruth: Further Reflections," 140; Goitein, "Women as Creators of Biblical Genres," 1–34. LaCocque, *Ruth*, simply writes that "the book of Ruth is a feminine book from beginning to end" (5) and agrees that the author is probably a woman (38), an opinion gradually formed from an earlier agnostic position expressed in *The Feminine Unconventional* (110–11). Phyllis Trible simply describes the book as "A man's world tells a woman's story." Trible, *God and the Rhetoric of Sexuality*, 166. Already in 1972 Samuel Sandmel considered the female authorship of Ruth. Sandmel, *The Enjoyment of Scripture*, 25. See also Kalmanofsky, *Dangerous Sisters of the Hebrew Bible*, 157.

10. The possibility of female "storytellers" operative in Ruth should be considered in context with the singers of 1 Samuel 18:7, et. al. and perhaps the ballad singers of Num 21:27–30. Meyers described this context when she wrote, "Women who were singers, instrumentalists, composers, dancers, keeners, and even reciters of proverbs and sayings from a sapiential corpus all exhibited expressive skills in public venues." Meyers, "Mother to Muse," 73. To Meyers' list we simply suggest adding "storyteller."

11. See also, James Loader, who believes that "the story's perception of social reality is so delicately attuned to the nuances of practical female experience that the authorship of

and irony) are embodied and communicated to an audience. In the mid part of the twentieth century, S. D. Goitein[12] led the search for a female storyteller by suggesting several characteristics pertaining to literature that originate in a female culture. Fokkelein van Dijk-Hemmes has revisited those characteristics and suggests that their presence is the result of a dominant "F" voice.[13] If we are going to plausibly attribute female authorship to the Naomi Story[14] we should expect to find that:

1. The text should contain traces of an intent which is less than normally androcentric.

2. There should be talk in it of a (re)definition of reality from the female perspective, so that,

3. The narrative contains definable differences between the view of the male and the female figures.[15]

The above three characteristics are certainly operative in the Naomi Story.[16] The audience experiences the story, having access to the thoughts and feelings of the female characters.[17] The action of the story is carried by the

a woman seems more likely." Loader, "A Woman Praised by Women," 698.

12. Goitein, "Women as Creators of Biblical Genres," 1–33.

13. Van Dijk-Hemmes, "Traces of Women's Texts in the Hebrew Bible," 106–7. Jacqueline Lapsley suggests three strategies for reading, and presumably for uncovering the F perspective in the stories: 1) attending to women's words, 2) attending to the narrator's perspective, 3) attending to the textual worldview. Lapsley, *Whispering the Word*, 2. Timothy Lim considers the characteristics for identifying a female voice established by van Dijk-Hemmes and Athalya Brenner too elastic, and suggests, as far as the book of Ruth is concerned, that gender perspective be determined by noting the gender of the speakers in the dialogues within the book. Since those speeches are roughly equal (26 female speeches; 21 male speeches), Lim concludes, "the book represents both male and female perspectives." Lim, "The Book of Ruth and its Literary Voice," 282.

14. Van Dijk-Hemmes, "Traces of Women's Texts in the Hebrew Bible," 31–32.

15. These characteristics are suggested, mindful of Carol Meyers timely warning against the over separation of male/female spheres. Meyers, "'Women of the Neighborhood' (Ruth 4:17)," 114–15.

16. Carol Meyers suggests six characteristics, in a text from the Hebrew Bible, that point to a woman's voice: 1) a woman's story is being told, 2) a wisdom association is present, 3) women are agents in their own history, 4) the agency of women affects others, 5) the setting is domestic, and 6) marriage is involved. Meyers, "Returning Home: Ruth 1:8 and the Gendering of the Book of Ruth," 109–10.

17. Irmtraud Fischer writes, "It can be assumed that the author was past the middle of her life. This becomes clear through Naomi, who is the main figure (although not the hero) of the story. Most of the things happening are being watched from her viewpoint

female characters.[18] The dilemma driving the plot of the story is a female concern (1:9).[19] The pivotal threshing floor scene presents a female interpretation of a sexual encounter with a male.[20] And it is the women of the community that are positioned to offer blessings at the end of the book (4:14–17a), giving to women the primary agency in (re)defining the future.[21]

The death of the male characters at the beginning of the story sets the stage for a F story. That F point of view is continued in the dialogue of the story. In her discourse analysis of Ruth, Ilona Rashkow observes that "discourse is often viewed as a form of domination" and the "converse of speech, silence is equally meaningful since the literary character who is denied discourse often experiences narrative suppression as well."[22] The discourse in the Naomi Story (and book of Ruth) is dominated by F voices and gives expression to a F point of view within the context of a M culture. This position of dominance can be illustrated by examining Naomi–Ruth dialogue and Ruth–Boaz dialogue. Rashkow writes, "with Naomi, Ruth is determined and assertive, but of relatively few words; with Boaz, Ruth maintains a higher level of formality but is quite articulate . . . Ruth's discourse empowers her to replace marginality and insecurity by wealth and a more stable status."[23] The power and dominance in discourse within the Naomi Story is especially clear when contrasted to the dialogue in the Bathsheba story of 2 Samuel 11. There, Bathsheba, although clearly a major character

---

and almost all persons concerned in the book are related to her." Fischer, "The Book of Ruth," 34.

18. Ostriker, "The Book of Ruth and the Love of the Land," 344.

19. Though we consider much of the city gate scene in chapter 4 a scribal addition to the Naomi Story, even here the event is filtered through the female concern to find security as expressed in 1:9, although the action is certainly dominated by male characters.

20. This female perspective was, perhaps unwittingly, articulated (although in a somewhat sexist manner) by Theophile Meeks when he described the threshing-floor scene as an example of the "wily ways of a woman to get her man." Meeks, "Translating the Hebrew Bible," 333. We suspect the encounter might would be described differently if narrated by Boaz.

21. James Loader says of the episode in 4:13–17, "the male perspective just is not there. What is told here is told from a *female* perspective." Loader, "A Woman Praised by Women," 692. Irmtraud Fischer writes, "The worldview in the book of Ruth is thoroughly female." Fischer, "The Book of Ruth," 33. Likewise, Carol Meyers encourages recognition of the female gender perspective of the story, even if the gender of the author is unknowable. Meyers, "Returning Home," 89.

22. Rashkow, "Ruth," 28.

23. Ibid., 29.

in the story, has no direct speech or dialogue and is cast in a submissive role, a pawn caught in the abuse of political power wielded by David.

Of special interest in expressing the F point of view is the naming episode at the end of the Story (4:17). As often as not, women give names to children (62% of the naming episodes) in the Bible.[24] The naming of a child (as well as the naming of places or objects commemorating an event) can be construed as a ritual act. "Because a name in the biblical world was not simply a means of identification but rather signified the essence of a person, the anthroponymic (name giving) process meant establishing the vitality of a new life."[25] Carol Meyers notes in cases where fathers participate in the naming: "the few instances of men naming children may be the result of the male perspective, which attributes to the father the function of name-giving when the names may have actually been given by the mother."[26] In the naming episodes of the Hebrew Bible, the more independent and powerful the woman, the more active and trending toward exclusive is her involvement in naming offspring. This makes the occurrence in the Naomi Story all the more significant for, "this is the only instance of a group of women naming a child. In so doing, they signify solidarity with the new mother."[27] Female solidarity with Naomi is not incidental but planned and developed by the storyteller right from the opening of Act One. In fact, all the naming episodes in the Naomi Story are by women:

- Naomi changes her own name to Marah (in conversation with other women)
- Naomi enquires of Ruth and Ruth reveals Boaz's name
- The village women name the child born to Ruth

Interestingly, in the naming episode concluding Act Five, the mother is Naomi, not Ruth. And notice, the son named is Obed—Servant. In naming the baby, the women direct the future by naming the present. A servant has been presented to Naomi and her dilemma is solved.

The F point of view is reinforced by the male characters in the story. In contrast to the women heaping blessings upon our heroines, the male characters are not present when Naomi is welcomed back to Bethlehem

24. Meyers, *Households and Holiness*, 42.

25. Ibid., 43; see also, Bohmbach, "Names and Naming in the Biblical World," 35.

26. Meyers, *Households and Holiness*, 42.

27. Meyers, "Everyday Life in Biblical Israel," 195.

18

(1:19); are suggestively more than a little unpleasant, and even threatening, co-workers in the field (2:9).[28] The husbands and sons; Elimelech, Chilion, and Mahlon are present only as names and the genealogies at the end of the book were probably not part of the Naomi Story.[29] Even Boaz, the most prominent male character in the story, lacks independent thought and is present as a pawn, acting, he thinks, on his own, while, in reality Naomi and Ruth (as well as the audience) know all along that his reactions have been anticipated and planned.

All of this suggests that the Naomi Story was performed in front of female audiences, sympathetic to the plight of the female characters in the story and aware of the manipulations required to find security in a male dominated economy. It's not hard to imagine how such a presentation, including the irony, sarcasm, wordplays, and character development would be received with knowing nods of approval among a female audience.

The contrasts between a male and female perspective that are suggested by the three criteria listed by van Dijk-Hemmes are made plain and powerfully embodied by the gender of the performer. Applied to the Naomi Story, which pivots so dramatically in the sexuality of the threshing floor scene, the social and physical power of sexuality is utilized by the performer in order to influence the audience in a desired manner. Van Dijk-Hemmes suggests: "Even if, as in the case of Ruth, the interplay between the narrator and public can only be advanced as a hypothesis it is nevertheless highly plausible that this story is indeed a collective creation of women's culture, a story shaped by the cooperation between (a tradition of) wise women narrators and their actively engaged (predominantly F[emale]) audience."[30]

Yet, recognition of the story's feminine ownership has had little impact on the way commentators present Ruth. Understandably, most commentators are concerned with the literary reiteration of the story that has come to find its home in the Hebrew Bible. But, the literary reiteration of the story, taking the story away from its female owners[31] and placing it in the control

28. If we admit the city gate scene as part of the Naomi Story, in which Boaz figures prominently in the assist of the female characters. Other males are present as unnamed group of elders (4:2) and selfishly reticent benefactor (4:6).

29. Some have even seen Elimelech's immigration to Moab as an act of betrayal, abandoning his fellow countrymen in time of their greatest need. Hendel, "Ruth," 258. Agnethe Siquans counters this view by claiming that the poverty of Naomi, not inherited wealth is woven into the story, "Foreignness and Poverty in the Book of Ruth," 446–48.

30. Van Dijk-Hemmes, "Ruth," 138–39.

31. Campbell considers that this oral story may have even been part of a musical

of (most likely) male scribes, fundamentally affected the subversive nature of the Naomi Story upon which the book of Ruth was based.[32] Within the context of female musical performances in ancient Israel, Carol Meyers considers the social dynamics involved in a female subculture of ancient Israel and writes, "Normal hierarchies favoring males are suspended and subverted by the communicative flow of the expressive act, in which female performers have control by virtue of the focus on them—on their words and their actions. Women musicians thus exert social control during the performance event, not only because of the function of the event in the political and personal aspects of the community—the events discussed here are hardly pure entertainment—but also by the intrinsic appeal and aesthetic qualities of the expressive acts."[33]

If women storytellers exerted a similar influence as did their musical counterparts, then transferring the story from the domain of a female performer to a (most likely) male scribe represents a significant moment in the production of the Naomi Story as the book of Ruth now preserved in the Hebrew Bible. Consider the following, also by Carol Meyers: "Most of the producers of scripture were elite, urban males such as priests and members of the royal bureaucracy, probably addressing other men; . . . Their goals and interests rarely included the concerns or practices of women . . . The perspective of the producers of scripture was for the most part national and communal, not familial and domestic."[34]

But, the remaking of the story into the male domain has been incomplete and uneven for the presence of the female culture is still observable. In the paragraphs that follow, we attempt to recapture that subversive quality of the female ownership of the Naomi Story.

repertoire sung by ancient female bards (*Ruth*, 18–23).

32. Meyers writes, "Performance is not only an activated instance of skill and creativity; it is also a mode of communication involving an audience. The dynamics of the performer-audience communicative flow can themselves have a favorable impact on women's status in society." Meyers, "Mother to Muse," 76. If this is so, and we believe it to be, then usurping that performance by a male performer can certainly affect that "favorable impact."

33. Ibid.

34. Meyers, *Households and Holiness*, 7.

Mother's House

The project of the Naomi Story is reinforced by Naomi's opening directive to her daughters-in-law. Naomi, grief-stricken and destitute, sees no hope for either herself or for her daughters-in-law while in her company, so she admonishes them to return to their "mother's house (1:8). This is an unusual phrase in the Hebrew Bible and may give a hint to the sarcastic, subversive character of the story's project. Naomi seems to intentionally avoid using the more usual "father's house" hinted at in 1:9. The phrase, "mother's house," appears elsewhere only in Gen 24:28 and Song of Songs 3:4 and 8:2.[35] A related term "her house" is used in Prov 31:21, 27. The usage in Song of Songs appears to refer specifically to the bedroom of a woman's mother and so symbolizes a safe and secure environment for the expression of female sexuality.[36] If this, not so subtle, reference to female sexuality is also present in the use of the term in Ruth 1:8, it functions as a foreshadowing to the pivotal Act Three of the story in which Ruth's sexuality becomes the means by which the desired security of 1:8 is achieved. It's worth noting that in all other biblical narrative, in which widows return home, they always return to a "father's house."[37] In fact, the surprising appearance of the "mother's house" seems to have been objectionable to those responsible for various recensions of the LXX and the Syriac, preferring "parent's house" or "father's house."[38] When the term "mother's house" is used in the Hebrew Bible, it invariably appears within the context of a woman's story in which "women are agents of their own destiny" and "the agency of women affects others."[39] The use of "mother's house" here, in 1:8, reinforces the female orientation of the project of the Story and provides "powerful evidence for the presence of a female text."[40] The term helps set the stage for the sarcasm that will be used so effectively in the Naomi Story.

35. André LaCocque considers both Ruth and Song of Songs to have been written by a female author and so the "mother's house" usage in these two books reflecting a female point of view. LaCocque, *Ruth*, 44. See also LaCocque, *Romance, She Wrote*; and Meyers, "'To Her Mother's House,'" 39–51.

36. Rashkow, "Ruth," 29.

37. Gen 38:11; Num 30:17; Deut 22:21; Judg 19:2, 3. See Campbell, *Ruth*, 64.

38. Campbell, *Ruth*, 60; see also Meyers, "Returning Home," 92.

39. Meyers, "Returning Home," 109.

40. Ibid., 114.

Female Character Development

The female oriented project of the Naomi Story is reinforced by the manner in which identity is assigned to the main female characters of the story. In finding security in the house of a husband, Naomi and Ruth must each assume an identity—an identity that casts Naomi and Ruth as archetypes for all women (see 1:6; 3:14; 4:11, 13). The question of identity is brought to the attention of the audience repeatedly through questions and naming episodes (1:19–21; 2:5; 3:9, 16; 4:17). Of Naomi, Ilana Pardes writes, "despite her limited textual life span (we get to know her only as an aged woman), she is 'fraught with development,' . . . to a degree no other female character in the Bible reaches."[41] An analysis of character development within Ruth is invited by the very names assigned to the major characters in the book.[42] A. Graeme Auld agrees that at least some of the names in the book of Ruth are "chosen to illustrate the characteristics of the actors [sic *characters*] of the drama."[43] Naomi's marriage to Elimelech ("My God is King") ends in desperateness when he dies (punished by God), and so, in a very *un*royal and *un*divine manner, proving unable to help Naomi, leaving her destitute in a foreign land. Naomi's two sons, Mahlon ("Obliterated") and Chilion ("Eliminated")[44] also die (also punished by God), causing Naomi ("Pleasant" or "Sweet") to ask that her name be changed to Mara ("Bitterness").[45] Naomi's daughter-in-law Orpah ("Cloud [little or disappointing water]")[46] leaves to return to her "mother's house" (1:9) while her second daughter-in-law, Ruth ("Satisfy [with abundant water]" or "Drench"),[47] decides to accompany Naomi back to Bethlehem ("House of Bread"), her native home which she left years before because of famine. There, and through Naomi's

41. Pardes, *Countertraditions in the Bible*, 108. See McKay, who sees the underdevelopment of female characters as a byproduct of the "perspective of male readers." McKay, "Eve's Sisters Re-Cycled," 171; also, Brenner, "Some Observation," 192–208.

42. LaCocque, *The Feminine Unconventional*, 114.

43. Auld, *Ruth*, 260.

44. A variety of similarly repulsive names are offered by commentators. A sense of rhyme is important to retain in whatever translation is used. See Sasson, *Ruth*, 19.

45. Naomi's name change provides the occasion for the rabbis to, in Kates' words, see in her both a figure of suffering and a challenge to any simplistic notion of divine justice." Kates, "Transfigured Night," 53.

46. Or perhaps "back [nape] of neck" signifying Orpah's turning around or turning back to her mother's house. See Aschkenasy, "From Aristotle to Bakhtin," 227.

47. LaCocque, *Ruth*, 40. Some rabbinic exegesis offers alternate meanings for Orpah and Ruth, yet with similar contrasts. Beattie, *Jewish Exegesis of the Book of Ruth*, 192.

cunningness, Boaz ("Strength" or "Strength is in Him"[48]) is unwittingly manipulated by means of Ruth's sexuality, to secure a future for Naomi and Ruth while the near kinsman (the unnamed "So-and-So or "Mister What's His Name"),[49] from whom help would be expected for the widowed Naomi and Ruth, declines to extend any offer of help, valuing the women only as potential assets or liabilities to his own fortune.[50] The parade of names is complete when a son is born to Ruth. Named by the neighborhood women, and presented as a son for Naomi, Obed ("Servant")[51] brings to a satisfactory conclusion the project introduced by Naomi in 1:9 and in a manner that allows a complete subversion of the male bias that was, on the surface, designed to create security for the widowed and orphaned, but in reality led to the desperate condition in which Naomi and Ruth found themselves. The creative use of personal names for the characters in the story adds to the dramatic development and provides an additional spice of interest to the sarcastic gender subversion in the story.[52]

Character development is also accomplished through labels assigned to the characters. This will be seen clearly with the Ruth character as she progresses through a number of social identifications. At this point, however, we note a label used strategically throughout the Story that further evidences the female point of view. The Naomi Story opens describing the plight in which Naomi finds herself. Her husband and two sons are dead; she and her daughters-in-law are seemingly alone and in need. Twice, Naomi has been mentioned by name (1:2, 3). We know her already as: Naomi, widow, Bethlehemite, mother, sojourner. Yet, in 1:5 Naomi appears as *the woman*. We would expect the storyteller to refer to Naomi again by name (as in 1:2, 3),[53] but instead we have *the woman*. Could it be that is quite

---

48. Strouse and Porten, "A Reading of Ruth," 64.

49. Or "Such and Such," as LaCocque, *Ruth,* 41; see also, "Mister Whoever," Campbell, *Ruth,* 141; Davis, "Beginning with Ruth," 13, or her more colloquial, "Joe Schmoe"; Davis and Adams Parker, *Who Are You, My Daughter?,* 97.

50. We will argue later that the inclusion of Mr. So-and-So was not part of the original Naomi Story. Even so, the name of this short sighted figure fits the pattern of naming for the rest of the characters in the story.

51. Some suggest short for Obadiah, "Servant of God," although here it is Naomi who stands to be served, not God.

52. Phyllis Trible calls Ruth a human comedy. Trible, *God and the Rhetoric of Sexuality,* 166.

53. And indeed several English translations insert her name (NIV, GNB, CEV) at 1:5 sensing the awkwardness presented in the MT.

literally what the storyteller had in mind! Naomi is *the woman*. Her plight is typical of all women so that she is most accurately labeled: *the woman*. Focus on "the woman" is further sharpened in 1:6 where the storyteller uses singular verbal forms (she returned, she heard) when plural forms (they returned, they heard) would be expected.[54] Twice, further the storyteller uses this typical designation to describe the characters and action of the story. *The woman* (this time Ruth) has transgressed and appeared on the threshing floor (3:14) causing the plot of the story to take a sharp turn and a resolution to the drama is secured when a blessing is pronounced on the woman (4:11) and Ruth becomes his *woman* (4:13).[55]

A Story By Women For Women

The Naomi Story is not only about a woman, or two women, it is about relationships between women.[56] The story is about the way in which women construct relationships with one another to solve a common dilemma (1:9) while navigating difficulties imposed on them by God (1:13, 29) and social convention. The story is about a female communal experience best told to a female community. And so the story itself seems to call for a communal reception—an audience.

A performative oral presentation of the Naomi Story presupposes an audience interaction.[57] In all likelihood, the Naomi Story was performed by female performers for female audiences.[58] As we have already seen, several commentators have acknowledged this probability.[59] That implicit audience

54. And as supplied in LXX.

55. Parallel to "young woman" (הנערה) of 4:12 and so best translated "woman" not "wife."

56. Ilana Pardes has noted that this story is the only one in the Hebrew Bible in which women are said to "love" each other. Pardes, *Countertraditions in the Bible*, 102.

57. Although he doesn't extend the description to a performance analysis, André LaCocque writes; "I am convinced that Ruth is a brilliant polemical performance under the guise of an antique and innocuous tale." LaCocque, *The Feminine Unconventional*, 84–85. James Notopoulos describes well the interaction between poet and live audience. Notopoulos "Homer and Cretan Heroic Poetry," 239–40.

58. Writing about women musical performers in ancient Israel, Meyers has already posited the existence of guilds composed by women who "exercised exclusive control over group functions." Meyers, "Mother to Muse," 75. We simply suggest that this notion of guild be expanded to include dramatic performances suitable to the story of Ruth.

59. Fischer, "The Book of Ruth," provides a dissenting voice and is not convinced by arguments positing an oral performance and suggests that "an originally oral tradition is

comes close to the surface of the story in 2:1, 3:14, and 4:12.[60] The audience seems to be addressed directly, "providing information that permits the audience to relish what is developing while the characters are still in the dark."[61] The recognized presence of an audience allows us to investigate the interaction between the storyteller and the audience. Some have already noted the manner in which the storyteller builds the plot, both in what is explicit and in what is left ambiguous,[62] allowing elements of the story to grow "in the fertile minds of the audience."[63] Campbell has identified a series of word *inclusios* occurring throughout the book of Ruth, venturing that the audience may have "participated in crafting these delightful *inclusios* during the period of the oral transmission of the story."[64] Campbell's suggestion is significant for our present investigation. The suggestion implies a performance of the Naomi Story in which the audience was actively engaged in the unfolding of the drama as it was being told.

It's at the highly sexually charged[65] and pivotal[66] threshing floor scene that we see evidence of the audience's presence most dramatically. In the grey light of dawn, following their night together, Boaz stirs himself and says: "Let it not be known that the woman came to the threshing floor." Prefaced by a finite form "he said" (ויאמר) which, elsewhere in Ruth, always frames a direct quote, the natural question arises: to whom is Boaz talking? If he was addressing Ruth, we would expect Boaz to say: "Let it not be known that *you* came to the threshing floor." Some have seen the grammatical difficulty resident in Boaz's statement and have preferred to understand his statement as self talk.[67] But, this ignores the framing: "He

---

not to be presumed" (34). Fischer is of the opinion that the book of Ruth represents an "authentic female voice, perhaps even through the formulations of a male author" (33).

60. Also in 4:7, though we suspect this scene is part of the literary redaction of the Naomi Story.

61. Campbell, "Ruth Revisited," 58.

62. Sasson, *Ruth*.

63. Campbell, "Ruth Revisited," 61.

64. Campbell, *Ruth*, 14.

65. Joshua Berman describes well the linguistic evidence leading to the conclusion that "Ruth 3, as a story of great restraint in the face of sexual desire is very old indeed." Berman, "Ancient Hermeneutics and the Legal Structure of the Book of Ruth," 33.

66. Björn Reinhold attempts to make the case that Ruth 3 has intertextual links to Genesis 1–2, and the "starting point of human history" without mentioning the erotic qualities of the threshing floor episode. Reinhold, "Ruth 3," 117.

67. Hubbard, *Ruth*, 220.

said." When self talk is indicated (as in 4:4), the infinitive is used (לאמר). So, to whom is Boaz talking? The audience. The audience is being addressed directly, in a fashion similar to the speech of the chorus in 1:19 and 4:14–15, and in the shortened version of the city gate scene, 4:11–13. The audience, their assumptions of social propriety, and their understanding of what has just taken place on the threshing floor, have become part of the story. The audience has become co-conspirators with Naomi, Ruth, and Boaz.

The Naomi Story: A Subversive Tale

The Naomi Story was propelled by a search for a resolution to a uniquely female predicament in eighth to sixth century Judah: security in the house of a husband (1:9). That search came to resolution through the female manipulation of a male dominated system of property rights. To borrow a term used by Jacqueline Lapsley; the Naomi Story is a "counter tradition,"[68] a subversion of a dominant cultural economic form. Nehama Aschkenasy describes this counter tradition eloquently when she writes:

> Ruth may be read as romantic comedy with carnivalesque undertones, rooted in the seasonal celebration of nature and its cycles, and thereby connected to festivities outside the boundaries of respected society. It offers a humorous, even rebellious critique of law and authority that has been coated with a story of historical and covenantal significance to the people of Israel, yet its comedic mode and carnivalesque spirit have not been totally suppressed . . . The humor in Ruth, especially in its deception of a patriarch, offers a topsy-turvy moment in which the woman is licensed to manipulate the powerful man and teach him how to behave.[69]

One might also read the humor in Ruth through Mikhail Bakhtin's Marxist lens and become more aware of the tale's subversive and antinomian aspects, of the intent of its comic voice to destabilize society with its rigid laws and offer validity to the multiplicity of

---

68. Amply illustrated by Lapsley, *Wispering the Word*, 3; and Pardes, *Countertraditions in the Bible*; see also Ostriker, "The Book of Ruth and the Love of the Land," who uses "countertext" to describe "a text embedded in Scripture that forms a counter-current to certain dominant biblical concepts and motifs . . ." (344). The notion of muted groups and differing orders of perception developed by Shirley Ardener is also applicable. Ardener, *Perceiving Women*, xi.

69 Aschkenasy, "From Aristotle to Bakhtin: The Comedic and the Carnivalesque in a Biblical Tale," 280.

voices and groups existing in society, especially to two minority groups. We have on the one hand the antiestablishment groups who, in the time of the tales composition, fought against the likes of Ezra and Nehemiah for the acceptance of foreign wives. On the other hand is the disenfranchised half of Israel, the women, who are allowed in this story to assert themselves, take center stage, and freely fashion their own destiny—a privilege mostly afforded to men in the biblical narratives.[70]

Aschkenasy's comments assume the existence of a subculture, or a muted female culture within the dominant male culture. Commenting on the status of women as characterized in the law codes of the Old Testament, Phyllis Bird writes women occupied the role of a "legal non-person; where she does become visible it is as a dependent, and usually an inferior, in a male-centered and male-dominated society."[71] The establishment of a female point of view, represented in the Naomi Story, stands in stark contrast to the generally recognized status of women in Israelite society of the early to mid-Second Temple period. Alice Ogden Bellis suggests that the post-exilic period was a "low period for women"[72] but Tamara Eskenazi is of the opinion that women in Second Temple Yehud may have enjoyed greater legal and economic privileges owing to a heightened sensitivity to ethnic purity and communal solidarity.[73] Should this be the case, the Naomi Story becomes even more interesting as a subversive counter-cultural drama.

Subversion

The design of the Naomi Story is to engage the audience and, in the process, to change the audience. In her analysis of the intertextuality between the story of Tamar (Genesis 38) and Ruth, van Wolde makes a compelling argument, leading to the conclusion that both stories are about challenging boundaries and changing the identity of insiders and outsiders.[74] Both stories take place within a firmly established network of mores and power structures presumably well known by the respective audiences. And in both stories, pivotal episodes subvert those previously accepted mores and

70. Ibid., 280–81.
71. Bird, "Images of Women in the Old Testament," 56.
72. Bellis, *Helpmates, Harlots, and Heroes*, 28.
73. Eskenazi, "Out of the Shadows," 31.
74. Van Wolde, *Ruth en noomi*, 28.

power structures causing the audiences to rethink their own acceptance of the way things are. The unveiling of Tamar and the moment of recognition on the threshing floor (3:8) allow the reader to see differently. Ruth and Tamar function as "eye-openers," to "unveil the audience."[75]

Consider what one commentator wrote about the episode in Ruth 3:6–13. "In a story where so many customs and conventions have already been stretched, readers are led to wonder whether this time they will be stretched to the breaking point."[76]

As darkness engulfed the threshing floor, providing cover for Ruth's nocturnal visit, the subversive nature of the episode is brought into clear light. If nothing else, the plan conceived by Naomi and acted upon by Ruth, if successful, would achieve a degree of security for both women through marriage to a wealthy benefactor. But it is a subversive plan, destroying the "Cinderella-like" qualities of the story by making clear to all that the male actors are pawns, predictably moved about by the designs of the women in the story. The appearance of male power and prestige is uncovered for what it is, a thin veil behind which resides an opportunity for female achievement. Ruth is an "anti-Cinderella" subverting the sexism of the fairytale.[77] As such, Ruth may very well stand in an Israelite stream of tradition that certainly includes Tamar, but perhaps also Bath-sheba, Esther, and the proverbial Worthy Woman (Proverbs 31:10; Ruth 3:10) herself.

Boaz's invitation, suggesting that Ruth spend the night with him on the threshing floor is far from innocent. Boaz tells Ruth to "stay the night" (3: 13) employing the same verb used earlier by Ruth to express her commitment to Naomi (1:16). Sakenfeld concludes that this repetition of language used by Ruth, committing herself to Naomi, argues against any sexual overtones here in chapter 3.[78] But is this conclusion necessary or even preferable? Could it be that Boaz's request for sexual favors in chapter three, and so admitting the power Ruth holds over him, is intended as an ironic and subversive conclusion to the plan begun back in chapter two? Boaz thinks he is a man of power, standing, and great influence. In reality, and as the audience knows full well, he is an unwitting pawn in someone else's designs.

75. Ibid.

76. Sakenfeld, *Ruth*, 54.

77. This is similar to the notion of role differentiation espoused by Berquist, "Role Differentiation in the Book of Ruth," 36.

78. Sakenfeld, *Ruth*, 64.

The purpose of the subversion deserves consideration. LaCocque makes a compelling argument asserting that the book is an interpretation of Torah.[79] Could it be that the subversive nature of the book was intended to consider the inequities and short comings of the application of Torah in the sixth century BCE? If so, could it be that the Naomi Story functioned as a civil rights protest in which the women of the group asserted their demands for a measure of equality presently denied them by a male dominated economic structure that sought to legitimize its privilege based upon a particular application of Torah?[80] LaCocque puts it like this: "More profoundly, the Law is no longer a means of control and power (at times of manipulation), but the instrument of peace, reconciliation, and equality."[81]

The subversive project of the Naomi Story has become subverted by book of Ruth.[82] The project or purpose of the book of Ruth is described well by LaCocque: "it is possible to perform the Torah in a creative and flexible manner, opposing the suspicious and rigid ultraconservatism of the integration party [represented by Ezra-Nehemiah]. Moab can also have a place in Israel; . . . The sexual audacity of . . . Ruth the Moabite . . . must be judged leniently."[83]

Ruth a Femme Fatale?

The Naomi Story pivots on the developing relationship between Ruth and Boaz. The characterization of Boaz as "near kinsman" (2:20) invites a consideration of the Ruth Boaz relationship within the context of the levirate custom (Deut 25:5–10) and sexual mores as expressed in Leviticus 18 and 20. On the surface it appears that the levirate custom violates the norms of Leviticus 18 and 20 and the continued childlessness of the couple in Lev 20:21 negates the very purpose of the levirate custom. Further, in Lev 20:21 "the brother / sister-in-law relationship is called נדה, a strong term used as a euphemism for the pollution generated by a menstruant. Hence, this verse can be read as a polemic against the levirate law. Nonetheless, within the

79. LaCocque, *Ruth,* 27.

80. LaCocque characterizes Ruth as "antiestablishment" (ibid.).

81. Ibid.

82. Georg Braulik considers the project of the literary version of Ruth a critique to Deuteronomy 23–25. "The Book of Ruth as Intra-Biblical Critique on the Deuteronomic Law," 18–19.

83. LaCocque, *Ruth,* 20–21.

broader biblical context levirate arrangements override the relevant incest prohibition, probably because they provide for the preservation of paternal lineage, demarcation of family property, continuation of the deceased male's memory, and social survival in general."[84] The proscriptive texts of Leviticus 18 are addressed to males and see the female as the object of the illicit act. The consent or lack of consent by the female object does not seem to figure into the regulation. In Leviticus 20 the female is presented as less passive with the female the active subject of verbs in verses 12 and 17. The various regulations concerning sexuality expressed in biblical law (Lev 18, 20) or proscribed in prophetic texts (Ezek 22) may be understood as regulating behavior to maintain social order, a male patrimony that considered female sexuality a commodity and at times dangerous.

This male bias informing sexual mores is reflected in narratives as well. Athalya Brenner suggests that perhaps a male fantasy of daughter seducing father may "partially explain the series of narratives that begins with Lot and his daughters, continues with Tamar and Judah, and culminates in Ruth and Boaz."[85] Brenner suggests, "This trend in the three-part wife-sister series, reinforces the narrative ambiguity concerning father-daughter incest: the daughter is seductive, the father innocent; the story is repeated [and enjoyed?], then softened and sublimated."[86]

Claus Westermann considers the episode of Lot's daughters within the context of narratives describing Hagar (Genesis 16), Rebekah (Genesis 17), and Tamar (Genesis 38) writing, "These acts of revolt against prevailing standards of morality and customs have always the same goal: it is a question of having one's own child and thereby assuring the women their only possible future."[87] By attaching the future well-being of the women involved to the hope of male offspring, Westermann acknowledges the dominant patrimony of the Israelite social order but, attempts to moderate that bias for a few lines later he writes that, these extraordinary actions, initiated by the female characters in the stories, show that, "women had greater importance in patriarchal times than is generally acknowledged."[88] Westermann's

84. Brenner, *The Intercourse of Knowledge*, 115–16.

85. Ibid., 102. It is interesting that in all three of these narratives, the action is initiated by the female, whereas in the legal and prophetic texts the norm is to assume male initiative.

86. Ibid., 103.

87. Westermann, *Genesis 12–36*, 315.

88. Ibid., 315.

conclusion seems unwarranted. These episodes are powerful because of their abnormality. They are unusual and deviant, not expressions of social normality.[89] It is hard to escape the conclusion that the drama of dangerous sexuality in these stories is meaningful only in a patrimonial social order. The stories do help illustrate the social meaning of male and female sexuality. Expressions of male sexuality and female sexuality help define social boundaries and networks.[90] Brenner writes, "the gendering of human sexual behaviours, be the behaviours socially acceptable or otherwise, is governed by this naturally divinely ordained male authority for the purpose of regulating societal survival, which is equated with continuity"[91] and "deviation from norms is viewed as damaging to the social texture."[92] Legislation governing sexual behavior and narratives describing sexual mores in the Hebrew Bible demonstrate, "a deep concern for patriarchal values: paternity, 'seed,' male honor and shame, male control over females, and hierarchic order."[93] Consequently, the sexual intrigue and manipulation initiated by Naomi and executed by Ruth, as a dramatic turn in the Naomi Story, functions as a subversive commentary on the generally accepted male authority and patrilineal structure of society and not just a private love affair. Naomi and Ruth, manipulate the system in order to achieve their own goals independent of social expectations.

By and large, within the Hebrew Bible men are depicted as sexually autonomous whereas females are governed by the dominant males to whom they are related.[94] Female sexual autonomy is unacceptable. Therefore, Naomi's conspiracy with Ruth, acted upon by Ruth, and told within a circle of a female audience is counter-cultural. Through the names assigned to the male characters of the episode, "Strength" or perhaps "Quick" (Boaz) and "So-and-So" (if indeed the unnamed next of kin was part of the Naomi Story) an element of sarcasm and humor is inserted into the very serious business of social subversion.[95]

---

89. Perhaps involving older goddess stories? Gunkel, *Genesis*, 197–99.

90. Brenner, *The Intercourse of Knowledge*, 151.

91. Ibid., 132.

92. Ibid., 133.

93. Ibid., 152.

94. Pressler, "Sexual Violence and Deuteronomic Law," 112.

95. Female initiated sexual deviation is woven into "the trope of 'Israel's apostasy.'" Brenner, *The Intercourse of Knowledge*, 135.

Athalya Brenner suggests a summary conclusion of female sexuality in the Hebrew Bible,

> What I am trying to point out is that, in a corpus of literature that depicts female sexual behavior as suspect at best, dangerous and destructive to the fabric of society if not tightly controlled at worst, signs of female independent behavior—be such behavior of a sexual nature or otherwise—would be branded as 'harlotry' in order to transpose such defiant phenomena decisively to the realm of the undesired and socially marginalized.[96]

> In short, HB [Hebrew Bible] males are depicted as having at least a modicum of independent, autonomous potential for social-sexual behaviours motivated by desire. HB females are reduced for the most part to biological, procreativity oriented sexual behavior—if they want their behavior to be approved of, and unless they inhabit the magical poetic garden of love (in the SoS [Song of Songs]).[97]

The threshing floor encounter is not just a matter between one woman and one man, but is surrounded by a fabric of social expectations that, in the telling of the story, appear thread worn and frayed. The Naomi Story told by and to women, turns this on its head, viewing these social expectations from a subversive point of view.

The City Gate

Act 4 of the Naomi Story provides a subversive commentary on the male use of female sexuality. Esther Fuchs has described the social assumptions so prevalent in many Hebrew Bible narratives.

> The institution of motherhood is a powerful patriarchal mechanism. Male control of female reproductive powers in conjunction with patrilocal and monogamous marriage (for the wife), secures the wife as her husband's exclusive property and ensures the continuity of his name and family possessions through patrimonial customs and patrilineal inheritance patterns. The institution of motherhood as defined by the patriarchal system guarantees that both the wife and her children will increase his property during his lifetime and perpetuate his achievements and memory after his death.[98]

96. Ibid., 151.
97. Ibid., 178.
98. Fuchs, "The Literary Characterization of Mothers," 129.

According to Fuchs, the strength of the male imposition is seen by making the women want what benefits the male. "It must be understood that by insisting on woman's unmitigated desire for children and by making sure that the female characters dramatizing this desire are either wives or widows, the biblical narrative promotes a patriarchal ideology."[99] "By projecting onto woman what man desires most, the biblical narrative creates a powerful role model for women. The image of the childless woman (barren wife or widow) who evolves from vulnerability and emptiness to security and pride by giving birth to sons offers a lesson for all women."[100]

If indeed Fuchs is correct, it is remarkable that Naomi and Ruth resist this trend. They offer a lesson for all women by their use of male desire to accomplish their own purposes. Fuchs goes on to state, "The literary constellation of male characters surrounding and determining the fate of the potential mother dramatizes the idea that woman's reproductive potential should be and can be controlled only by men."[101] Here too, the Naomi Story is subversive. While the male characters of the story believe they are controlling the sexuality of the women in the story, in reality, as the audience and the female characters of the story know, it is the women who are in control, not only of male sexuality but of the institutions governing sexuality.

Once more a description offered by Fuchs is helpful in illustrating the subversive quality of the Naomi Story,

> We must conclude that although the procreative context is the only one that allows for a direct communication between woman and Yahweh (or his messenger), and although motherhood is the most exalted female role in the biblical narrative, the biblical mother-figures attain neither the human nor the literary complexity of their male counterparts. The patriarchal framework of the biblical story prevents the mother-figure from becoming a full-fledged *human* role model, while its andocentric perspective confines her to a limited literary role, largely subordinated to the biblical male protagonists.[102]

In the Naomi Story, it is Naomi and Ruth who receive the greatest character development. Boaz never attains the complexity of the Naomi

99. Ibid., 130–31.
100. Ibid., 130.
101. Ibid., 129.
102. Ibid., 136.

character and male sexuality is for procreation, an heir for Naomi. In the Naomi Story, the female deception is designed to achieve a female benefit: security. The deception is particularly successful in that it uses the male patrilineal system and makes the male characters (including a not so subtle self-congratulatory male sexual prowess) unwitting accomplices in securing the female causes articulated by Naomi at the beginning of the story. The subversiveness of the Naomi Story is not that it challenges the male dominated system, but that it manipulates the male dominated system to achieve female goals, while allowing the male characters the delusion that they are in charge.

Muted but not Silenced

The subversive nature of the Naomi Story is illustrated by a description of the Hebrew Bible provided by Lapsley,

> The patriarchal nature of the text [Hebrew Bible] must be squarely faced by both women and men, and readers must recognize the extent to which the values and norms embedded in the Bible are distinctively masculine, although they are most often presented as universally valid. The particularity of women's lives and experience are only marginally represented in the Bible, and women are not infrequently presented as objects of male activity and as subordinate to the desires and designs of men.[103]

The Naomi Story turns this description on its head. In the Naomi Story, it is the search for family and security by the female characters that drives the plot. The male characters are supporting only, designed to either assist or frustrate the project of the women. And finally, the desires and designs propelling the story are certainly conceived by and enacted on by the female characters and significantly, validated by the climactic naming episode, again voiced by female characters, bringing the drama to a conclusion.

Naveen Rao calls the book of Ruth "an alternative scripture" that provides a "subaltern reading about the lives of the widowed, landless, migratory masses who have been conveniently avoided, disregarded and pushed into anonymity."[104] While Rao has in mind to characterize Ruth in opposition to the ethic of exclusion expressed in Ezra and Nehemiah, we

---

103. Lapsley, *Whispering the Word*, 7.

104. Rao, "The Book of Ruth as a Clandestine Scripture," 115.

agree with her sensitivity to the counter textual nature of the Naomi Story and seek to explore the muted or resistant voices still echoing in Ruth. Importantly, those voices, pushed into anonymity, have not faded altogether. There are voices that resist this bent. "Sometimes these 'voices of resistance' are muted and the reader must strain to hear them, but they are nonetheless an intricate part of the richness of the text."[105]

Lapsley is of the opinion that there are stories in the Bible (Exodus and Ruth) "where women's values surface as saving values."[106] Were these value sets intended by the authors of these texts? Lapsley writes, "We cannot know, but in the end the question is not especially relevant."[107] At this point we must disagree. In the Naomi Story, becoming the book of Ruth, we find it is possible to know and it does matter. The transformation from oral performance to written presentation and the change in value set that transformation entails is an important part of the history and character of the book of Ruth. For the Naomi Story, this transformation means taking a story, the plot of which is driven by a particular concern of women in eighth-century-BCE Judah, and changing that story into a statement about the ethnic boundaries of the post-exilic Jerusalem community. That is, the "women's values" were intentionally usurped. The social power resident in the oral performance by which a female culture reinforced the legitimacy of its own concerns, is usurped to serve other purposes. Purposes not primarily concerned with those original female values. The nature of that change, how, and why, that change took place is a very relevant step in understanding both the Naomi Story and the book of Ruth.

The subversive nature of the Naomi Story is retained but redirected in the book of Ruth. First, as a Moabite, Ruth represents a subversion of a post-exilic communal identity defined by ethnic exclusion. While Ruth's ethnicity is important in the Naomi Story, it is magnified in the book of Ruth and serves as Ruth's identifier six times (1:4, 22; 2:2, 6, 21; 4:10). Ruth is not just a foreigner, but she is a foreigner from an ethnic group, elsewhere in biblical literature, despised and refused entrance into the Israelite community.

> No Ammonite or Moabite shall be admitted to the assembly of the
> LORD. Even to the tenth generation, none of their descendants
> shall be admitted to the assembly of the LORD, because they did

105. Lapsley, *Whispering the Word*, 8.

106. Ibid., 10.

107. Ibid.

not meet you with food and water on your journey out of Egypt.
Deut 23:3–4. (NRSV)

Further, Ruth, a member of this despised ethnic group, is praised (1:8; 3:10) for her faithfulness and kindness (חסד)—a particularly important quality, used to describe fidelity to God or God's fidelity to Israel. Significantly, Ruth equals, if not exceeds, the faithfulness and kindness demonstrated by the consummate ethnic insider—Boaz (2:20). The book of Ruth, subverts this ethnic discrimination by making Ruth, the Moabitess, the provider of food for the Israelite, Naomi. Imtraud Fischer contrasts the subversive point of view in Ruth to the ethnic exclusiveness of Ezra–Nehemiah,

> Therefore the book of Ruth pleads for differentiated judging of the criterion for admission to the congregation, which also includes a differentiated view of integrating alien women by marriage. The female exegete is critical of her male colleagues who, in the books of Ezra and Nehemiah, take an altogether disapproving view of mixed marriages (Ezra 9–10; Neh. 13:23–27), with an explicit reference to the Moabite passage of Deut. 23:4–7 in Neh. 13:1–3.[108]

The book of Ruth is subversive by applying the levirate custom to Ruth, a non-Israelite.[109] The custom is enacted in an effort to preserve the name and lineage of a deceased Israelite male, who dies without offspring, by requiring the deceased male's next-of-kin to marry the widow and, hopefully, father a son in the name of the deceased male (Deut 25:5–10).[110] Commentators have understood that this is the custom behind the actions of Naomi and Ruth in both the threshing floor scene (chapter 3) and the city gate (chapter 4).[111] But the custom appears to have been subverted and subverting.

The book of Ruth refers to the levirate custom two times (1:11–13; 4:1–10). In the Naomi speech of 1:11–13 she claims that she is too old to produce more sons for her daughters-in-law. The sense is that the supposed sons would be for the benefit and security of Orpah and Ruth. In Ruth 4:1–10 the custom surfaces again, but notice, the purpose has changed.[112]

108. Fischer, "The Book of Ruth," 36–37.

109. Not all agree that the levirate custom is involved in the Naomi Story. See Sasson, *Ruth*, 126; and Gordis, "Love, Marriage, and Business in the book of Ruth," 246–52.

110. Genesis 38 and the story of Tamar (undoubtedly referenced in Ruth 4:12) is the only other biblical narrative referring to the custom.

111. LaCocque, *Ruth*, 47; Hubbard, *Ruth*, 109.

112. We include the whole passage here, although we are of the opinion that only

In 4:1–10, concern is not to produce offspring for the deceased, but to provide for Naomi. The chapter four passage is entangled with the laws of redemption (Lev 25:23–34), focusing on the field owned by Naomi. Ruth's role in chapter four is to give a future to Naomi. In fact, the offspring born to Ruth and Boaz is "a son born to Naomi." (4:17). These two laws: the levirate (Deut 25:5–10) and redeemer (Lev 25:23–24) are nowhere connected in the biblical legal codes. The Ruth author allows the character of Ruth to conflate the two legal principles in the threshing floor scene in order to motivate Boaz to marry her and so provide for Naomi's wellbeing, as well as her own. In effect, this conflation subverts the androcentric bent of the two customs.

> The halakhah, which the Torah exegete who composed the book of Ruth puts into the mouth of the exegete Ruth, aims at the secure living of women who are only granted a marginal position in a patriarchal society. The halakhah given by Ruth interprets both laws for the benefit of *women* and thus can be called 'feminist.' Ruth contradicts the androcentricity of the levirate, which does not focus on the widow but only on the deceased *husband*. She also contradicts the androcentricity of the concept of redemption that primarily deals with the man who owns land and the patriarchal family.[113]

The subversive reinterpretation of these customs favoring the female characters in the story, is reinforced through the discredited dissenting view provided by the narrow minded and self-centered Mr. So-and-So (4:5) who is not even granted a real name and who stands in contrast to the god-fearing Boaz (3:10). The elders and townspeople confirm the position taken by Ruth and so further reinforce the reinterpretation of the Torah offered by the book of Ruth.

> The author regards levirate marriage and redemption as a duty of solidarity for women, even for foreign women. In her eyes it is not a legal institution beneficial only for men, even if they are already deceased. Therefore it is not at all reasonable to assume that the author had not known the legal regulations of Deuteronomy, or that she had simply forgotten a notice of birth for Mahlon. From her viewpoint the law favors the living women, not the dead men.[114]

---

a truncated form of 4:1–10 was original to the Naomi Story. That truncated form still involved the levirate custom.

113. Fischer, "The Book of Ruth," 40–41.

114. Ibid., 41.

Subversion assumes connections to a cultural standard that is now open for question. Connections between the Naomi Story and the Torah are invited by the storyteller herself. Explicit references to Rachael, Leah, and particularly Tamar (4:11–12) invite the audience to observe the Naomi Story with the tales of these ancestresses in mind. When these connections are made, the subversiveness of the Naomi Story is expressed in reversals to the Torah stories.

1. The Naomi Story begins with a "famine in the land" (1:1). The famine is the backdrop that will eventually integrate the foreigner, Ruth, into Israel. In Genesis, famines do just the reverse. In Genesis, famines put women in danger of being integrated into the genealogy of a foreign king (Gen 12:10; 26:1).

2. In 1:14, Ruth is said to "cling" to Naomi. She leaves the "house of her mother" in order to cling to Naomi. This sounds reminiscent, but just the reverse of the action depicted in Gen 2:24 and the description of Abraham in Gen 12:1–4.

3. Although not explicit, the Naomi Story may also have made connections between Ruth and Rebecca. The blessing offered to Ruth in 2:10 brings to mind a similar blessing offered to Rebecca in Gen 24:27. In an unusual fashion, Ruth is compared to Rebecca, both of whom are said to have "seed" (זרע, often translated "offspring"; Ruth 4:12; Gen 24:60) a normally masculine attribution. Like Tamar, Ruth has integrated into the Israelite family and has become elevated to the status of Leah and Rachel.

4. A reference to Lot's daughters (Gen 19:33–35) may also have been in the mind of the Naomi Story storyteller. Lot's two daughters find themselves in a predicament similar to that engulfing Ruth and Naomi. The daughters complain that, "there is no man to come in to us . . ." (Gen 19:31). In order to secure children, they encourage their father to drink to excess and while he is intoxicated senseless, and on two consecutive nights, Lot's daughters have intercourse with their father, both becoming pregnant by him. And interestingly enough, the son born to the oldest daughter is named, Moab—the father of the Moabites (Gen 19:37). This tawdry story of the Moabite origin (and the Ammonites—springing from the child born to Lot's youngest daughter), is turned around and made part of the Israelite heritage through Ruth.

5. In 4:15, the chorus declares that Ruth is better than seven sons. It is interesting that the short genealogy of 4:17b, mentioning three generations is matched by the long genealogy of 4:18–22 with its ten generations, making Ruth indeed equal to, if not better than, seven sons.

In becoming the book of Ruth, the subversive voice of the Naomi Story has been muted, but certainly not silenced.

Where to Be Found?

It isn't enough to posit the Naomi Story as an oral substrate to the book of Ruth. As we were reminded earlier in this chapter, oral performance is conditioned by the communal interests of its attentive audience. For longetivity, the story requires audience buy in. If we are going to really understand the oral substrate, the Naomi Story, we need to discover all we can about the community in which the Naomi Story circulated. According to Polak, a simple syntactical profile, closer to oral communication, results from a culture with limited literacy. Polak concludes 1–2 Samuel reflects a popular culture where orality remained the primary vehicle for transmitting tradition.[115] Robert Miller believes there is ample evidence from the ancient Near East supporting the existence of a tradition of oral performance: "audience—speaker interaction, variety of delivery modes ("genres"), court setting, serial performance, even the harp."[116] Can all of this be applied to the Naomi Story? Is there a popular culture employing an audience / speaker interaction tradition of performance into which we may place the Naomi Story?

Dijk-Hemmes posits the story of Ruth as a product of "women's culture," a creation of an "old prophetess or wise woman."[117] The story may have been part of the "repertory of a professional female storyteller."[118] If the Naomi Story was by women and for women, what can we know about when, how, and why the story (and presumably others like it) was told? Can we reconstruct a setting that was the likely forum for the telling or performing of the Naomi Story? Was the Naomi Story one way in which a women's point of view was given voice? In our search for answers to these questions,

115. Polak, "The Oral and the Written," 59–105.

116. Miller, *Oral Tradition in Ancient Israel*, 104.

117. Van Dijk-Hemmes, "Traces of Women's Texts in the Hebrew Bible," 106.

118. Ibid., 107.

we will be mindful of cultural layers that co-exist in any given society, allowing for the expression of various emphases (sometimes conflicting) within a dominant cultural structure. E. Showalter presents a cultural model that makes accessible, "the primary cultural experience of women as expressed by themselves," distinct from "roles, activities, preferences and rules of behavior prescribed for women."[119] The cultural approach, advocated by Showalter, allows the description of the women's culture as a "muted" group the boundaries of whose culture and reality overlap the dominant (male) group.[120] The muted ("gagged" as described by Sancisi[121]) female culture shares much with the dominant male culture but resides in the background often invisible but always present as a subversive potential ready to challenge the dominate formulation of reality with a "double voice"[122] informed by both the dominant and the muted cultural groups. That muted culture is present in the Naomi Story, embodied through the "women of Bethlehem."

The Women of Bethlehem

Groups of women, sisterhoods,[123] or companionships,[124] are mentioned throughout the Hebrew Bible (Gen 34:1; Num 25:1–5; Song of Songs 2:7) and are certainly present in the Naomi Story. Ruth gleans with the other young women (2:8, 23). The women of Bethlehem greet Naomi upon her return to Bethlehem (1:19), and the "women of the neighborhood" take part in an unusual naming event (4:17). In both of the framing events (1:19 and 4:17), the women's group expresses solidarity with Naomi through naming events. The significant function of the group in naming both Naomi and Obed argues that the women are more than casual acquaintances. In 4:17 the "women of the neighborhood" speak with one unified voice just as the "women of the neighborhood" acted in unison in Exod 3:22 (the only other occurrence of שכנות in the Hebrew Bible) and gave their valuables in response to the request made by the Israelite women.

---

119. Showalter, "Feminist Criticism in the Wilderness," 260.

120. Van Dijk-Hemmes "Traces of Women's Texts in the Hebrew Bible," 26; see also Ardener, *Perceiving Women*, xi–xii.

121. Sancisi-Weerdenburg, "Vrouwen in verborgen werelden," 18.

122. Showalter, "Feminist Criticism in the Wilderness," 266.

123. Kalmanofsky, *Dangerous Sisters of the Hebrew Bible*, 119–20.

124. Bledstein, imagines Tamar, daughter of David, as the genius behind the story. Bledstein, "Female Companionship," 132–33.

Even as the threshing floor (3:14) and perhaps the city gate (4:2) in the Naomi Story seems to be a "man's world," it isn't hard to imagine a similar setting where women gathered to grind grain, bake, weave, and care for children.[125] Or, in the case of the Naomi Story, greet newcomers (1:19) and welcome newborns (4:17). The skills necessary for all these activities and social engagements would be passed from one to another as would the news and gossip of the day, filtered by the common interests and point of view shared by the group. Carol Meyers comments, "Women's informal alliances, designated Women's networks, are not some hypothetical web. . .Such networks function in two domains: first, they link women (and thus their families) to other communities; and second they provide connections among women (and their families) in neighboring households in the same community."[126] The informal association[127] would easily give recognition to those more skilled in a particular craft, body of knowledge, or ability to tell a good story.[128] A wise woman[129] (Judg 5:29; 2 Sam 14:2; 20:16) could well have developed the Naomi Story as part of a "repertory of a professional female storyteller."[130] The most popular stories would be those that easily communicated common concerns of members of the group[131] and, to the degree that male dominated structures were perceived as the source of those concerns, a critique of those male structures.[132] And so it isn't hard to imagine the growing popularity of the Naomi Story. We find in the Naomi Story a subversive potential that, in its irony and sarcasm, offered ready challenge to the dominant patrilineal group in which the dilemma of the story (finding security in the house of a husband) was cast.

125. Meyers, "Family in Early Israel," 25–27. See also Meyers, "Households and Holiness," 16. A case can be made for understanding the בית אם ("house of the mother") as an example of the "woman's world" or at least a social institution viewed from a woman's point of view (Gen 24:28; Ruth 1:8; Song of Songs 3:4).

126. Meyers, "Everyday Life in Biblical Israel," 191.

127. Meyers, "Households and Holiness," 67–68.

128. Meyers, "Everyday Life in Biblical Israel," 201

129. Van Dijk-Hemmes, "Traces of Women's Texts in the Hebrew Bible," 106.

130. Ibid., 107.

131. Childbirth and rearing, the security of the family, would be prominent among those shared concerns. See Meyers, "Households and Holiness," 16.

132. Bow, "Sisterhood?," 205–6.

Conclusion: Subverting Subversion

The Naomi Story may have been too powerful a story to leave in the hands of the subversives. The Naomi Story has been subverted and co-opted into a literary construct with a quite different social function. The, most likely, female performer was replaced by a male scribe.[133] The female audience has given way to a literary elite, interestingly enough personified, in at least the opinion of one commentator, by a male character: Boaz.[134] And the definition of reality from a female perspective, illustrated well by the women's blessing of 4:14–17a, is, by the addition of 4:17b–22, remade into an apologetic for David and a male dominated system of social power.[135]

In some ways, by means of the literary remake of the story, the powerful and subversive Naomi Story has been absorbed into the male dominated power structures and transformed into a safe and respectable love story that lacks much of its original subversive power. But the nullification of the subversion could not be total. "But women as storytellers are now, I believe, as firmly entrenched in the social landscape of ancient Israel as are women singers of victory songs. Whether a male scribe, in recording the story, could silence the woman's voice in making the transition I seriously doubt."[136]

So, why attach the genealogy of Israel's most famous king to this particular story? Why did the literary author choose Ruth by which to make his point? The genealogy is attached to Ruth because the subversive character of Ruth is useful in presenting, in a positive manner, the subversive nature of the Davidic phenomenon. The glorious reputation of David is subversively applied to argue against an ultra-orthodox application of Torah that serves an exclusive power base illustrated in the marriage constraints of Ezra–Nehemiah. LaCocque recognizes that this application of Ruth to the

133. Lim argues that the literary voice of Ruth is mixed, masculine and feminine and that, "in its final form, the book of Ruth represents a thoroughly male perspective." Lim, "The Book of Ruth and its Literary Voice," 268, 282.

134. LaCocque, *Ruth*, 32.

135. Siquans considers the book of Ruth "written deliberately against a certain interpretation of Deuteronomy that can be found especially in the books of Ezra and Nehemiah." Siquans, "Foreignness and Poverty in the Book of Ruth: a Legal Way for a Poor Foreign Woman to Be Integrated into Israel," 445. But see LaCocque who considers the genealogy an integral part of the book. LaCocque, *Ruth*, 13, but concedes the genealogy does reflect "contemporary structures of power" *Ruth*, 11; i.e., a male dominated social power structure. Also Nielsen, *Ruth: A Commentary*, 4–5.

136. Campbell, "Ruth Revisited," 72–73.

service of the more famous David robs the "heroine of her due" but is not the result of "conscious chauvinism."[137] Conscious or not, the effect is the same. The reapplication of the Naomi Story, taking it from the world of Israelite women and placing it in the male dominated halls of social power, subverts the subversion of Naomi, but not completely and in the end it is the performative subversion that gives power to the story. The "chorus of women's voices"[138] can still be heard.

137. LaCocque, *Ruth*, 14.
138. Van Dijk-Hemmes, *On Gendering Texts*, 109.

3

The Naomi Story: A Performance Analysis

When the Naomi Story became the book of Ruth, the story changed. The purpose of the story changed. The nature of the story's popularity, the manner in which the story was told, and the audience for whom the story was meaningful, all changed. In short, the cultural place of the story changed. To fully understand and appreciate the performance of the Naomi Story, we need to appreciate the way performance serves cultural needs and helps to form a sense of communal identity. Performance can express and reinforce, as well as challenge, the inter-relational networks that weave the fabric of the community.

Cultural Memory

Our interest in the performance of the Naomi Story recognizes the important role that performance plays in cultural memory. Werner Kelber suggests that performance operates within the realm of cultural memory by recalling images of the past so as to transport them into the present (a preservative function) and to reconstruct those images of the past so as to integrate them into the present (an integrative function).[1] According to Kelber, memory "selects and modifies subjects and figures of the past in order to make them serviceable to the image the community wishes to cultivate of

1. Kelber, "The Case of the Gospels," 61.

itself."[2] Implicit in the suggestion of a performed Naomi Story and a written book of Ruth is the recognition of two separate (although perhaps overlapping) communities or sets of communal interests; one appropriate to the oral version and one appropriate to the written version. With each version, the images of the past are made serviceable to different communities or interests. The preservation and integration appropriate to the audience of the oral Naomi Story was not the same as that of the written book of Ruth and it is not at all correct to think that the story told about Naomi was simply transferred to a new medium and became the same story only now preserved in written form, titled Ruth. Something quite different is at work.

A Performance Tradition

How specific can we be in describing the oral performance if the written version of Ruth is not a simple medium transfer of that performance?[3] In answer to this question, let's first consider exactly what we intend to reconstruct. We cannot reconstruct an "original" performance but, a performance tradition. Each oral performance is a work in and of itself and becomes what Werner Kelber calls "equiprimordial" to all other oral performances.[4] Edward Campbell, also sensitive to the changes that may arise during the performance (perhaps singing) of the story, wrote, "Therefore while each performance was something new, a new creation, it was the same story."[5] That is, in one sense, there is no original performance from which all others derive but each performance is equiprimordial, original, in its own right. Therefore, if the book of Ruth is based upon the oral performance of the Naomi Story it is based upon a tradition of performance. We, therefore, cannot reconstruct the "original" Naomi Story but can in broad terms propose a reconstruction of an oral tradition upon which the literate version was based. Consequently, disagreement should be expected over some of the details of the performance tradition. Admittedly, any proposed reconstruction that we offer is hypothetical and can, at best, hope for plausibility

2. Ibid., 56.

3. Robert Miller suggests that some of the aspects of that performance event include: "audience–speaker interaction, variety of delivery modes ('genres'), court setting, serial performance, even the harp." Miller, *Oral Tradition in Ancient Israel*, 104.

4. Kelber, "In the Beginning Were the Words," 74.

5. Campbell, *Ruth*, 19. Susan Niditch is not convinced by either Campbell or a writer influential for Campbell: Lord, *The Singer of Tales*. Niditch, "Legends of the Wise and Heroines," 455–56.

approaching probability. Yet, we are willing to go further than others in postulating a performance. Nehama Aschkenasy, while offering an analysis of Ruth as comedic and carnavelesque, cautions, "I do not suggest that the Ruth narrator was in any way acquainted with the genre of comedy as practiced by the Greeks, nor do I propose that the narrator had in mind a stage production when composing the tale."[6] While Aschkenasy is undoubtedly correct in questioning any acquaintance with Greek genres, or that the Naomi storyteller envisioned a full scale theatrical production complete with staging, props, and costume, performance should not be limited to the stage and the analytical constructs of performance can usefully be applied to the Naomi Story without necessitating a stage production.

Further, the speculative nature of our reconstruction should not, in and of itself, dissuade us. There are ample precedents showing hypothetical reconstructions have been used with rich results. Perhaps best known is the reconstruction of Q by New Testament scholars. In fact, a recent comment on Q reconstruction suggests fascinating parallels with Ruth.

> Finally, recent scholarship on Christian origins has emphasized that the culture of the eastern Mediterranean was oral-scribal. Reading literacy was very low, which meant that most of the early Jesus people heard stories and sayings performed orally. Texts were composed by those few competent to write, but texts such as Q were composed to function more like a musical script for performance than a textbook to be read.[7]

Much like Q is conceptualized in the quote above, we seek to identify and describe the oral substrate of a performance tradition as it is now expressed in the book of Ruth. In attempting to reconstruct the performance tradition, we must recognize that the oral medium presents differently than the written medium. But, having said this, we are not without direction as to what that oral performance must have looked like.

We began this chapter with assistance from Werner Kelber. Once again, Kelber may offer help. In his investigation of the New Testament gospels, and the oral performances that preceded and co-existed for a time with the written pieces, Kelber has identified several characteristics of oral performance the remnants of which may yet appear in texts built upon

---

6. Aschkenasy, "From Aristotle to Bakhtin," 280.

7. Kloppenborg, Q: the Earliest Gospel, 35.

those oral substrates.[8] Several of his characteristics seem to be especially applicable to the Naomi Story.

- Scenic duality—a concentration on two characters at a time in the developing plot

- Focusing on individuals rather than general conditions

- Dialogues have give and take—antagonistic back and forth that makes the dialogue more unusual over the routine of everyday

These characteristics are certainly present in the book of Ruth, and more so in the Story of Naomi. These three characteristics will help us to frame the performance tradition we seek to identify and describe. How does the Naomi Story focus the audience's attention on the individuals involved, generally two characters at time, and in a fashion that emphasizes dialogue in moving the story forward?

The Naomi Story "Script"

The book of Ruth has the highest ratio of dialogue to narrative of any biblical book.[9] Fifty five of the eighty five verses in the book are dialogue (64%).[10] Expressed differently, the majority of the book of Ruth is discourse appearing in a narrative context. This discourse deserves particular attention.[11] Polak describes written discourse as "formal and planned."[12] Spoken discourse, on the other hand is "less formal than written language, and is often casual, in particular when used in the intimacy of the household and in a circle of friends and acquaintances (the conversational mood). In spoken discourse one meets more paratactic constructions, most sentences contain

8. Kelber, *The Oral and the Written Gospel,* 51–54.

9. Sasson, "Ruth," 320.

10. The dialogue percentage goes even higher if the genealogy at the end of chapter 4 is removed or if it is considered one syntactical unit instead of 4 verses (up to 68% dialogue). Timothy Lim calculates 69% dialogue in Ruth. Lim, "The Book of Ruth and its Literary Voice," 270. This compares with 42.71% dialogue in the Genesis narrative as determined by Radday and Shore, *Genesis: An Authorship Study,* 24–25. Arian Verheij reports 43.33% dialogue in the Samuel narrative, 34% dialogue in the narrative of 1–2 Kings and 21% dialogue in 1–2 Chronicles. Verheij, *Verbs and Numbers,* 32–36.

11. Discussions on the function of narrated dialogue in biblical texts can be found in: Bar-Efrat, *Narrative Art in the Bible*; Sternberg, *The Poetics of Biblical Narrative*; Savran, *Telling and Retelling*; Nieholl, "Do Biblical Characters Talk to Themselves?," 577–92; Polak, "Forms of Talk in Hebrew Biblical Narrative," 167–98.

12. Polak, "The Style of the Dialogue in Biblical Prose Narrative," 57.

fewer constituents, long noun phrases are rare, while reference by means of deictic particles and pronouns is frequent."[13] "It appears that this great variety in style is related to the nature of oral narrative and the special gifts and techniques developed by the storytellers over the generations. In oral narrative quoted discourse is an essential element . . . *Anthropologists who study these phenomena in their proper setting often highlight the theatrical talents of the oral narrator, who turns a character's discourse into an actor's performance, and the narrative, at least partly, into a play on stage.*" [italics added].[14] This idea of the oral narrator who turns the character's discourse into an actor's performance guides our construction of the Narrator/Storyteller in the script found in Chapter 6, the Performance Notes.

The dialogue in the book of Ruth is ideally suited to a storyteller's rendition of the Naomi Story. If the present book of Ruth includes compositions of written dialogue, previously performed by live actors engaged in conversation before live audiences, insights drawn from conversation analysis[15] and performance criticism will enrich our understanding of the written composition and the oral substrate from which the written composition was framed.

Conversation Analysis

Written discourse and spoken discourse tend to different syntactical constructions. Consequently, even if now reported in narrative, originally spoken discourse should display at least some of those syntactical particulars. In comparison to spoken discourse, Polak describes written discourse as tending to more complicated syntactic constructions:[16]

13. Ibid., 59.

14. Ibid., 94.

15. Conversation Analysis is an approach to the investigation of social interaction developed first by Harvey Sacks and his colleagues, Emmanuel Schegloff and Gail Jefferson. See Sacks, Schegloff, et al., "A Simplest Systematics for the Organization of Turn-Taking in Conversation," *Language*, 696–735 and Sacks, *Lectures on Conversation*. Insights from the discipline were applied usefully to the book of Jonah with an introduction to the literature of the discipline by Person, *In Conversation with Jonah*. An example of the application of the discipline to biblical dialogue is also found in Miller, *The Representation of Speech*; and Miller, "Silence as a Response," 23–43. A concise presentation of Conversation Analysis is found in Polak, "Negotiations, Social Drama and Voices of Memory in Some Samuel Tales," 49–50. See also, Hutchby and Wooffitt, *Conversation Analysis*; Drew, "Conversation Analysis," 71–102.

16. Polak, "The Style of the Dialogue in Biblical Prose Narrative," 57.

THE NAOMI STORY: A PERFORMANCE ANALYSIS

- More constituents

- Subordinated clauses

- Long noun phrases

- More nominal elements

Polak maintains that this style of narrated discourse appears in biblical texts from the Persian period and the end of the exilic period (Ezra, Esther, Daniel, 1–2 Chronicles) and slightly less so in texts from the exilic period (the prose narratives in Jeremiah) or the century preceding the exile (the Deuteronomistic history of the Judean kings in 2 Kings 11–22).[17]

In comparison, Polak characterizes spoken discourse as:[18]

- Less formal than written discourse

- Often casual (often signified by the presence of pronominals and deictics)

- Contains more paratactic constructions

- Sentences with fewer constituents

- Long noun phrases are rare

These characteristics are found in the quoted discourse of parts of Genesis (26:27; 42:2) and Samuel (1 Sam 10:14-16; 19:17)[19] and dominates in at least the first three chapters of the Book of Ruth.

Polak's analysis of dialogue in biblical narrative uses the characteristics of spoken discourse as a point of comparison to the written discourse.[20] We suggest that an intermediary step is required for analyzing the dialogue of Ruth.[21] The constructed, narrated dialogue in Ruth is reflective of a constructed, performed dialogue which, in turn, is reflective of normal conversation.

J. Maxwell Atkinson has pointed out that "an adequate understanding of how texts are produced and responded to may remain elusive so long as the issue is pursued without making close comparative reference to how

17. Ibid., 58–59.

18. Ibid., 59.

19. Ibid., 60–61.

20. Ibid., 57–58.

21. Polak seems to consider the possibility of performance characteristics in the narrated dialogue, but does not pursue this stage of development. Ibid., 94.

talk works."[22] That is, reported dialogues in written narrative bear some similarity or intentional dissimilarity to ordinary, everyday conversation.[23] In applying Atkinson's observation to the book of Ruth, we add that it is equally important to reference the formalized manner in which performance utilizes normal and ordinary talk. The constructed speech[24] now forming dialogues within the Ruth narrative was formed from performed speech presented as ordinary, everyday talk by actors before an audience that intuitively understood the artificially constructed nature of the dialogue they were witnessing. So, in Ruth, we have a twofold movement from ordinary conversation to performed conversation to narrated conversation.

Normal Conversation —> Performed Conversation —> Narrated Conversation

With only three exceptions (2:15; 4:4; 4:17)[25], all the dialogue in the book of Ruth is presented as direct speech representing exact quotations.[26] That is, the dialogue in Ruth invites a comparison to normal conversation.

Adjacency Pairs: Round, Exchange, Turn

The direct speech in the book of Ruth fits Cynthia Miller's description of "interactive reported speech"[27] and is easily configured into the script of a performance. Narrated conversation is fundamentally structured in terms of "contiguous, alternating turns of talk, known as 'adjacency pairs.'"[28] Adjacency pairs are broadly categorized into two groups: those with *Preferred Responses* or those with *Dispreferred Responses*.

> Preferred Response: The actions accepted or enacted in the second part of the adjacency pair are encouraged in the first part (*Request*

22. Atkinson "Two Devices for Generating Audience Approval," 230.

23. Dialogue appearing in narrative can be of several varieties: reported speech, represented speech, constructed speech, or narrated conversation. Miller, *The Representation of Speech in Biblical Hebrew Narrative*, 49, 50, 339–400. Polak, "Negotiations, Social Drama and Voices," 49–50. Person, *In Conversation with Jonah*, 28.

24. Ibid., 23.

25. 3:14 is often translated as indirect reported speech, but we will make the argument in six that it is in fact direct quoted speech, directed to the audience.

26. Cynthia Miller notes that direct speech is the "preeminent strategy for representing speech in the Bible." Miller, *The Representation of Speech in Biblical Hebrew Narrative*, 143.

27. Ibid., 235.

28. Ibid., 235.

/ *Acceptance*). Preferred second parts are generally brief utterances given without delay and are unmitigated.[29]

Dispreferred Response: The actions accepted or enacted in the second part of the adjacency pair are discouraged in the first part (*Request / Refusal*). The refusal can take a variety of forms in the response: delay, counterproposal, explanation of the dispreferred response, declination, and, at times, silence.[30]

The movement of plot or character development, through dialogue, can be observed in the progression of adjacency pairs. In conversation analysis,[31] adjacency pairs are grouped into expanding categories that carry the movement and development of plot or character. We will use the following designations:

- Round—an adjacency pair composed of speaker and response
- Exchange—a series of rounds
- Turn—the movement of plot or development of character evident in a series of exchanges

The direct dialogue serves the narrator by providing information advancing character development or plot to which the dialogue is linked even while the conversation partners advance their own exchange (question—answer). Sometimes the Request (A) or Response (B) of the adjacency pair includes informational elements not referred to or required by the other member of the pair, but is useful for the development of the character, plot, or project of the narrator. In this case, we may conclude that the audience is the addressee and it is for the audience's benefit that new informational items are introduced. The round of Ruth 1:8–10 provides a clear example.

The speech A of the round (Naomi's speech of 1:8–9) contains three distinct bits of information:

1. Go back each of you to your mother's house.
2. May the LORD deal kindly with you, as you have dealt with the dead and with me.

---

29. Person, *In Conversation with Jonah*, 17.

30. Miller, "Silence as a Response," 40–41.

31. A helpful introduction can be found in Sidnell, *Conversation Analysis*. See also, Polak, "Speaker, Addressee, and Positioning," 359.

3. The LORD grant that you may find security, each of you in the house of your husband.

The response B (response by Orpah and Ruth of 1:10) addresses only the first informational element:

1. No, we will return with you to your people

Information elements 2 and 3 from A are superfluous to the dialogue exchange between Naomi, Orpah, and Ruth. It may be concluded that information elements 2 and 3 of A, while in the performance addressed to Orpah and Ruth, are, in fact, directed to the audience. Informational elements 2 and 3 explain the rationale for information element 1 and articulate the project that will guide the development of the plot within the performance.[32] In this round, the dispreferred response B addresses the action requested in A (return) while remaining silent regarding the supporting rationale of request A (The LORD grant that you may find a home, each of you in the house of her husband). The dispreferred response B explicitly denies the first part of the request, and implicitly casts doubt on the viability of the second (the LORD deal kindly) and third (find a home in the house of a husband) part of request A. In this manner the cultural norm of female security obtained through attachment to a male household is highlighted as the project for the following drama. The degree to which the dialogue advances the linked context of the narrative, instead of the adjacency exchange between the dialogue partners, varies and is an important device for including the audience in the dialogue.

The second adjacency pair illustrates another manner in which the dialogue and the narrative can be linked. This round forms a Preferred Response but uses verbal silence and narrated action to form the response.

Round 2: Ruth 1:11–14

A. Turn back, my daughters, why will you go with me? Have I yet sons in my womb that they may become your husbands? Turn back, my daughters, go your way, for I am too old to have a husband. If I should say I have hope, even if I should have a husband this night and should bear sons, would you wait till they were grown? Would you therefore refrain from marrying? No, my daughters, for it is exceedingly bitter to me for your sake that the hand of the LORD has gone forth against me.

B. Silence: Implied Acceptance.

32. See also the discussion in Sternberg, *The Poetics of Biblical Narrative*, 688.

The response to the Invitation of A is supplied by a narration, not a speech. Given the extended and expositional style of the surrounding dialogue, the silence of this response is just as powerful as it is unusual.[33] Orpah's weeping, kiss, and return implies an explicit Preferred Response to Request A and an implicit Preferred Response to the rationale for the invitation of Request A (homelessness: the result of no male offspring from Naomi, a sign that the hand of the LORD is against Naomi). For the audience, no less than for the characters of the drama, a silent acquiescence to the desperate plight of a homeless, unattached female, occasions weeping and resignation.

But the silent resignation of Preferred Response B forms a backdrop to the explicit challenge to the social status quo in the third Adjacency Pair: Ruth 1:15–17.

Round 3: Ruth 1:15–17

Request A^1. See, your sister-in-law has gone back to her people and to her gods; return after your sister-in-law.

Dispreferred Response B^1. Entreat me not to leave you or to return from following you; for where you go I will go, and where you spend the night I will spend the night; your people shall be my people, and your God my God; where you die I will die, and there will I be buried. May the LORD do so to me and more also if even death parts me from you.

Dispreferred response B^1 selectively and incompletely responds to the invitation of A^1. The explicit refusal to "return" implicitly casts doubt on the validity of the premise informing the remainder of the invitation: that security is found in the house of a husband, a child of Naomi. The incomplete manner in which B and B^1 respond to A and A^1 allows the constructed conversation to illuminate the premises and social arrangements that function as the basis for the preferred action. The dialogue is constructed not to effect a desired action (returning) but to bring attention to and so make available for examination a cultural assumption (find a home, each

---

33. According to Ch. Rabin, quoted discourse in biblical narrative tends to use shorter clauses than the surrounding prose, reflecting perhaps "the brevity of most of the turns of human speech" composed of "sentences which tend to be short, with few subordinate clauses, and therefore also comparatively few conjunctions. The rhythm of human speech is staccato while that of biblical narrative is flowing." Rabin, "Linguistic Aspects," apud Polak, "The Style of the Dialogue in Biblical Prose Narrative," 54. This observation by Rabin is certainly contradicted by the dialogue narrated in Ruth and Polak demonstrates that Rabin's generalization is only valid for "(a) casual discourse, or (b) late pre-exilic and (post)-exilic narrative." Polak, "The Style of the Dialogue in Biblical Prose Narrative," 54.

of you in the house of her husband) that functioned as the rationale for the preferred action.

In these first three adjacency pairs in the book of Ruth, it becomes apparent that the dialogue is not ordinary, everyday conversation designed to effect the preferred social contract (return of the daughters-in-law to a male household).[34] Instead, the adjacency pairs are "constructed" both through the reported speech, but also through the edited silence of Preferred Response B to draw the audience's (whether readers or listeners) attention to selected cultural norms judged by the narrator or performer to be worthy of examination. The turn, or movement of plot, evident in this first exchange focuses the audiences' attention on the social conventions helping to create the plight of the characters.

The Performance Event

Understanding how the "script" and dialogue function in oral performance is only one step in investigating the performance of the Naomi Story. Performance involves a whole set of dynamics that come to life in the interaction between drama, actor, and audience. In the remainder of this chapter we consider some of those dynamics especially pertinent to the Naomi Story.[35] These concepts often have an analogous relationship to commonly used literary terms, such as plot, action, conflict, etc., but are specifically aimed at what happens off the page, when the story is enacted in some fashion.

Iconic and Dialectic Presentation

A performance, "gives us something and nothing to respond to."[36] The *something* a performance offers can be referred to as the iconic element of the performance: "the element offered to us for display."[37] Sound, color, movement; all of these are iconic elements heightened by the very fact that they are on display for spectators. *Iconic modes of presentation*, such as parades, political rallies, and other celebrator rituals present and celebrate

---

34. See however, Polak, "On Dialogue and Speaker Status in the Scroll of Ruth," 196–218; Polak, "On Speaker Status and Dialogue in Biblical Narrative: Part 1," 98–119.

35. David Rhoads has provided a helpful introduction to a number of performance dynamics. Rhoads, "Biblical Performance Criticism: Performance as Research," 165.

36. Bernard, *Theatrical Presentation*, 73.

37. Ibid.

what is, the status quo, a moment frozen in time that celebrates identity. The Naomi Story is an iconic presentation that was first embodied in the storyteller's movements, tonal qualities, and emotions, all of which formed the "something" that became borrowed by the biblical scribe.

The *nothing* offered by the performance is the dialectic element. This *nothing* is "the air that crackles from the interchange between one actor and another, between one moment and another."[38] It is the interplay between the place of presentation, the presenters, and the spectators. It is a give-and-take that requires both the actor and the spectator as participants. It can well be characterized as a 'nothing" for this aspect of performance gives nothing but instead calls out from the spectator a powerful response essential for the creation of the imagined reality of the performance. The sensory response to the iconic, that which can be seen and heard, expands into the imaginative response to the dialectic, that which is created when the storyteller/actor assumes the life of the character and the audience engages in the imaginative interplay along with the actor, particularly when characters engage in conflict and rising and falling tension, pulling spectators into the emotional and psychological world of their action. *Dialectic Modes of presentation* stress becoming and change. The storyteller must expertly blend the iconic and dialectic elements of the Naomi Story into her performance. In the Performance Notes of chapter six, these concepts are what inform the stage directions and explanations of the storyteller's behaviors.

The balance between iconic elements and dialectic elements determines the mode of presentation. The *something* and *nothing* offered to us by Naomi's storyteller pulls the listeners into the story. She relies on her knowledge that the spectators are not merely a group of individuals, but a community—a "we" with a shared identity. A relationship between the storyteller/actor, the characters of the story, and the audience emerges as a kind of feedback loop that relies on the shared knowledge of the story and its subversive qualities.

Audience

An oral performance of the Naomi Story presupposes an audience interaction.[39] On at least three, if not four, occasions, that implicit audience comes

---

38. Ibid., 74.

39. Although he doesn't extend the description to a performance analysis, André LaCocque writes; "I am convinced that Ruth is a brilliant polemical performance under

close to the surface in the literary version of the story. As already noted, the audience becomes explicitly present in at least: 2:1, 3:14, 4:7 (if indeed 4:7 was authentic to the Naomi Story), and 4:12.The interaction with the audience is just as significant as the interaction between actor, character, and drama. Two important performance concepts from theatre help to clarify the role of the audience in the Naomi Story.

Actor—Character—Audience

The actor-character-audience relationship we encounter in the story of Naomi is primarily characterized by direct presentation, or presentation where the performer acknowledges the presence of the audience and makes that acknowledgement explicit.[40] In many of the scenes, the actor-character-audience relationship goes beyond the recognition of the audience's presence, and extends to audience participation. This kind of direct presentation is an open form of exchange where the audience accepts the double nature of the presentation, knowing that the storyteller/actor is not the character, yet willfully and willingly suspending disbelief in order to facilitate entrance into the relationship being offered to the audience through the character. In this way, the audience and character are given entrance into an imagined reality that can powerfully impact the nature of the audience even after the performance is complete.

The character and the character's actions form the site where the storyteller/actor and spectator meet. The interplay of these two phenomena creates an imaginative space where the spectators share beliefs, values, and feelings of belonging. Whether it is the storyteller taking us into the fields of Moab, the gates of Bethlehem, or the threshing floor itself, these spaces, with their connection to reality, are where cultural memory is celebrated and where a group identity is established, sustained, and transmitted.

Audience Identity

It is important to remember that performance is used to *reconstruct* the past in such a way as to assist in forming or sustaining a *concrete social identity* for its spectators, with the goal of creating a commitment or *obligation* to a

---

the guise of an antique and innocuous tale." LaCocque, *The Feminine Unconventional,* 84–85.

40. Ibid., 11.

specific ideal, value, or belief. Just as in the theatre and drama, a common ground (shared values) is established between presenter, presentation, and spectators in what is known as the communal audience, the Naomi Story seeks to promote an audience identity in which the values, language, and thoughts of all involved are as identical as possible. And this identity is an intentional project of the Naomi storyteller. The storyteller wants to help shape the audience; to create values and priorities, to help spectators think of themselves in a specific fashion.

Active Audience

The movement that occurs when a performance changes a passive audience into active participants is a critical aspect of the storyteller—spectator relationship in the Naomi Story. The storyteller assumes she is performing for a communal audience, i.e., a group of "people whose total social experience is at one with each other and the presenters."[41] "In the fully formed communal audience, the values, language, and thoughts of all involved in the theatrical experience are identical, or as close to identical as possible. This kind of community makes multiple communication possible. A common ground must be established between presenter, presentation, and spectator."[42]

The common ground between storyteller and audience, materials, history, and memory of the story, creates this active, communal relationship between the two. The spectator is engaged on multiple levels; indeed is required to be engaged. As Marco De Marinis suggests about the process of spectatorship, "there is no doubt that the sensory faculties of the perceiving subject are called upon to sustain an effort, to which, for both quantity and quality, there is no equivalent in any other artistic field."[43] At the very core of drama (as it occurs, or happens, for an audience) there is a continuous give-and-take, or interplay between audience and presentation that can occur along a spectrum from the emotional and intellectual to full participation. "Initially, the give-and-take occurs between the physical activity of presentation and the sensitized organs of perception in an audience. Gradually the sensory response expands into the imaginative. Entertainment is thus a precondition to other specific responses. Something must be held between

---

41. Beckerman, *Dynamics of Drama,* 135.

42. Doan and Giles, *Prophets, Performance and Power,* 101.

43. De Marinis, "Dramaturgy of the Spectator," 107.

the presenter and the receiver. Such and such an action, being entertained, should effect entertainment in the audience."[44]

This is precisely what Michael Goldman refers to as the important connections between drama and life and those features of life "we're likely to regard as intensely difficult, issues that bear on self and meaning, on persons and texts, on identity and community,"[45] leading to our active participation. In the telling of the Naomi Story, the storyteller and audience are merged in an imaginative space that accommodates life and drama in a deeply meaningful experience. The creation of an active audience, a situation in which the storyteller's listeners are drawn into the story, is enhanced if the audience is already familiar with the story. We know this is the case with our Naomi storyteller and the audience she gathers to hear the story. Our storyteller relies on having what is known as a closed audience, which makes it possible for her to use performance choices (iconic and dialectic modes of presentation) that are tailored to her audience.

The Closed Audience

"Closed performances anticipate a very precise receiver and demand well-defined types of 'competence' (encyclopedic, ideological, etc.) for their "correct" reception. This is mostly the case with certain forms of genre-based theatre: political theatre, children's theatre, women's theatre, gay theatre, street theatre, musicals, dance theatre, mime, and so on. In these cases, of course, the performance only 'comes off' to the extent that the real audience corresponds to the anticipated one, thus reacting to the performance in the desired way."[46] As you will see in our script for the telling of the Naomi Story in chapter 6, we assume a closed audience with precisely the kind of competence our storyteller requires. The closed audience, or audience-in-the-know is essential to the storyteller's ability to work in short hand, or to use gestures and expressions that are immediately recognizable to the audience. Closed audiences facilitate an ironic exchange between the storyteller and the spectators.

---

44. Beckerman, *Dynamics of Drama,* 145.

45. Goldman, *On Drama,* 6–7.

46. De Marinis and Dwyer. "Dramaturgy of the Spectator," 100–114.

The "Project" of the Naomi Story

The project of a performance is a combination of the character's intention and motivation. More than simply what a character wants, however, the project also includes the ways in which a character seeks to achieve desired goals.[47] The project of the Naomi Story is clearly presented, through Naomi, in 1:9: "The LORD grant that you may find security, each of you in the house of your husband."

Finding security in the house of a husband will dominate the remainder of the performance, and gives structure to the resolution of the performance in 4:14–17a.[48] Tension is created as the project moves through unanticipated and unconventional means in pursuit of resolution. And this tension is what provides a sense of the subversive to the performance. Security will be found—and it will be found in the house of a husband. But the manner in which that security becomes realized gives the lie to the notion of patriarchal power for it is through the subversive planning of Naomi and Ruth that Boaz becomes the source of security, totally unaware that his actions were anticipated and connived.[49] Woven into this project is a question of identity. In finding security in the house of a husband, Naomi and Ruth must each assume an identity—identities that in some ways function as archetypes for all women (see 1:6; 3:14). The question of identity and who has the ability to create identity, is brought to the attention of the audience repeatedly through dialogue and naming episodes (1:19–21; 2:5; 3:9, 16; 4:17).

The project of the Naomi Story sets the trajectory of the story and is worded so as to make the conclusion quite surprising. The security wished for by Naomi will be found in the house of a husband. This reference is quite normal and consistent with the frequently found "father's house," a name given to the common nuclear social unit dominated by a male and governed by male concerns. Yet, in the Naomi Story, this project has a subversive undertone to it, for it is preceded in 1:8 by Naomi's directive to her daughters-in-law that they return to the "house of their mothers."

---

47. Beckerman, *Dynamics of Drama*, 70.
48. Doob Sakenfeld, "The Story of Ruth," 225–26.
49. See also Williams, *Women Recounted*, 84.

Precipitating Context: 1:1–6

The Naomi Story begins in the fields of Moab. Later in the Story (4:11–12), the storyteller invites connections to other biblical narratives and we can assume that the same invitation is present here in the precipitating context of the Story. The precipitating context generally includes background information that is either found in other scenes or parts of the story, or is part of shared information from legend, myth, and other socially and culturally shared information.[50] And in the case of the Naomi Story, Moab is more than a location east of Judah. The primogenitor of Moab was conceived in incest (Gen 19:36–37), the women of Moab were remembered as seductresses (Num 25:1–4), and Moabites were forbidden entry to the assembly of YHWH (Deut 23:2–4).[51] Moab is a place of dangerous sexual seduction and Ruth personifies that threat. How would this precipitating context be received by a female audience? The connection between the memory of Moabite seduction and the seduction that will unfold on the threshing floor seems more than accidental.

The significance of the place of the precipitating context is reinforced by the significant places throughout the remainder of the story. Naomi left Bethlehem (*house* of bread), traveling to the *fields* of Moab in order to escape a famine. The men of her family meet tragedy in the fields of Moab and Naomi is forced to return to Bethlehem with a Moabite girl. Naomi will be provided food from the *fields* of Bethlehem through the agency of Ruth the Moabitess (2:2). Finally, a resolution to the problem of the Story's project is achieved on the *threshing floor*—a liminal spot that is neither *house* nor *field*—a transitional place—used only rarely and, by its very nature, presupposes movement from somewhere (field) to somewhere (house *with* bread). By Boaz's own admission (3:14), the threshing floor was not a place for women, or at least only for women selling their sexuality (Hosea 9:1). The irony would not be lost. Naomi, the Israelitess, found no relief, either in the house of bread or the fields of Moab, but only through the agency of the Moabitess on the threshing floor. How would all this play out by a woman for women? On the threshing floor, the "woman" is a tool for male use. Naomi and Ruth turn this upside down and make the man, Boaz, a tool

---

50. Beckerman, *Dynamics of Drama*, 51.

51. Even the oppressive and enslaving Egyptians are granted more welcome than the Moabites (Deut 23:7).

for accomplishing female purposes, even if Boaz maintains the fiction that he is acting independently and on his own initiative.

Narrator /Storyteller

The narrator is invisible in the book of Ruth. The book lacks any inserts, editorial comments, or self-references so that the narrator becomes an observer to the story every bit as much as the audience. The narrator of the book of Ruth does not direct the audience to form conclusions about the unfolding action or the characters involved. The hidden narrator allows latitude in point of view which, while at times creating ambiguity, permits greater interaction on the part of the audience.

In contrast, the role of the storyteller in the Naomi Story is much more visible, even prominent. Since oral performance only happens when embodied, the Naomi Story is dependent upon the presence, the physical embodiment of the storyteller, in a way the book of Ruth is not dependent upon the narrator. The storyteller serves as a bridge between the lived world of the audience and the performed world of the Naomi Story. She has a foot in both worlds, allowing some of the same kind of ambiguity and latitude as afforded by the narrator in the book of Ruth, but much more present as a guide, sharing the joy of discovery with the audience. Self-references (the absence of which hide the narrator) are not required by the storyteller in the oral presentation for her presence is obvious, a ghostly presence evident still in the literary version, through the use of deictics, dicitur, audience direct address, and strategic repetition.

The Chorus

The chorus appears in three episodes in the Naomi Story. Already, Frederic Bush recognized this function for the women of 4:14.[52] Helen Bacon establishes an idea of the Chorus in the Greek theatre that is worth considering here, especially if we consider an active and participatory audience for the storyteller during a presentation of the Naomi Story. Bacon writes, "the musical form of the Athenian drama, in particular its ever present chorus, reflects the fact that it was created and flourished at a time when the Greek world, although it was beginning to move toward the predominantly literate culture that found its culmination in Alexandria, was still largely condi-

52. Bush, "Ruth 4:17," 6; and Porten, "The Scroll of Ruth," 25.

tioned by the traditions of a primarily oral culture of its remote and recent past."[53] She goes on to argue, "Greek audiences would have experienced the choruses of Greek drama as a natural and necessary form of human interaction which they had witnessed and participated in since childhood, a social reality, rather than the artificial artistic convention they seem to us."[54] If, as we suggest, the oral substratum of Ruth contains a performed story by women for women, then the generally accepted idea that all drama was first choral (oral), the evolution of the chorus must be seen as an integral part of the action. In this same context, the role and function of the chorus as part of a closed audience experience where the storyteller can rely on the intimate knowledge of the spectators sets the stage for an exclusive and subversive opportunity. Or, as Aristophanes suggests through the character of Dionysus in *Frogs*, the chorus performs a much-needed public service that is key to the welfare of the city.

Comedy

The Naomi Story invites comparison to the Genesis stories of Rachael, Leah, and Tamar. The formal characteristics of these stories are comedic in nature and, in Ruth, include: trickery, comic plot structure, dialogue, reversal, hiddenness / surprise, and sexuality.[55] Just like the stories of Rachel, Leah, and Tamar found in Genesis, the Naomi Story subverts the status quo, undercutting the patriarchal order to achieve female goals. Nehama Aschkenasy agrees that "More than any other biblical story or cycle of tales, the book of Ruth belongs to the dramatic genre" and can easily be adapted for the stage.[56] Aschkenasy suggests several dramatic possibilities for Ruth but offers a caveat by observing, "The obvious difference between Ruth and classical or Shakespearean drama is that Ruth was meant to be read, not performed"[57] and "nor do I propose that the narrator had in mind a stage production when composing the tale."[58] But was this always the case? Could those dramatic possibilities be remnants of a pre-literate stage of the story that was indeed meant to be performed? And if this oral substratum

---

53. Bacon, "The Chorus in Greek Life and Drama," 6.

54. Ibid.

55. Jackson, *Comedy and Feminist Interpretation of the Bible*, 180.

56. Aschkenasy, "The Book of Ruth as Comedy," 31.

57. Ibid., 31.

58. Ibid., 44.

does exist can it be reconstructed and made visible in a way to allow for that performance? Aschkenasy leads us to suspect that this reconstruction may indeed be possible for she goes on to state it is "appropriate to study Ruth in the light of theories of drama, both ancient and modern."[59] Adrien Bledstein has already suggested that "reading Ruth through the filter of imagining the book as written by a wise woman with a sense of humor and irony changes what we see."[60] Perhaps we can do more than just imagine and appreciating the Naomi Story as comedy opens our eyes to the sophisticated social power resident in the story's first telling.

In no way are we suggesting that what came to be known as traditional forms of theatrical comedy (Old and New Greek Comedy, Aristophanic Comedy, Shakespearean comedy, etc.) are formally present in the Naomi Story or the Book of Ruth. However, as Aschkenasy suggests, looking at the Naomi Story and the Book of Ruth in light of those forms may bring useful insight to our understanding of the complex stories behind these stories. For example, we know that sometime in the late fourth century BCE, a new style of Greek comedy developed.[61] This New Comedy focused more on the plot of the play and often employed recurring stock characters such as cooks, soldiers, pimps, and the cunning slave, among others. The Chorus became less important to the plot and plays seem to settle on an established five-act structure. The subject of New Comedy also differed and was more concerned with everyday people and their relations with family, other classes, and foreigners.[62] Aristotle suggests Comedy developed out of those who led the phallic procession. More specifically, the part of the chorus in Old Greek Comedy probably developed from a band of revelers, who danced, sang, and amused the crowd with obscene buffoonery and personal satire. These processions were connected to a fertility ritual in the worship of Dionysus whose tragic aspect was connected to the flowering and then inevitable death of all things, and whose comic aspect focused on the fertility of the natural world. Sex was an essential part of the celebration, for the culmination of the ritual was a symbolic marriage aimed at the magic stimulation of the soil; hence, in early Greek comedy, as in most

---

59. Ibid., 32.

60. Bledstein, "Female Companionship," 117.

61. For a thorough examination of the history of Greek Comedy, see, Heath, "Aristotelian Comedy," 344–54.

62. Adapted from Cartwright, http://www.ancient.eu/Greek_Come.

modern comedies and novels, marriage and presumptive procreation form the proper ending of the tale.[63]

The connections to the plot, given circumstances, project, and outcomes of the Naomi Story are almost a comic trifecta. From the context of time in terms of harvest and threshing, Ruth's fertility and ability to provide a child for Naomi, family relations based on gender and class, subversion of social systems, and ending with the marriage of Ruth to Boaz as a way of restoring balance to Naomi's world (to Woman's world), we suggest that we are clearly in the realm of performed comedy.

Erotic Desire

There are several motivators that an author or performer can use to effectively engage the reader or audience. Curiosity about an event in the past can motivate the reader of history. Pleasure and the desire to "feel good" leads audiences to concerts, plays, and quiet evenings with a good book. Ego, vanity, or adventure can all be tapped into by a performer to bring the audience into the performance. The storyteller of the Naomi Story has used, with great skill, an audience's desire for adventure or romance. Desire is the engine that propels the action within the Naomi Story. The audience's desire for stability, security, a future, justice, and on more than one occasion, romance provides the hook, keeping the audience engaged in the development of the story. Even the book of Ruth, a remake of the oral performance, is "a carefully constructed drama written by a writer of great literary talent, who causes the emotions of the reader to fluctuate between hope and despair . . ."[64] The story moves to a "dramatic climax"[65] absorbing Boaz, Ruth, and the desire of their relationship[66] into the resolution of the project introduced in 1:9. But this is not the only example of the storyteller's use of desire to engage the reader / audience. The interwoven ambiguity (4:8),[67] suspense, and suggestive language[68] that relies, at times, on older

---

63. http://legacy.owensboro.kctcs.edu/crunyon/e261c/05–GreekDrama/Aristophanes/Comedy.html.

64. Derby, "A Problem in the Book of Ruth," 185, translating and quoting from Garsiel, "The Development of the Plot," 66–83.

65. Beattie, "The book of Ruth as Evidence for Israelite Legal Practice," 265.

66. Pollack, "Notes on Megillat Ruth—Chapter 4," 185.

67. Derby, "A Problem in the Book of Ruth," 180.

68. Korpel, "Theodicy in the Book of Ruth," 340.

and possibly more familiar stories and traditions (Genesis 38;[69] Song of Songs 7:12[70]) is designed to create a sense of desire on the part of the audience that becomes an important performative element of the threshing floor scene in chapter three.

The Naomi storyteller has crafted the story to allow the audience to project desire into the story and so identify with characters in the story. The audience feels the pain and bitterness of Naomi and Ruth. The audience is suspenseful and doesn't want to be found out on the threshing floor. The audience cheers the success of the characters, and feels satisfaction at the secure outcome and "happily ever after" way the story ends. The common device throughout the book is the use of desire to move the reader from one episode to the next.

In the dramatic unfolding of Ruth, transitional episodes are magnified in importance, propelling the reader from scene to scene. It is quite clear that the pivotal moment in the drama is the threshing floor encounter described in Ruth 3: 6–13.[71] That moment has been explained in numerous ways, including a "striptease"[72] and a highly erotic scene that is interrupted by Ruth's ethical appeal.[73] Attempting to survey the possibilities resident in the encounter, one recent commentator wrote: "Lacking textual controls, imagination may lead readers in wildly different directions: a steamy tryst between mutually desiring persons . . . a beautiful but needy Ruth forcing herself to relate to a rough, pot-bellied, snaggle-toothed (but rich) old man. . . .a wily, scheming Ruth cooperating with Naomi to compromise and thus force the hand of the most handsome and wealthy bachelor of the community. The very reticence of the text leads readers to supply additional details . . ."[74] One commentator chose to characterize the scene as an "ambiguous encounter in the night" so that "the reader often cannot know precisely what is happening."[75]

69. Van Wolde, "Texts in Dialogue with Texts," 8–24.

70. Korpel, "Theodicy in the Book of Ruth," 340. Bjorn Reinhold attempts to find inter-textual connections between Ruth 3 and Genesis 1–2. Reinhold, "Ruth 3," 111–17.

71. Fewell and Gunn, *Compromising Redemption*, 47.

72. Van Wolde, *Ruth en Noomi*, 82.

73. Fischer, "The Book of Ruth," 45.

74. Sakenfeld, *Ruth*, 57. See also de Fraine, *Ruth*, 154. Bos, "Out of the Shadows," 64.

75. Linafelt and Beal, *Ruth and Esther*, 46. Shadrac Keita and Janet Dyk recognize the ambiguity in the Ruth text but put forth a different evaluation concerning the eroticism woven into the story. Keita and Dyk, "The Scene at the Threshing Floor," 26–29.

Ambiguous as it may be, rabbinic exegesis seems to have sensed that the erotic was not far below the surface of the episode and spared no effort in explaining the encounter of 3:6–13 otherwise. Beattie summarizes rabbinic comment on the threshing floor encounter by writing, "The Rabbis clearly felt that the scene at the threshing-floor, in which Ruth and Boaz spent the night together, needed a careful exegesis lest the reader might conclude that they might actually have engaged in sexual intercourse."[76] The Syriac version of Ruth 3 eliminates the suggestive sentence in verse 9 and the Targum seeks to reduce the erotic nature of the account by granting Boaz a ripe old age of 80. These alterations would be unnecessary had there been no suggested erotic offense to begin with.[77] Certainly, several vectors of social power come to meet at this threshing floor encounter. Commentators have examined the legal backdrop to the episode,[78] and the gender issues resident in the encounter,[79] but the power of the erotic has yet to be fully considered in the performance tradition of the threshing floor encounter. Ruth 3:1–18 is acknowledged by commentators as a pivotal episode in the book of Ruth[80] and is no less important in the Naomi Story. In this pivotal episode, the nature of the action, prescribed by Naomi in 3:4, effected by Ruth in 3:7, and reacted to by Boaz in 3:8–9, serves to draw together desire, sexual power, and subversion in one powerful dramatic moment.

The specific nature of the desire propelling the action of Ruth 3:6–13 can now be examined more closely.[81] The threshing floor episode, in its

76. Beattie, *Jewish Exegesis of the Book of Ruth*, 179. Murphy is also of the opinion that "sexual intimacy is not envisioned in the episode." Murphy, *Wisdom Literature*, 93. See also the discussion of the *ketib* and *qere* of 3:3,4 in Irwin, "Removing Ruth," 331–38 in which it is suggested that the verbal forms are intended to remove or at least minimize the role of Ruth in the nocturnal visit to the threshing floor by making Naomi the subject of the verb "I will go down" (v. 3) and "I will lie down" (v. 4) (337).

77. Samaritan tradition also recognizes the elicit sexual encounter at the heart of the story of Ruth. Anderson and Giles, *Tradition Kept*, 253.

78. See for example, Matthews, *Judges and Ruth*, 235–237; Sakenfeld, *Ruth*, 59–60; LaCocque, *Ruth*, 21–28; Berman, "Ancient Hermeneutics and the Legal Structure of the Book of Ruth," 22–38.

79. Kates, "Women at the Center," 185–198; Donaldson, "The Sign of Orpah," 130–44.

80. A. Boyd Luter and Richard Rigsby have argued that the episode at the threshing floor participates as the "central focus" and part of the inner chiastic layer pointing to that focal point within the book. Luter and Rigsby, "An Adjusted Symmetrical Structuring of Ruth," 15–28. See also the earlier treatment that also considers the centrality of the threshing floor episode by Bertman, "The Symmetrical Structure of Ruth," 165–68.

81. Sasson, *Ruth*, 71.

literary rendition, is constructed with vocabulary (ידע, שכב, גלה, כנף) that is "indicative of the sexual tension at play here."[82] One commentator notes that in this episode, "never is there any indication of the consummation of sexual relations, yet the choice of words keeps that possibility always before the reader."[83] The story heightens the tensions by imposing "great restraint in the face of sexual desire."[84] Indeed, it may be that the whole function of the episode is to heighten that desire, for the threshing floor setting is steeped in sexual connotations (Hosea 9:1) and sexual imagery may include even the characters[85] involved—Ruth risking a sexual encounter (metaphorically expressed by grinding: Job: 31:9–10; Lamentations: 1:15), and Boaz, an "ox who will not be muzzled" (Deuteronomy 25:4).[86]

The performance or dramatic telling of the threshing floor episode is ripe with erotic imagination that could be used effectively by the performer. Earlier we considered the likelihood that the Naomi Story is the work of a female artisan. That simple gender identification is not enough. The Naomi Story is the work of a female artisan and *not* a male artisan. Brenner points out that texts presenting a female voice can be identified, not by hiding female sexuality, but by recognizing that sexuality and weaving it into the story of the text.[87] In the use of desire as a motivator within the presentation of Ruth, the distinction and contrast seems important. Consider the following by James Loader: "There is a clear *polarization* of male and female perspectives in the story, the subtle handling of which reveals a *critical* point of view adopted by the storyteller. This in turn exposes not only a differentiation of the interests and values of women and men within the

---

82. Berman, "Ancient Hermeneutics and the Legal Structure of the Book of Ruth," 33.

83. Sakenfeld, *Ruth*, 54. Fischer writes, "If this is not instruction [Naomi's instruction to Ruth in 3:1–5] to seduce the man, it is at least a plan to give Boaz the opportunity to seduce Ruth." Fischer, "The Book of Ruth," 30.

84. Berman, "Ancient Hermeneutics and the Legal Structure of the Book of Ruth," 33. See also *Ruth* Midrash Rabbah, 70–71.

85. Berman, "Ancient Hermeneutics and the Legal Structure of the Book of Ruth," 34–35.

86. Berstein, "Two Multivalent Readings in the Ruth Narrative," 15–26. See also the post-biblical usage of "the place where the attendant threshes" in reference to female genitalia, Niddah 41b *Tohoroth*, 285 and "threshing" (שרד) to refer to male sexual activity, Pesahim 87b *Mo'ed* 2, 461; et. al.

87. Brenner, "Naomi and Ruth," 144.

given extra-literary society, but indeed the *controversial* manifestation of the female perspective verses the dominant male one."[88]

The feminine perspective in the Naomi Story is itself "controversial" and subversive. The book embodies the subversive side of desire as the engine by which to propel the reader / audience. Just before the concluding genealogy, events are so dominated by the perspective of Naomi and the townswomen that Loader can conclude, "Without being denied, the male, collective and clan interests are merely ignored."[89] The subversion is complete. The interests of the male perspective need not even be bothered with—they can simply be ignored.[90] The male perspective can be ignored because gender roles have been effectively deconstructed thereby allowing for the possibility of a new and changed reconstruction of roles.[91]

Bride-in-the-Dark

The Naomi Story brings to the attention of the audience a way to understand her story by the mention of Rachel (Genesis 19), Leah (Genesis 29), and Tamar (Genesis 38) in Ruth 4:11–12. Common to the narratives of all four women is the "bride in the dark" or "bed-trick" motif.[92] The "bed-trick" or "bride-in-the-dark" motif is a turn of events in which a man is surprised by an unexpected bed-partner or a substituted partner.[93] The connection to the bed-trick of Rachel, Leah, and Tamar is unwittingly made by the elders and townspeople of Bethlehem in 4:11–12, who cannot know the full impact of their words. But, as the audience knows, the prayer for offspring from the LORD is going to be answered through an unorthodox means—just like Rachel, Leah, and Tamar. Within the comic structure of Ruth, the bed-trick occurs at a pivotal juncture—a *Saturnalia*—or "a moment of chaos, characterized by breaking of all boundaries, by making merry, and by eating and

---

88. Loader, "A Woman Praised by Women," 698.

89. Ibid., 699.

90. Bledstein captures the sense of subversion when she writes, "She [Ruth's author] anticipates, through narration, Jeremiah's later vision: 'Yahweh has created a new thing on earth: female surrounds a mighty man.' (Jer. 31.22)." Bledstein, "Female Companionships," 133.

91. Berquist, "Role Differentiation in the Book of Ruth," 36.

92. Nielsen, *Ruth*, 92; see also Black, "Ruth in the Dark," 20; Fisch, "Ruth and the Structure of Covenant History," 430–31.

93. Black, "Ruth in the Dark," 20.

drinking excessively."[94] Led by the "Lord of Misrule," a role filled by Boaz, this moment of disruption is key in the unfolding of Naomi's plan.[95]

Who Are You?

Identity is important in the Naomi Story. Beyond providing descriptions for the characters in the story, the identities assigned, when applied to an evolving dramatic plot, become designations of social boundaries. As the Naomi Story progresses, a series of questions is presented that serve as markers, signaling a change in Ruth's identity.[96] In 2:5, Ruth has caught Boaz's attention, but a social barrier is presented as Ruth is identified as a member of a lower social class, a "worker-girl." Later, (3:9) in reply to a question, secretly asked, Ruth speaks her name (the first time anyone speaks Ruth's name) identifying herself as a "maidservant," a member of a higher social standing than a worker-girl and perhaps a suitable marriage partner. In 3:10 Boaz calls her "my daughter." Ruth has become an individual, not just a member of a social class. Several verses later (3:16), Naomi also uses "my daughter" to ask who is approaching in the dark. The use of the phrase "my daughter" indicates that Naomi knows who is coming—but she doesn't know the outcome of Ruth's nocturnal visit to the threshing floor or Ruth's current social state. Several translations attempt to capture this social flux in 3:16 and so the translation "How did it go with you . . . ?" (NRSV) and the "How is it with you . . .?" (JPS). Ellen Davis has perhaps captured the sense the best when she translates Naomi's question: "Who are you now, my daughter?"[97]

A Child is Born

A central feature of the plot moving the Naomi Story is the transition from childlessness to motherhood. All the women at the beginning of the story are childless. Namoi is bereaved of her sons and husband while Ruth and Orpah have dead husbands and no children. The unlikelihood of change

94. Aschkenasy, "The Book of Ruth as Comedy," 34.

95. Contra Moshe Bernstein, who while recognizing the ambiguity resident in the threshing-floor scene, argues that the noble character of Ruth and Boaz precludes any sexual encounter on the threshing-floor. Bernstein, "Two Multivalent Readings in the Ruth Narrative," 17–20.

96. Davis, "Beginning with Ruth," 18–19.

97. Ibid., 19.

motivates Orpah to leave her mother-in-law and return to her people and to her gods (1:15), while Ruth casts her lot with Naomi, famously adopting Namoi's home, people, God, and burial place (1:16–17). Significantly enough, Ruth doesn't mention offspring as part of her imagined future.

Just as at the beginning of the story, Ruth and Naomi share the condition of barrenness, at the end of the story both women share the role of mother. Ruth gives birth to a son because the, "LORD gave her conception" (4:13), but Naomi takes the child, places him on her lap and becomes his nurse (4:16). The women of the village jubilantly declare "A son has been born to Naomi" (4:17). As pointed out by Ilana Pardes, "this is a radical violation of the formula according to which the son is born to the father."[98] This remarkable conclusion to the drama, ending in the female naming episode of the child in 4:17, with the father not even present, brings the opening childless condition to a positive conclusion in a manner that specifically addresses the concerns of the female characters of the story. The patrilineal structure in which Naomi and Ruth find themselves is subverted and the well-being of the women is secured. The project of the drama is resolved and, in comedic fashion, the status quo remains but changed forever.

98. Pardes, *Countertraditions in the Bible*, 106.

4

The Naomi Story Becoming the Book of Ruth

Ruth is a subversive book.[1] In some ways, the story resides on the boundaries. The story involves women on the edge of economic survival, stretching ethnic identities, and challenging gender propriety. Many have written about the subversiveness of the story's plot, contending that the story comments on legal precedent, social conventions, and literary traditions.[2] André LaCocque, considering the story of Ruth in context with Jonah, Esther, the Joseph story, and Job, writes, "With respect to the setting, the understated language on religious matters, the synergism of human agents with God and often the latter's conspicuous absence, the role of the underdogs and women in bringing about (partial) fulfillments of *Heilsgeschichte*—all point to a common stock of *subversive* authors."[3]

In this chapter, we turn our attention to an aspect of Ruth's subversiveness that has not received much notice. The book, itself, is a subversion of

---

1. Alicia Ostriker labels Ruth a "countertext" forming a "counter-current to certain dominant biblical concepts and motifs." Ostriker, "The Book of Ruth and the Love of the Land," 344. Alice Ogden Bellis describes Ruth as a subversive woman in a subversive book, but considers the subversion a result of Ruth's ethnic identity. Bellis, *Women's Stories in the Hebrew Bible,* 183–84. We will see in the coming analysis that the subversion of Ruth extends beyond ethnicity.

2. Ostriker, "The Book of Ruth and the Love of the Land," 353; LaCocque, *Ruth,* 5. Agnethe Siquans suggest that, in the story, it is the power of Torah that is able to transform society and its members. Siquans, "Foreignness and Poverty in the Book of Ruth," 452.

3. LaCocque, *The Feminine Unconventional,* 93.

a previous story. The book of Ruth has subverted the Naomi Story. The Naomi Story was appropriated and refashioned by a segment of sixth century Israelite society that gave to the Naomi Story a new purpose and a new theme. The Naomi Story was subverted into the book of Ruth.

Date

In tracing the journey from the Naomi Story to the book of Ruth, we need to establish a date for the composition of the book. Scholarly disagreement in ascribing a literary form to the book of Ruth involves disagreement in assigning a date for the book which, in turn, proves pivotal for understanding the theme and purpose of the story. The following illustrates the nature of the choices: "Either the tale is pre-exilic apologue or it is postexilic parable. Apologue sets an ethical model; its purpose is edification and confirmation of world. Parable questions ideology; it subverts world."[4] Currently, most proposals for dating the book of Ruth gather around one of two options.[5] Either, commentators suggest a pre-exilic date for the book, suggesting that the book was written to answer criticisms of David's mixed ancestry[6] (one writer even suggesting the book was written by David's friend and confidant—Nathan[7]) or, a post-exilic date that suggests the book was part of a movement countering positions of nationalistic and ethnic exclusivity like those expressed in Ezra–Nehemiah.[8] If our suggestion is correct, that the book of Ruth is a post-exilic composition based upon a pre-exilic Naomi Story, we should expect to find characteristics of both a pre-exilic (the

4. Ibid., 91.

5. LaCocque argues persuasively that the date assigned to the book of Ruth is highly significant for understanding the meaning of this "little literary jewel." Ibid., 84.

6. Hubbard, *Ruth*, 46; Nielsen, *Ruth*, 29. Jacob Licht is of the opinion that the book of Ruth is a "presentation of disagreeable fact [David's mixed ancestry] in the best possible light." Licht, *Storytelling in the Bible*, 125. Edward Campbell also posits a pre-exilic date (perhaps associated with the reforms of Jehoshaphat in the middle of the ninth century) but without considering the book an apologetic for the line of David. Campbell, *Ruth*, 28. Tod Linafelt believes the book of Ruth is "to be read as an interlude between Judges and Samuel." Linafelt and Beal, *Ruth and Esther*, xviii.

7. Gow, *The Book of Ruth*, 207–10.

8. A proposal for a post-exilic date for Ruth is most common among older historical critical scholars. See, for example, Fohrer, *Introduction to the Old Testament*, 251. Yitzhak Berger considers allusions to 1 Samuel 25 in Ruth. Berger, "Ruth and Inner-Biblical Allusion," 253–72; and Auld has listed a number of links between Ruth and 1 Samuel, "Reading Kings on the Divided Monarchy," 338.

Naomi Story) and a post-exilic composition (the literary remake) in the book. Perhaps the most thorough examination of information relevant to Ruth's social and legal setting, and, most importantly, an assessment of the book's vocabulary and orthography, was conducted by Ziony Zevit, leading him to conclude, "that Ruth was written sometime between 600 and 500 B.C.E., perhaps during the last part of this period, ca. 525–500 B.C.E."[9] In the analysis that follows we will accept Zevit's arguments and consider the book of Ruth a mid-sixth century literary witness to a performative event, a story told and retold since at least the eighth century BCE.[10]

The transition from an oral Story to a written Book is more than a change in modality. When the Naomi Story became the book of Ruth, the oral substrate of the oral performance was overlaid with material that changed the theme and purpose of the Story. Concurrent with the change in theme and purpose was a change in the social place, audience, location, and the social influence of the story.[11] Why and how did all this happen?

9. Zevit, "Dating Ruth," 594. Athalya Brenner places the composition of the Book of Ruth in Second Temple times, perhaps just a little later than Zevit. Brenner, *The Book of Ruth*, 119–63. Katrina J. A. Larkin is of the opinion that linguistic arguments are inconclusive for determining a date for the book of Ruth. Larkin, *Ruth and Esther*, 20. Larkin goes on to comment, "that the very inconsistency of the [linguistic] evidence might point to a long period of transmission before the story reached its present form." Larkin, *Ruth and Esther*, 20. Lisa Wolfe also places the authorship of the book in the "dialogue of the postexilic, restoration community of the sixth-to fifth-century Jews." Wolfe, *Ruth, Esther, Song of Songs, and Judith*, 2. LaCocque also agrees with the post-exilic dating for the book, *The Feminine Unconventional*, 84; see also Campbell, *Ruth*, 19–24. Mats Eskhult argues that "it is clear that the idea of 'the many Aramaisms' in Ruth is ill-founded, and still worse is the conclusion that these alleged Aramaisms point to a late date." Eskhult, "The Importance of Loanwords for Dating Biblical Hebrew Texts," 16. Polak's proposal for an oral substrate dating from at least the eighth century BCE that received a scribal revision for chapters one through three during or near the eighth century BCE and during the sixth century for chapter four, is, in broad terms, consistent with Zevit's proposal.

10. More recently a later date has been supported by Lau, *Identity and Ethics in the Book of Ruth*.

11. We are not suggesting that the usurpation of the Naomi Story by the book of Ruth was sudden, immediate or complete. Undoubtedly the two versions co-existed for a time, in different segments of society. Only as the social conditions addressed by the Naomi Story and the book of Ruth changed, did the Naomi Story fade and the book of Ruth grow in popularity.

Primary Oral or Primary Literate Society?

To understand the change from the Naomi Story into the book of Ruth, we need to contextualize that change within a larger change from a primarily oral society to one that was primarily literate. A simple syntactical profile in texts (as observed in Ruth, particularly in chapters 1–3), closer to oral communication, stems from a culture with limited literacy. In addition to parts of Ruth, the syntactical profiles of 1–2 Samuel and some of the Patriarchal cycles reflect a popular culture where orality remained the primary vehicle for transmitting tradition.[12] Polak discusses the presence of the spoken form in narrative material:

> Many tales, and even entire narrative cycles, are characterized by the *high number of clauses consisting of a predicate only, or of predicate with one single argument, the low number of clauses in hypotaxis, and the low number of expanded noun chains.* . . .This style is characteristic of such narrative cycles as, e.g., the tales of the Patriarchs, of Samuel, Saul, and David, of Elijah and Elisha. In other words, *even though in their present form these cycles belong to written literature, they are based on a substrate of oral literature.*[13]

> It appears that this great variety in style is related to the nature of oral narrative and the special gifts and techniques developed by the story-tellers [sic storytellers] over the generations. In oral narrative quoted discourse is an essential element . . . Anthropologists who study these phenomena in their proper setting often highlight the theatrical talents of the oral narrator, who turns a character's discourse into an actor's performance, and the narrative, at least partly, into a play on stage.[14]

Orality and literacy must have existed side by side in ancient Israel.[15] Joachim Schaper argues that, "Israel, throughout its entire history—as far as we know it—was a literate society . . ."[16] Yet, he cautions, "literacy in the sense of being able to both read and write substantial pieces of literature, was, as far as I can see, a skill restricted to a very small class of people, not

12. Polak, "The Oral and the Written," 59–105.

13. Polak, "The Style of the Dialogue in Biblical Prose Narrative," 62–63.

14. Ibid., 94.

15. See Ro, "Socio-Economic Context," 601; also Harris, *Ancient Literacy*; Young, "Israelite Literacy," 239–53; Schniedewind, "Orality and Literacy in Ancient Israel," 327–32; Schaper, "Exilic and Post-Exilic Prophecy and the Orality/Literacy Problem," 324–42.

16. Schaper, "The Living Word Engraved in Stone," 10.

just in the early period of the monarchy but right up to and including the time of the exile."[17] For Schaper, this is a pivotal observation and directs the manner in which he considers social memory in Israel, for, as he states, "the way memory operates in a primary oral society is very different from the way it works in a literate society."[18] An expression of that difference, cited by Schaper, is articulated by Walter Ong, ". . . oral societies live very much in a present which keeps itself in equilibrium or homeostasis by sloughing off memories which no longer have present relevance."[19] The Naomi Story and the book of Ruth functioned as expressions of social memory. If Ong is correct, the transition from the Naomi Story to the book of Ruth would have been marked by conditions which made the Story no longer relevant or, at least, the book of Ruth of more immediate relevancy to the engaged audience. The relevancy of the Naomi Story depends on the following four social conditions:

1. A patrilineal male privilege expressed in land holdings and female identity / social place achieved through attachment to a male.[20]

2. Shared female solidarity / identity experienced as a subset within male biased dominant social institutions.

3. Sexual tension that recognized the female as both desirable and dangerous to the male. Female sexuality may be expressed and available as a tool for the female and as a prized possession for the male.

4. A mechanism for the transmission of the story, presumably within the female subset.

When the above four conditions no longer exist, or are not relevant as social givens, the Naomi Story loses its power, or, in Ong's terms, becomes a sloughed off memory. Perhaps, it's better to say that transformation of the Naomi Story to the book of Ruth, marked movement from one social subgroup to another in which the concerns and interests, the relevant memories changed. Orality and literacy existed side by side in ancient Israel and assumed different levels of primacy within different social subgroups. The

17. Schaper, "A Theology of Writing," 103.

18. Schaper, "The Living Word Engraved in Stone," 10.

19. Ong, *Orality and Literacy*, 46.

20. Carol Meyers argues that patriarchy be replaced by a concept of heterarchy, allowing a complex of formal and informal social power arrangements within ancient Israel. Meyers, "Hierarchy or Heterarchy?," 250–51.

differences between the function of memory in a primary oral and a primary literate society explain some of the characteristics we now find in the book of Ruth superimposed upon the Naomi Story.

William Schneidewind, describes the eighth through seventh centuries BCE as a time when literacy "flourished" in Judah, at least in comparison to the "less fertile ground" provided in the early Iron Age.[21] This flourishing of writing coincides with a social change, the urbanization of Judah in which writing "was a regular part of a burgeoning government bureaucracy" and the use of writing "by new social classes (military, merchants, craftsmen) is indicated by inscriptional evidence relating to government bureaucracy, economic globalization, and religious ideology."[22] Schneidewind's observation about new social classes and social change is reminiscent of Lenski's taxonomy applied to "advanced agrarian societies" (Ruling Class, Governing Class, Retainer Class, Priestly Class, Peasant Class, Merchant Class, Artisan Class, Unclean and Degraded Class, and Expendable Class).[23] The rise of new social classes and social change suggests that literacy is mobile, moving between social subgroups.

The fluidity of evolving social subgroups and the oral or written forms of memory transmission utilized by each argues against an oral-written dichotomy as a binary opposition in the description of ancient Israelite society, particularly when only the product of written transmission is favored as a way of knowing that ancient society.[24] There can be movement between oral and literate subgroups within a society. Michael Floyd argues that the oral—written binary be expanded and applied to three aspects of prophetic (and we would add non-prophetic) documents: composition, transmission, and performance.[25] An analysis of all three as oral or written events will better assist in understanding the social dynamics of the biblical texts.

21. Schniedewind, "Orality and Literacy in Ancient Israel," 328. Ian Young argues that there was a limited amount of literacy in ancient Israel. He contends that, "the writing and reading mentioned in the biblical text often has the meaning of "commissioning the writing" or being "read to." Young, "Israelite Literacy (Part 1)," 248–49.

22. Schniedewind, "Orality and Literacy in Ancient Israel," 329.

23. Lenski, *Power and Privilege*, 190–296. See also Michael Floyd's historical review and critique. Floyd, "Write the Revelation!," 108–25. Floyd is undoubtedly correct in warning against a social developmental model or oral–literate prophecy that favors (even if unintentionally) some form of Eurocentricism, but to remove all competition for social power from oral and written forms of prophecy does not seem to tell the whole story.

24. Ibid., 123.

25. Ibid., 123–24.

The notion of subgroups within a given society, utilizing different methods of communication and social memory, is addressed by Ehud Ben Zvi when he writes, "It is worth noting that at the present discussion clearly leads to an image of 'restricted, high literacy' and 'general orality' as two deeply interwoven social phenomena."[26] Orality and literacy co-exist and do so unequally in various subsets within a society. As the Naomi Story moved from one social location to another, so, too, its form, function, and even medium changed. Johannes Ro, mindful of social subgroups, asks a question that has direct application to the story of Ruth. "Would the absence of literacy among the very poor have meant that they lacked the categories to formulate, orally, a kind of theology of liberation? I think not."[27] The Naomi Story may have been a vibrant expression, a voice that, because of its power, was destined to become usurped and transformed in the service of a social group not originally intended. The movement of the Naomi Story from one social subgroup to another, during a time of social change, set the stage for the transition from the Naomi Story to the book of Ruth and the editorial layering that changed the purpose, theme, and relevant social memories now associated with the book of Ruth.

Oral and Written Authority

Did the book of Ruth garnish more social authority, simply because of its written form, than was attached to the Naomi Story? How did the transition from an oral medium to a written medium impact the influence of the story in post-exilic Yehud? Much of the discussion about the extent and prominence of literacy in ancient Israel rightfully considers examples of literacy uncovered by archaeologists (i.e.: Lachish Letters—Letter 3— the "Letter of a Literate Soldier,"[28] the Siloam Inscription) or references to writing in the biblical text including: Isa 65:6; Jeremiah 36; 51:60–64; Ezek 2:8–3:3; 13:9; Hab 2:1–5; Zech 5:1–4; Mal 3:16; Ps 56:8; 69:28; 139:16; Neh 13:14; Exod 32:32; Deut 7:10.[29] These references are dominated by record-keeping, itemizations, commemorations, and similar small entries that are suited to a static, unchanging presentation. If, as some have suggested, God

---

26. Ben Zvi, "Introduction: Writings, Speeches, and the Prophetic Books," 23.

27. Ro, "Socio-Economic Context of Post-Exilic Community and Literacy," 609.

28. Na'aman, "The Distribution of Messages," 179.

29. Schaper, "Exilic and Post-Exilic Prophecy and the Orality / Literacy Problem," 325–27.

is represented as a divine book-keeper, "oral record-keeping is thus considered less durable and less reliable than book-keeping."[30] Following this line of reasoning, written transmission is considered more reliable and given greater social authority than oral memories. This is exactly what Schaper argues—that written texts were granted more authority than oral texts. God is presented as writing, lending divine authority to the text. Shaper writes, "The writing down, [of the Decalogue] performed by God himself, *provides the material basis for the immutability of the commandments . . .*"[31]

If we apply this evaluation of social authority to the Naomi Story and the book of Ruth, are we to conclude that the book of Ruth was granted more authority, simply because it was written? From the portrayal of God writing it does not follow that writing itself is deemed more authoritative than orally delivered messages. For, in many of the same prophetic texts mentioned above, those that portray God as book-keeper, God also speaks and delivers oral messages that have no lack of authority. Ian Young concludes that, among prophetic texts, the transition from oral to written occurred when "the oral narratives of the prophetic schools became useful to the literate circles of the royal court."[32] A similar usefulness must be speculated to have occurred in the transition of the Naomi Story to the book of Ruth from one social group to another. We must therefore ask, what are the benefits to a specific group that are accomplished by the written form of Ruth?

Could it be that static communications (lists, registries, commemorative texts) were well suited to writing, while at the same time other types of communication (epic, directive, song, oracle) demanded the presence of the speaker in order to effect authority. The connection between speaker and message is alluded to by E. F. Davies in his discussion of Ezekiel 2–3. There, the prophet swallows the text and "becomes (to our eyes, at least) virtually indistinguishable from what he ate."[33] Oral presentation had no less authority than the written; it simply was more intimately connected with the authority and skill of the presenter. Performance is only embodied by a performer, while a text tends to develop a life of its own. The projected authority of a text is actually a projection of authority by those deemed

---

30. Ibid., 328.

31. Ibid., 336.

32. Young, "Israelite Literacy (Part 1)," 252–53.

33. Davies, *Swallowing the Scroll*, 135. Schaper points out that this movement, from orality to textuality to orality, is also apparent in Deut 5:22 and 6:6–9. Schaper, "Exilic and Post-Exilic Prophecy and the Orality/Literacy Problem," 332.

gatekeepers of the text while performance admits no gatekeeper apart from the performer.[34]

Spectrum of Naomi–Ruth

If the book of Ruth is a remake of a presentation lifted from Israelite female culture, it may be useful to think of the transition from performance to literature as the movement along a spectrum from one set of concerns and purposes to another. The subversive nature of the female performance of the Naomi Story is maintained by the literature, only now directed toward subverting the ethnic and nationalistic perception of Torah (illustrated by Ezra, Nehemiah) by an inclusive and non-ethnic, universalistic understanding of Torah. By relying on the Naomi Story, the writer of the book of Ruth appropriated the popularity of the Naomi Story and transformed that popular tale of gender subversiveness into a message of Torah as love.

Female Performance	Scribal Literature
Female audience	Male audience
Concern with female security	Concern with national identity
Subversive feminine	and urban continuity
	Torah is love

It is clear that, in the Naomi Story, ethnic communal identity is not the issue. The precipitating context begins with the plight of Naomi, an Israelite widow. Ruth is readily acknowledged as a Moabitess, even after her offer to renounce her own ethnic communal identity in favor of adopting that of Naomi. While gleaning in the fields, it isn't Ruth's ethnicity that causes concern, but her gender (2:15–16). On the threshing floor, an episode that pivots the whole drama to resolution, the issue is not that a *Moabitess* is present, but that *the woman* is present (3:14). Polak suggests that dialogue embedded in biblical narrative can serve as social drama in which the "participants in this drama represent two sides in social, cultural, religious or ethnic oppositions."[35] This comes close to describing the core dialogues in Ruth. The dialogues between Naomi, her daughters-in-law, and particularly

---

34. Ibid., 336 quoting Ben Zvi, "Introduction: Writings, Speeches, and the Prophetic Books," 13. See also Polak, "The Oral and the Written," 59–105.

35. Polak, "Negotiations, Social Drama and Voices," 47. See also Turner, *From Ritual to Theatre.*

between Naomi and the good people of Bethlehem draw the listener's attention to matters of gender defined social power. For the Naomi Story, the predicament revolves around gender issues. In 4:15, Ruth, (the woman), is worth more than seven sons.

This concern for gender gets turned around in the book of Ruth. The genealogy added onto the Naomi Story at the end of the book, describing ten generations of Israelites, compared to the three generations of 4:17, leads the reader to now conclude that the *Moabitess* is indeed more worthy than seven *Israelites*. In the book of Ruth, the repeated use of "the Moabitess" to identify Ruth signals quite clearly that gender issues have become subsumed under a more pressing ethnicity question. Loyalty and kindness (חסד) can be found outside the Israelite camp.

If women storytellers exerted a similar influence as did their musical counterparts (ballad singers, mourning women), then transferring the story from the domain of a female performer to a (most likely) male scribe represents a significant moment in the transformation of the Naomi Story into the book of Ruth as now preserved in the Hebrew Bible. Consider the following: "Most of the producers of scripture were elite, urban males such as priests and members of the royal bureaucracy, probably addressing other men; . . . Their goals and interests rarely included the concerns or practices of women . . . The perspective of the producers of scripture was for the most part national and communal, not familial and domestic."[36]

In other words, the project of the Naomi Story has met with the goals and interests of a new community. That new community left an imprint on the Naomi Story, making it into the book of Ruth. But, as van Dijk-Hemmes and others have noted, the remaking of the story by the male domain has been incomplete and uneven, for the presence of the female culture is still observable under the national imprint.[37]

Movement from a Female Voice to a Male Voice

The transition from the Naomi Story to the book of Ruth is more than a change from an oral to a scribal medium.[38] The transition from the Naomi Story to the book of Ruth is more than an alteration of the plot or charac-

36. Meyers, *Households and Holiness: The Religious Culture of Israelite Women*, 7.

37. Van Dijk-Hemmes "Traces of Women's Texts in the Hebrew Bible," 26.

38. See the discussion by Martii Nissinen regarding similar questions posed to prophetic literature in Nissinen, "The Dubious Image of Prophecy," 26.

terization of the actors (although both did change). On a more fundamental level, the *voice* of the story changed and the imposition of a male voice upon the now, more muted, female voice characterizes the transition from the Naomi Story to the book of Ruth. Although, he questions an original and dominating female perspective, Timothy Lim is convinced that "in its final form, the book of Ruth represents a thoroughly male perspective."[39]

Various cultural theoretical approaches have been developed to help formulate feminist literary criticism and provide explanations for gender differences within texts. A cultural model, as developed by E. Showalter, makes accessible, "the primary cultural experience of women as expressed by themselves," distinct from "roles, activities, preferences and rules of behavior prescribed for women."[40] The cultural approach allows the description of the women's culture as a "muted" group the boundaries of whose culture and reality overlap the dominant (male) group.[41] The muted ("gagged" as described by H. Sancisi-Weerdenburg[42]) female culture shares much with the dominant male culture but resides in the background, often invisible, but always present as a subversive potential ready to challenge the dominate formulation of reality with a "double voice"[43] informed by both the dominant and the muted cultural groups. If placed in this framework, the Naomi Story existed as an expression of support and solidarity within the muted female culture, while, at the same time, recognized as a subversive potential by the dominant male culture. It's that subversive potential that made the Naomi Story attractive to those interested in forming the book of Ruth, harnessing that potential and applying it in a new direction.[44]

This sort of shift from a female culture to a male culture has been observed elsewhere. Ria Lemaire notes that, in Europe of the Middle Ages, the "transition from oral traditions to written culture led to an increased marginalization of the cultural traditions of women" as the written culture became monopolized by a "men's culture."[45] Fokkelien van Dijk-Hemmes

---

39. Lim, "The Book of Ruth and Its Literary Voice," 282.

40. Showalter, "Feminist Criticism in the Wilderness," 260.

41. Ardener, *Perceiving Women*, xi–xii.

42. Sancisi-Weerdenburg, "Vrouwen in verborgen werelden," 18.

43. Showalter, "Feminist Criticism in the Wilderness," 266.

44. Can the same be observed in the Israelite prophetic movement as it also moved from the aural to the written? For an entry to the literature see, Lange, "Literary Prophecy and Oracle Collection," 248–75.

45. Lemaire, *Passions et Positions*, 190.

thinks, "it seems probable that a comparable process occurred in ancient Israel"[46] and it is within this cultural shift that the Naomi Story became the book of Ruth.

Framing Processes, Social Movements, and the Transition from Naomi to Ruth

If the book of Ruth was used as a counterpoint to an ethnically and religiously defined social identity present in the post-exilic Judean community as expressed in Ezra–Nehemiah, the book was an expression of a self-conscious social movement. Perhaps, a consideration of the dynamics of social movements can help shed light on the transition of the Naomi Story to the book of Ruth, or at least, give us language, a way of thinking, that may help us understand the function of the book of Ruth in that post-exilic social movement.

Framing Processes

Within contemporary sociological theory, framing processes are understood as the processes enabling individuals and groups to interpret and understand the "world at large."[47] "Frames help to render events or occurrences meaningful and thereby function to organize experience and guide action."[48] "Framing functions in much the same way as a frame around a picture: attention gets focused on what is relevant and important and away from extraneous items in the field of view."[49] In other words, much like good theatre, frames create shared ways of thinking about the world and about the self.[50] The Naomi Story focused attention on gender inequalities and the particularly female way in which security was achieved. The book

---

46. Dijk-Hemmes, "Traces of Women's Texts in the Hebrew Bible," 28.

47. Goffman, *Frame Analysis*, 21. An overview can be found in Noakes and Johnston, "Frames of Protest," 1–29.

48. Benford and Snow, "Framing Processes and Social Movements: An Overview and Assessment," 614. See also Hunt, Benford, et al., "Identity Fields," 191; Johnston, "Verification and Proof in Frame and Discourse Analysis," 62–91. Framing theory seems especially applicable to the Naomi Story book of Ruth transition, for framing concepts are grounded in communication processes. See Oliver and Johnston, "What a Good Idea!," 187–88.

49. Noakes and Johnston, "Frames of Protest," 2.

50. Johnston, "Verification and Proof in Frame and Discourse Analysis," 64.

of Ruth, refocused, or reframed attention, considering the appropriate role of ethnic boundaries in formulating a communal identity. Those promoting an ethnic and religious inclusivity like that found in the book of Ruth, constructed a way of thinking about communal identity that was ethnically pluralistic and considered fulfillment of the law apart from religious ritual. They framed reality differently than that framed by those promoting a narrow ethnic purity as found in Ezra–Nehemiah. We see in the two bodies of literature, the book of Ruth on one hand and Ezra–Nehemiah on the other, two different ways of constructing a shared self-identity, two social visions of reality in competition with one another.

Frames identify a social problem, the persons or structures responsible for the injustice, and a vision for resolution. In terms of framing processes, creating and acting upon this shared self-identity involves three component tasks: diagnostic framing, prognostic framing, and motivational framing.[51] The book of Ruth touches on all three. In the book of Ruth the ethnic boundaries between insiders and outsiders as articulated in Ezra and Nehemiah are blurred by assigning to David (the consummate Israelite insider) characteristics that make him an outsider (Moabite ancestry).[52] Further, "goodness" (the assumed quality of insiders) is attributed to the Moabitess (3:10). It was incumbent upon the movement actors, in our case those wishing to define the post-exilic Jerusalem community in terms of ethnic plurality and "goodness" (חסד) apart from ritual, to construct a view of reality (a frame) that was coherent, convincing, and compelling.[53] To accomplish this, the Naomi Story, easily revised to the book of Ruth, fit the bill. The Naomi Story already had a circulation and popularity, because it preserved a socially relevant memory, among at least a muted subgroup, the women, of sixth century BCE. Yehud. At the same time, the story signified a challenge to the status quo. It represented a subversive power that could be redirected, now to challenge notions of ethnicity where formerly it challenged accepted notions of gender.[54]

51. Snow and Benford, "Ideology, Frame Resonance and Participant Mobilization," 197–200.

52. Douglas Lawrie is not convinced that communal identity is the concern of the Book of Ruth. He writes, "It is hard to believe that the example of Ruth . . . a 'paragon of virtue' could have served as an argument against Ezra's policy regarding foreign wives." Lawrie, "Narrative Logic and Legitimized Interposition in the Book of Ruth," 96.

53. See Westby, "Strategic Imperative, Ideology, and Frames," 218.

54. Da Silva, "Ruth, plaidoyer en faveur de la femme," 252.

Commentators have sensed this communal function of the story in helping to create a group identity. Irmtraud Fischer observes, "What is narrated [the Ruth story] as a seemingly *private* story of life is to be read *politically*."[55] Through strategic labeling, both forms; the Naomi Story ("the woman") and the book of Ruth ("the Moabitess"), help create a sense of identity, a "we" verses "they." The story expressed what was politically relevant in easily identifiable terms that were immanently relatable. The story, common to the experience of members of the subgroup, also addressed issues on a social structural level.

The value of story in promoting social movements has long been affirmed by social theorists.[56] The effective story links the diagnostic, prognostic, and motivational elements required in framing a social identity by drawing audience participation into the interpretive process. The effective story resonates with people's every day experiences—it must ring true.[57] The effective story carries the authority of lived experience, yet includes ambiguities that require the investment of interpretive work on the part of the audience to anticipate the normative conclusion to which the story is driving.[58] The effective story draws the audience into the telling of the story. Certainly, the book of Ruth, as did the Naomi Story before it, satisfies these conditions. The dilemma of the story, as well as the scenes employed for the movement toward resolution, were part and parcel of the audience experience.[59] And the ambiguity resident in the pivotal threshing floor scene was certainly sufficient to draw the audience into the world of the story.[60]

55. Fischer, "The Book of Ruth," 48. Fischer's comment brings to mind the phrase "the personal is political" used effectively in discussing gender politics by Millett, *Sexual Politics*, 24–25. See also Margolis, "Redefining the Situation," 332–47.

56. See, White, "The Value of Narrativity," 5–27; Abbott, "From Causes to Effects," 428–55; Emirbayer, "Manifesto for a Relational Sociology," 281–317; Davis ed., *Stories of Change*; Snow, "Framing Processes, Ideology, and Discursive Fields," 380–412; Polletta, *It Was Like a Fever*.

57. Polletta, Chen, et al., "The Sociology of Storytelling," 123. See also Gamson, "How Storytelling Can be Empowering," 187–98; Ewick and Silbey, "Narrating Social Structure," 1328–72.

58. Polletta, Chen, et al., "The Sociology of Storytelling," 111.

59. Frank Polak suggests something close to this when he describes the "vividness of the dialogue" giving voice to opposing interests in a social drama. Polak, "Negotiations, Social Drama and Voices," 47.

60. See, too, Matthews, "The Determination of Social Identity in the Story of Ruth," 49.

Cultural memory is often expressed in narratives that describe and unite a community. Both shaped by and shaping that community, narratives can provide a sense of identity in the form of a collective past. Narrative recalls the past in order to establish an identity in the present and a vision for the future. The Naomi Story and the book of Ruth nestle themselves in that larger flow of tradition. The recall of past traditions and heroes plays an important role in both the Naomi Story and the book of Ruth. The mention of Rachel, Leah, Tamar, and the genealogies added at the end of the book help provide "narrative fidelity,"[61] connecting the frame (either gender or ethnic identity) to the larger communal narrative of myth and foundational assumptions. The relatively few and select number of tales becoming communal narratives, drawn from the vast pool of possibilities produced by the members of a society, suggests that a complex set of negotiations is a work in order to produce cultural memory.[62] Within the biblical narrative, the book of Ruth has an important role to fill negotiating a social identity of post-exilic Israel.

Editing the Book of Ruth: A Thin Veneer

The book of Ruth is the product of a series of strategic edits layered over the Naomi Story. The way Frank Polak describes select other biblical narratives is equally applicable to the book of Ruth. "The writing authors who penned these tales were intimately acquainted with the oral performance of the narrators/singers of tales and the stylistic norms of the performance, and accepted these norms as guidelines for composition in writing. Possibly some of the longer tales in the lean, brisk style were dictated by the narrator/singer for the sake of persons with interest."[63]

Nehama Aschkenasy agrees that the oral substrate is still visible just under the lines of the book of Ruth.[64]

---

61. Noakes and Johnston, "Frames of Protest: A Road Map to a Perspective," 12.

62. Polak, "Negotiations, Social Drama and Voices of Memory in Some Samuel Tales," 46.

63. Polak, "Orality: Biblical Hebrew," 934. See also Notopoulos, "Homer and Cretan Heroic Poetry: A Study in Comparative Oral Poetry," 225–50.

64. This type of editing is known elsewhere in the history of biblical texts. A relatively thin layer of sectarian editing was applied to the pre-SP group of texts from Qumran resulting in the Samaritan Pentateuch. See Anderson and Giles, *The Samaritan Pentateuch: An Introduction to Its Origin, History, and Significance for Biblical Studies*, 59–68.

While following the trajectory of comedy or even the carnivalesque genre, this form has been reshaped by the biblical narrator into a covenantal story. The elements of crude physical humor, the transformation of the figure of authority into an intoxicated, bumbling fool, and the women's double talk bringing down the lofty semantics of divine reward are secondary to the tale's overarching theme of redemption. Yet, these iconoclastic, rebellious, ironic perspectives are only thinly disguised and are still powerfully present, giving the tale its vigor and elasticity and its ability to speak to different generations without changing cultural views.[65]

The project of the Naomi Story is summarized in 1:9 "The LORD grant that you may find a home, each of you in the house of her husband." The project of the book of Ruth is expressed in the genealogy of David at the end of chapter four and the oft repeated identification of Ruth as a Moabite. Lisa Wolfe describes the purpose of the book of Ruth by saying, "it [the book of Ruth] engages precisely the issues that were hotly debated during the time: What is the definition of a foreigner? Are the 'people of the land' of Judah and Israel Jews if they didn't go off to exile? Are the people who came back to Judah from exile Jews if they didn't originally come from Judah?"[66] When did the social memory preserved in the book of Ruth become useful and serve a social function for the group promoting it? To some degree that group can be characterized by describing the conditions operative in the book of Ruth:

1. Elevates the role of David and so affirms the centrality of a past idealized politic for the construction of a present and projected future communal self-definition.

2. Deemphasizes ethnicity as a boundary for community identity by allowing a Moabitess to express loyalty / goodness (חסד) who is granted more worth than seven (ethnic Israelite) sons.

3. Promotes a sense of stable social order based upon male privilege and social status, while at the same time recognizing the role of the female as child bearer in enhancing that male status. Boaz returns social stasis to the disruption by which the story began by exerting his communal authority and reincorporating unattached females into a male dominated familial structure.

65. Aschkenasy, "From Aristotle to Bakhtin," 281.
66. Wolfe, *Ruth, Esther, Song of Songs, and Judith*, 5.

Just as the Naomi Story reflected cultural interests and priorities, the book of Ruth can be contextualized by the values and priorities it promotes.

Text and Context

The change from the Naomi Story to the book of Ruth not only changed the story itself, but changed the context in which the story was placed and understood. The social connections to the story changed. Texts are read in context and the context often determines the thematic possibilities apparent in a particular text. As the book of Ruth, the Naomi Story no longer finds its home in the informal associations of women busy with the chores and routines of domestic life in an agrarian society. As the book of Ruth, the Naomi Story has been re-contextualized and is now read within a different set of communal interests and priorities.[67] Lisa Wolfe makes a straightforward and foundational observation; "Understanding the book of Ruth relies greatly on what literary label one assigns to it."[68] When it comes to the book of Ruth, there has been no shortage of labels or associations assigned. Katrina Larkin has read Ruth in the context of two additional "short stories" from the Hebrew Bible: Esther and Joseph (Genesis 37–50). This "triumvirate" provides the context for her reading of Ruth in which enforced residence in an alien land and the working out of divine providence figure as major themes.[69] Alternatively, Agnethe Siquans suggests that Ruth has connections with other books in the Former Prophets and with Wisdom writings, especially with the strong woman of Proverbs 3:11.[70] Following a different tack, A. Meinhold contextualizes Ruth with Psalm 132, assuming a composition in a pre-deuteronomic era.[71] Others

---

67. This is illustrated well by noting the various positions within the canon that the Book of Ruth has occupied. See Dearman and Pussman, "Putting Ruth in Her Place," 84.

68. Wolfe, *Ruth, Esther, Song of Songs, and Judith*, 5.

69. Larkin, *Ruth and Esther*, 11. Edward Campbell characterizes Ruth as a historical short story. Campbell, *Ruth*, 3–5. LaCocque calls Ruth a novella, a "history-like story" (LaCocque, *Ruth*, 9), similar to the description offered by Hermann Gunkel, which moves focus away from historical reporting and toward character development. Gunkel, "Ruth," 65. Campbell refers to Ruth as a Hebrew short story that has no historical claim. Campbell, "The Hebrew Short Story," 92.

70. Siquans, "Israel braucht starke Frauen und Männer," 20–38.

71. Meinhold, "Theologische Schwerpunkte im Buch Ruth und ihr Schwergewicht für seine Datierung," 129–37.

suggest alternative contexts.[72] LaCocque persuasively argues that the theme of Ruth is that, "it is possible to perform the Torah in a creative and flexible manner, opposing the suspicious and rigid ultraconservatism of the integration party [represented by Ezra–Nehemiah]. Moab can also have a place in Israel;. . ..The sexual audacity of . . . Ruth the Moabite. . .must be judged leniently."[73]

Midrash Rabbah, *Ruth*, 2.14 agrees.

> For what purpose then was it [Ruth] written? To teach how great
> is the reward of those who do deeds of kindness.[74]

Despite the wide ranging disagreement, we conclude the book of Ruth takes its place in "the field of tension between Law and commandment" in the post-exilic world illustrated by Ezra–Nehemiah.[75] The scribe, authoring this literary remake of the Naomi Story, chose his source material well. In promoting a view of law (a loving faithfulness), extending beyond the commandments, the scribe needed a source that was widely known, readily attachable to a renowned Israelite hero, but also a source that could retain its subversive undertone in the process, all the while readily identifiable with the audiences' lived experiences. That subversive undertone persists even in the literary remake and is ultimately dependent upon the presence of provocative desire moving the Naomi Story and the book of Ruth from episode to episode.

Bellis considers Ruth within the context of "parallels between it and the story of Tamar and Judah (Gen. 38)" and in this context views it a story

---

72. Georg Braulik understands the book of Ruth as a critique on Deuteronomic law. Braulik, "The Book of Ruth as Intra-Biblical Critique on the Deuteronomic Law," 1–20. Michael Goulder sees Ruth as a "homily on Deuteronomy 23–25." Goulder, "Ruth," 307–19.

73. LaCocque, *Ruth*, 20–21.

74. Midrash Rabbah, *Ruth*, 2.14. Yet, throughout the Midrashim and in the introductory poem, the rabbis recognize that the Deuteronomic pattern of reward and punishment is not at all clear or consistent in Ruth. The opening statement of the book, "In the days the judges judged" is rendered, "Woe to the day the judges are in need of being judged" and so recognizes a disruption and subversion of the expected moral norm. See also, Kates, "Transfigured Night," 49. Elimelech, too, personifies this tragic state, for he is portrayed, not as a simple farmer who flees famine in order to find food for his family. Instead, Elimelech is portrayed as a leader of the community, upon whom others relied, and who betrayed that trust out of pure self-interest. For this betrayal he is punished by death (Midrash Rabbah: *Ruth*, 1.5).

75. LaCocque, *Ruth*, 30.

about ethnicity.[76] Bellis agrees with André LaCocque, "Tamar the Canaan-
ite becomes Ruth the Moabite, and Judah's sons and Judah, himself, become
'So and so' [the unnamed kinsman who refuses to buy Naomi's field]."[77]
Bellis believes the story's intent was to "challenge those who objected to
foreign women."[78]

Mieke Bal considers yet another context.[79] Allusions within the text
of Ruth itself (4:11–12) invite contextualization with the Rachael and Leah
story in Genesis 29–30. Bal contends that the comments by the elders in
4:11–12 (and so the author voicing the moral of the story) acknowledge,
"the rightness of the women's subversion when they equate Ruth to the position of Rachael and Leah together."[80]

Intertextuality

The contextual variety inviting the company of Ruth's story suggests wide
recognition of the power of the story. The book of Ruth presents many possible connections, but demands others. Like the Naomi Story before it, the
book of Ruth makes explicit links to Israelite ancestresses; Rachel, Leah
(4:11), and Tamar (4:12). Ruth, and her somewhat questionable nocturnal
exploits, are assigned honor by association with these heroes from the past.
These very explicit linkages, are supported by additional connections to the
plots, settings, and precipitating problems found in the patriarchal stories.[81]
While some of these similarities may simply stem from a common cultural
stock, some of the shared characteristics seem more peculiar. Below are
several of the more unusual shared characteristics:

- Relocation because of famine (Ruth 1:1 // Gen 12:26)

- Family survival endangered by childlessness (Ruth 1:5 // Genesis
  16–17; 25:21; 29:31; 30)

- Protection of a woman through whom a family line is achieved (Ruth
  2:8, 9, 22 // Gen 12:17; 20:3, 6; 26:7–11; 34:1–31)

76. Bellis, *Helpmates, Harlots, and Heroes*, 184.

77. Ibid., 184 (apud LaCocque, *The Feminine Unconventional*, 99–100). See also
LaCocque, *The Feminine Unconventional*, 105.

78. Bellis, *Helpmates, Harlots, and Heroes*, 189.

79. Bal, *Lethal Love*, 85.

80. Ibid.

81. Robert Hubbard suggests even more possible motifs from Ruth also found in the
patriarchal stories. Hubbard, *Ruth*, 40.

- Female sexual initiative pivotal in plot resolution (Ruth 3:7–15 // Genesis 38)

- Marriage to a foreigner leading to a ruling dynasty (Ruth 4:13, 17b–22 // Genesis 38; 41:45, 50–52)

- Conception as a divine gift (4:12, 13 // Gen 21:1–2; 25:21; 29:31; 30:17; 30:22, 23; and also 1 Samuel 1:19–20)[82]

The parallels from the patriarchal stories noted above, are, in the book of Ruth, boldly aligned with the Moabitess in a way that must also bring to mind: Gen 19:36; Numbers 21–23; 25:1; and Deut 23:3.

Mark Leuchter is of the opinion that the story of Tamar in Genesis 38 is an implicit complaint against the Judahite monarchy. If this is indeed the case, an intriguing similarity exists between the Genesis 38 story and the book of Ruth. The parallels that exist between Ruth and Tamar in Genesis 38 have been noted by others.[83] The difference in the two tales is that while Genesis 38 presents a complaint against (but significantly not a rejection) of the Judahite monarchy, Ruth has been recast, with the revisions to chapter four, presenting the Davidic line in a positive light.[84] Leuchter describes the view expressed in Genesis 38: "Kingship is not pitted against rural culture but is claimed by it, positioned as an institution that draws sacral legitimacy through its connection to agrarian life."[85] Certainly, the same is true in Ruth. Of Genesis 38, Mark Leuchter writes:

> If the narrative is a metaphor for the uprooting of the rural Judahite population, then Judah's mistreatment of Tamar parallels the monarchic administration's mistreatment of the hinterland and its institutions. The conclusion of the narrative, which sees Tamar give birth to David's ancestor Perez, drives home the author's polemical point: the future of the Judahite kingdom will be secured only if

82. While parallels between Ruth's conception and conception stories in Genesis and 1 Samuel are certainly evident, so, too, is one major difference. In the Genesis and Samuel episodes, God or YHWH: visits, grants a prayer, opens a womb, remembers, or hearkens. In Ruth 4:13, YHWH takes a much more active and direct role by actually "giving" conception.

83. See Van Wolde, "Texts in Dialogue with Texts," 8–12.

84. Carlos Bovell also points to a hoped for restoration of the Davidic dynasty as a key in understanding the book but points not to the genealogy at the end of the book, but to, what he sees as a, chiastic structure in the opening of the book (1:1–6). Bovell, "Symmetry, Ruth and Canon," 190.

85. Leuchter, "Genesis 38 in Social and Historical Perspective," 227.

the royal administration, like Judah himself, admits the errors of its ways and ends its assault on the institutions of the hinterland.[86]

It is fascinating to consider Leuchter's suggestion that the Tamar in Genesis 38 is a recast taken from an "old myth regarding a woman of the same name who symbolized the principle of the land's numinous fertility in rural lore."[87] In this respect, the Tamar story of Genesis 38 represents the same sort of "covering" or reusing of an older story as we see in the literate recasting of the Naomi Story.[88] Both may have taken a well-known story from popular culture and recast it, giving it a spin and purpose decidedly political in intent.

Ruth: Genealogies and Identity

Connections are important in the book of Ruth. For one commentator at least, the marriage between Ruth (descended from Lot) and Boaz (descended from Abraham) repairs the long split patriarchal house and concludes the Ruth corpus as "*Heilsgeschichte* in miniature."[89] It does seem clear that the book of Ruth, unlike the Naomi Story, has a "looking before and after"[90] in which the genealogies at the beginning and the end of the book are not secondary appendages[91] but necessary mechanisms connecting the patriarchs with the royal house of David. These connections are part of the process by which a communal identity was presented by the Ruth author. Ingeborg Löwisch makes the case that the traditions given expression in the creation story, the exodus, and genealogies "refer to Israel's origins and

---

86. Ibid., 225.

87. Ibid., 226. Katherine Doob Sakenfeld, based upon information gleaned from the genealogies of Ruth, Chronicles, and Genesis argues that the Ruth tradition shows greater affinity to Genesis than to Chronicles. Sakenfeld, "Why Perez?," 416.

88. Leuchter, relying on the analysis conducted by Frank Polak, characterizes Genesis 38 as an "intermediate style, that is, a form of expression generally oral in character but containing periodic flourishes of complex characteristics." Leuchter, "Genesis 38 in Social and Historical Perspective," 215.

89. Fisch, "Ruth and the Structure of Covenant History," 435.

90. Ibid., 435.

91. The unity of that final product is well documented in an article by Stephan Bertman in which he clearly described the symmetrical design of Ruth. The classic chiastic structure, as identified by Bertman, has few anomalies (2:1; 2:15–18; 4:13), none of which detract from the "unifying plan" or "architecture." Bertman, "Symmetrical Design in the Book of Ruth," 168.

emergence in order to identify resources and formulate identities."[92] The same can be said for the book of Ruth which uses a dynastic origin story to help formulate an identity for a post-exilic community. A comparison between the genealogies in the book of Ruth and those found in Chronicles, Ezra, Nehemiah may prove instructive in understanding that communal identity.

The references to women in the Chronicles genealogies "follow specific linguistic patterns and feature distinct themes. They build a corpus of *female-gendered genealogies* that establishes one of several counter-traditions subverting the normative layer of the overall text unit."[93] Why then do those genealogies, concerned with the house of David, not include Ruth?[94] This despite the fact that the genealogies of Judah and the house of David (1 Chron 2:3–4:23) contain the highest concentration of female entries in all the genealogies appearing in 1 Chronicles 1–9. It is also worth noting that the genealogies of Judah and David also contain a high number of non-Israelites (2:16–17; 2:34–36). In fact, the Chronicler, "does not moralize against the important roles that non-Israelites played in his people's past. Quite the contrary, he calls attention to them."[95] As a female, non-Israelite, Ruth's absence from the Chronicler's genealogy is conspicuous. Genealogies are constructed to help "reconstruct identity over periods of change."[96] Ruth's absence from the genealogies of Chronicles may simply indicate that her mention did not facilitate the kind of community identity the Chronicler was intent on constructing.[97] But, if the community identity created by the Judah genealogies is inclusive and multi-layered in terms of "gender as well as in terms of ethnicity and class,"[98] it seems as though the inclusion of Ruth in the ancestry of David would be of benefit, adding to the weight of the other Canaanites, Ishmaelites, Arameans, Egyptians, and Moabites already included in the Judah genealogies. Ruth, as female and Moabite, was important to the community identity being fashioned through the genealogies

---

92. Löwisch, "Genealogies, Gender, and the Politics of Memory," 228.

93. Ibid., 228.

94. Sarah, too, is absent from the genealogies of 1:1—2:2.

95. Knoppers, *1 Chronicles 1–9*, 302.

96. Löwisch, "Genealogies, Gender, and the Politics of Memory," 230.

97. See Geoghegan, "Israelite Sheepshearing and David's Rise to Power," 63.

98. Löwisch, "Genealogies, Gender, and the Politics of Memory," 238. See also Knoppers,"Intermarriage, Social Complexity, and Ethnic Diversity in the Genealogy of Judah," 30.

appearing in the book of Ruth, but not to the community identity fashioned through the genealogies appearing in Chronicles, Ezra, and Nehemiah.[99] As contemporary to Chronicles, Ezra, and Nehemiah, the book of Ruth recommends interracial marriage at the same time Chronicles, Ezra, and Nehemiah oppose it, going so far as to recommend existing marriages be annulled (Neh 13:23–27). The Nehemiah author refers to Solomon (Neh 13:26) as support for the proscribed ethnically exclusive social actions, but the author of Ruth refers back to ancient heroes as well—David, and the already seen episodes from Genesis to counter the arguments of Chronicles, Ezra, and Nehemiah. "Thus she [author of Ruth] quotes texts from Genesis in order to tell her new story. She consciously refers to the commandments of the Torah, treating them in an unusual way in order to point out a new view of legal regulations. In her argument she refers to the tradition, yet she actualizes it—and especially in favor of women."[100]

Conclusion: Subverting the Subversive—From Oral to Written

The movement from oral presentation to written document has been observed elsewhere in ancient texts. Although the book of Ruth, written in sixth-century Yehud, comes from a quite different social context than the gospels of first and second century Palestine, the oral-literate dynamics present in the New Testament gospels may be illuminating in our consideration of the movement from the oral performance of the Naomi Story to the book of Ruth. Concerning the rise of the written gospel, Kelber writes, "Strictly speaking, therefore, the gospel [genre] arises not from orality *per se*, but out of the debris of the deconstructed orality."[101] Does the same happen with Ruth? Does the literate version of Ruth arise from the deconstructed oral version of Naomi—or in other words is the book of Ruth a subversion of the subversive Naomi Story?[102]

99. The assumption we make here is that the Ruth omission from the Chronicles genealogies was intentional. It is certainly possible that the Chronicler simply did not know about the Ruth story.

100. Fischer, "The Book of Ruth," 46.

101. Kelber, *The Oral and the Written Gospel*, 94–95.

102. A similar process is considered in application to the Hebrew prophetic literature by Nissinen, "The Dubious Image of Prophecy," 26–41. "The more scripture represented the true word of God and its interpreters the intermediaries of God, the more dubious the traditional prophetic performance became . . . they [the prophets] were despised rather than appreciated by the learned circles and were therefore probably driven to the

Just as the written gospels of the New Testament were not necessary or inevitable outcomes of their oral precursors, so, too, the written Ruth is not a necessary development of the oral version of the Naomi Story. The Book of Ruth is a creative event that uses cultural memory (the Naomi Story) for a specific purpose. In fact, Kelber asserts that the written gospels were not designed to preserve the oral traditions about Jesus—but to put an end to them.[103] Perhaps, the book of Ruth does the same—it usurps the Naomi Story by stealing its subversive power and applying it to a project different than what was intended by the oral performers. As with the gospels of the New Testament, the Book of Ruth may have efficiently, whether intentionally or not, brought an end to the performance tradition of Naomi and so effectively subverted the subversion.[104]

---

margins of society." (41). Armin Lange makes a similar observation: "The demise of aural prophecy is thus accompanied by an increasing prominence of literary prophecy." Lange, "Literary Prophecy and Oracle Collection: A Comparison between Judah and Greece in Persian Times," 260. See also Hornsby, "Ezekiel Off-Broadway," 2.1–2.8; Sherwood, "Prophetic Performance Art," 1.1–1.4.

103. Tom Thatcher, commenting on Kelber's position writes, "Matthew, Mark, Luke and John were not seeking to preserve and perpetuate the voices of their oral predecessors, but rather to silence them." Thatcher, "Beyond Texts and Traditions," 24. Doan and Giles suggest a very similar dynamic at work among the Hebrew prophets and their written legacy. Doan and Giles, *Prophets, Performance and Power: Performance Criticism of the Hebrew Bible*, 22–24. See also Schaper, "The Death of the Prophet," 66.

104. This is just the opposite of how Bauckham considers the book of Ruth a corrective to an overly male dominated perspective found within the biblical books. Bauckham, *Is the Bible Male?*

PART 2

5

Reconstructing the Naomi Story

In the reconstruction below, we present the Naomi Story in five acts. We are not the only, or the first, commentators to conceive of the story in terms of acts or scenes. Jacob Licht analyzed the book of Ruth, suggesting that it is constructed in four scenes connected by minor scenes[1] and Lisa Wolfe suggests that "one possibility is to view Ruth as a play in four acts, corresponding to each of the four chapters."[2] Shimon Levy considered the dramatic form of the book and suggests twelve distinct scenes.[3] We differ from those who have preceded us in several key regards. First, our concern is not primarily with the book of Ruth, but the Naomi Story on which the book was based. Consequently, in the reconstruction to follow, the city gate scene is truncated, composed of 4:2, 3, 9–12, the section we believe closer to the act as presented in the Naomi Story. That act was modified considerably, by the writer of the book of Ruth, changing it into the episode now found in 4:1–12. Second, we have attempted to be mindful of the role of the narrator in telling the Naomi Story. Throughout the book of Ruth there are several verses that appear to be redundant in the information they offer the reader or summary in nature. If understood as "scene changers" or scene openers and closers, the redundant or summary verses assume a new function. They

1. Licht, *Storytelling in the Bible*, 126–27.
2. Wolfe, *Ruth, Esther, Song of Songs, and Judith*, 6.
3. Levy, *The Bible as Theatre*, 85. The structure we suggest is similar to Levy's divisions, but we distinguish between Act and Scene as well as openers and closers.

signal to the audience a change of scene and serve to organize the dialogue in the story. The Naomi Story can be structured as follows:

1:1–6—Narrative Introduction
1:7–22—Act 1: Where is Security to be Found?
    1:7   Scene 1 opener: In the Fields of Moab
    1:19a— Scene 1 closer
    1:19b— Scene 2 opener: Returning to Bethlehem
    1:22— Scene 2 closer
2:1–23—Act 2: Gleaning in the Fields
    2:1   opener
    2:23   closer
3:1–18—Act 3: The Threshing Floor
    3:1   opener
    3:18   closer
4:2, 3, 9–12 Act 4: At the City Gate
4:13–17 Act 5: A Son is Born to Naomi
    4:13   opener

Naomi Story / Book of Ruth[4]

Sections, in the Book of Ruth, appearing in bold represent material believed to have been added to the Naomi Story or altered (sometimes only in prominent English translations) in order to achieve the purpose of the literary author, that being to serve as a counter-voice to the ethnic exclusivity represented by Ezra and Nehemiah.

Naomi Story	Book of Ruth
Introduction: 1:1–6	Chapter 1
In the days of the judging of the judges, there was a famine in the land, and a certain woman of Bethlehem in Judah went to live in the fields of Moab, she and her husband and two sons. 2 The name of the woman was Naomi and the name of her husband was Elimelech, and the names of her two sons were Mahlon and Chilion; they were Ephrathites from Bethlehem in Judah.	In the days **when the judges ruled**, there was a famine in the land, and a **certain man** of Bethlehem in Judah went to live in the **country** of Moab, **he and his wife** and two sons. 2 **The name of the man was Elimelech and the name of his wife Naomi, and the names of his two sons were Mahlon and Chilion**; they were Ephrathites from Bethlehem in Judah.

4. Text based on NRSV.

They went into the fields of Moab and remained there. 3But Elimelech, the husband of Naomi, died, and she was left with her two sons. 4These took Moabite wives; the name of one was Orpah and the name of the other Ruth. When they had lived there for about ten years, 5both Mahlon and Chilion also died, so that the woman was left without her two sons or her husband.

6Then she started to return with her daughters-in-law from the fields of Moab, for she had heard in the fields of Moab that the Lord had had consideration for his people and given them food.

Act 1: 1:7–12

7So she set out from the place where she had been living, she and her two daughters-in-law, and they went on their way to go back to the land of Judah. 8But Naomi said to her two daughters-in-law, 'Go back each of you to your mother's house. May the Lord deal kindly with you, as you have dealt with the dead and with me. 9The Lord grant that you may find security, each of you in the house of your husband.' Then she kissed them, and they wept aloud. 10They said to her, 'No, we will return with you to your people.' 11But Naomi said, 'Turn back, my daughters, why will you go with me? Do I still have sons in my womb that they may become your husbands? 12Turn back, my daughters, go your way, for I am too old to have a husband. Even if I thought there was hope for me, even if I should have a husband tonight and bear sons, 13would you then wait until they were grown? Would you then refrain from marrying? No, my daughters, it has been far more bitter for me than for

They went into the **country** of Moab and remained there. 3But Elimelech, the husband of Naomi, died, and she was left with her two sons. 4These took Moabite wives; the name of one was Orpah and the name of the other Ruth. When they had lived there for about ten years, 5both Mahlon and Chilion also died, so that the woman was left without her two sons or her husband.

6Then she started to return with her daughters-in-law from the **country** of Moab, for she had heard in the **country** of Moab that the Lord had had consideration for his people and given them food.

7So she set out from the place where she had been living, she and her two daughters-in-law, and they went on their way to go back to the land of Judah. 8But Naomi said to her two daughters-in-law, 'Go back each of you to your mother's house. May the Lord deal kindly with you, as you have dealt with the dead and with me. 9The Lord grant that you may find security, each of you in the house of your husband.' Then she kissed them, and they wept aloud. 10They said to her, 'No, we will return with you to your people.' 11But Naomi said, 'Turn back, my daughters, why will you go with me? Do I still have sons in my womb that they may become your husbands? 12Turn back, my daughters, go your way, for I am too old to have a husband. Even if I thought there was hope for me, even if I should have a husband tonight and bear sons, 13would you then wait until they were grown? Would you then refrain from marrying? No, my daughters, it has been far more bitter for me than for you, because the hand of the Lord has turned against me.' 14Then they wept aloud again. Orpah kissed her mother-in-law, but Ruth clung to her.

15 So she said, 'See, your sister-in-law has gone back to her people and to her gods; return after your sister-in-law.' 16But Ruth said,
'Do not press me to leave you or to turn back from following you! Where you go, I will go; where you spend the night, I will spend the night; your people shall be my people, and your God my God. 17Where you die, I will die— there will I be buried. May the Lord do thus and so to me, and more as well, if even death parts me from you!' 18When Naomi saw that she was determined to go with her, she said no more to her.

19 So the two of them went on until they came to Bethlehem. When they came to Bethlehem, the whole town was stirred because of them; and the women said, 'Is this Naomi?' 20She said to them, 'Call me no longer Naomi, call me Mara, for the Almighty has dealt bitterly with me.
21I went away full, but the Lord has brought me back empty; why call me Naomi when the Lord has dealt harshly with me, and the Almighty has brought calamity upon me?'

22 So Naomi returned together with Ruth, her daughter-in-law, who came back with her from the fields of Moab. They came to Bethlehem at the beginning of the barley harvest.

Act 2: 2:1–23

2Now Naomi had a kinsman on her husband's side, a respected worthy man,

you, because the hand of the Lord has turned against me.' 14Then they wept aloud again. Orpah kissed her mother-in-law, but Ruth clung to her.

15 So she said, 'See, your sister-in-law has gone back to her people and to her gods; return after your sister-in-law.' 16But Ruth said,
'Do not press me to leave you or to turn back from following you! Where you go, I will go; where you **lodge**, I will **lodge**; your people shall be my people, and your God my God. 17Where you die, I will die— there will I be buried. May the Lord do thus and so to me, and more as well, if even death parts me from you!' 18When Naomi saw that she was determined to go with her, she said no more to her.

19 So the two of them went on until they came to Bethlehem. When they came to Bethlehem, the whole town was stirred because of them; and the women said, 'Is this Naomi?' 20She said to them, 'Call me no longer Naomi, call me Mara, for the Almighty has dealt bitterly with me.
21 I went away full, but the Lord has brought me back empty; why call me Naomi when the Lord has dealt harshly with me, and the Almighty has brought calamity upon me?'

22 So Naomi returned together with Ruth **the Moabite**, her daughter-in-law, who came back with her from the **country** of Moab. They came to Bethlehem at the beginning of the barley harvest.

Chapter 2

2Now Naomi had a kinsman on her husband's side, **a prominent rich** of the family of Elimelech, whose name was Boaz. 2And Ruth said to Naomi, 'Let me go to the field and glean among the ears of grain, behind someone in whose sight I may find favor.' She said to her, 'Go, my daughter.' 3So she went. She came and gleaned in the field behind the reapers. As it happened, she came to the part of the field belonging to Boaz, who was of the family of Elimelech. 4Just then Boaz came from Bethlehem. He said to the reapers, 'The Lord be with you.' They answered, 'The Lord bless you.' 5Then Boaz said to his servant who was in charge of the reapers, 'To whom does this young woman belong?' 6The servant who was in charge of the reapers answered, 'She is Ruth who came back with Naomi from the fields of Moab. 7She said, "Please let me glean and gather among the sheaves behind the reapers." So she came, and she has been on her feet from early this morning until now, without resting even for a moment.'

8 Then Boaz said to Ruth, 'Now listen, my daughter, do not go to glean in another field or leave this one, but keep close to my young women. 9Keep your eyes on the field that is being reaped, and follow behind them. I have ordered the young men not to bother you. If you get thirsty, go to the vessels and drink from what the young men have drawn.' 10Then she fell prostrate, with her face to the ground, and said to him, 'Why have I found favor in your sight, that you should take notice of me, when I am a foreigner?' 11But Boaz answered her, 'All that you have done for your mother-in-law since the death of your husband has been fully told me, and

man, of the family of Elimelech, whose name was Boaz. 2And Ruth **the Moabite** said to Naomi, 'Let me go to the field and glean among the ears of grain, behind someone in whose sight I may find favor.' She said to her, 'Go, my daughter.' 3So she went. She came and gleaned in the field behind the reapers. As it happened, she came to the part of the field belonging to Boaz, who was of the family of Elimelech. 4Just then Boaz came from Bethlehem. He said to the reapers, 'The Lord be with you.' They answered, 'The Lord bless you.' 5Then Boaz said to his servant who was in charge of the reapers, 'To whom does this young woman belong?' 6The servant who was in charge of the reapers answered, 'She is **the Moabite** who came back with Naomi from the **country** of Moab. 7She said, "Please let me glean and gather among the sheaves behind the reapers." So she came, and she has been on her feet from early this morning until now, without resting even for a moment.'

8 Then Boaz said to Ruth, 'Now listen, my daughter, do not go to glean in another field or leave this one, but keep close to my young women. 9Keep your eyes on the field that is being reaped, and follow behind them. I have ordered the young men not to bother you. If you get thirsty, go to the vessels and drink from what the young men have drawn.' 10Then she fell prostrate, with her face to the ground, and said to him, 'Why have I found favor in your sight, that you should take notice of me, when I am a foreigner?' 11But Boaz answered her, 'All that you have done for your mother-in-law since the death of your husband has been fully told me, and

how you left your father and mother and your native land and came to a people that you did not know before. 12May the Lord reward you for your deeds, and may you have a full reward from the Lord, the God of Israel, under whose wings you have come for refuge!' 13Then she said, 'May I continue to find favor in your sight, my lord, for you have comforted me and spoken kindly to your servant, even though I am not one of your servants.'

14 At mealtime Boaz said to her, 'Come here, and eat some of this bread, and dip your morsel in the sour wine.' So she sat beside the reapers, and he heaped up for her some parched grain. She ate until she was satisfied, and she had some left over. 15When she got up to glean, Boaz instructed his young men, 'Let her glean even among the standing sheaves, and do not reproach her. 16You must also pull out some handfuls for her from the bundles, and leave them for her to glean, and do not rebuke her.'

17 So she gleaned in the field until evening. Then she beat out what she had gleaned, and it was about an ephah of barley. 18She picked it up and came into the town, and her mother-in-law saw how much she had gleaned. Then she took out and gave her what was left over after she herself had been satisfied. 19Her mother-in-law said to her, 'Where did you glean today? And where have you worked? Blessed be the man who took notice of you.' So she told her mother-in-law with whom she had worked, and said, 'The name of the man with whom I worked today is Boaz.' 20Then Naomi said to her daughter-in-law, 'Blessed be he by the Lord, whose

how you left your father and mother and your native land and came to a people that you did not know before. 12May the Lord reward you for your deeds, and may you have a full reward from the Lord, the God of Israel, under whose wings you have come for refuge!' 13Then she said, 'May I continue to find favor in your sight, my lord, for you have comforted me and spoken kindly to your servant, even though I am not one of your servants.'

14 At mealtime Boaz said to her, 'Come here, and eat some of this bread, and dip your morsel in the sour wine.' So she sat beside the reapers, and he heaped up for her some parched grain. She ate until she was satisfied, and she had some left over. 15When she got up to glean, Boaz instructed his young men, 'Let her glean even among the standing sheaves, and do not reproach her. 16You must also pull out some handfuls for her from the bundles, and leave them for her to glean, and do not rebuke her.'

17 So she gleaned in the field until evening. Then she beat out what she had gleaned, and it was about an ephah of barley. 18She picked it up and came into the town, and her mother-in-law saw how much she had gleaned. Then she took out and gave her what was left over after she herself had been satisfied. 19Her mother-in-law said to her, 'Where did you glean today? And where have you worked? Blessed be the man who took notice of you.' So she told her mother-in-law with whom she had worked, and said, 'The name of the man with whom I worked today is Boaz.' 20Then Naomi said to her daughter-in-law, 'Blessed be he by the

kindness has not forsaken the living or the dead!' Naomi also said to her, 'The man is a relative of ours, one of our nearest kin.' 21 Then Ruth said, 'He even said to me, "Stay close by my servants, until they have finished all my harvest."' 22 Naomi said to Ruth, her daughter-in-law, 'It is better, my daughter, that you go out with his young women, otherwise you might be bothered in another field.' 23 So she stayed close to the young women of Boaz, gleaning until the end of the barley and wheat harvests; and she lived with her mother-in-law.

Act 3: 3:1–18

3 Naomi her mother-in-law said to her, 'My daughter, I need to seek some security for you, so that it may be well with you. 2 Now here is our kinsman Boaz, with whose young women you have been working. See, he is winnowing barley tonight at the threshing-floor. 3 Now wash and anoint yourself, and put on your best clothes and go down to the threshing-floor; but do not make yourself known to the man until he has finished eating and drinking. 4 When he lies down, observe the place where he lies; then, go and uncover his feet and lie down; and he will tell you what to do.' 5 She said to her, 'All that you tell me I will do.'

6 So she went down to the threshing-floor and did just as her mother-in-law had instructed her. 7 When Boaz had eaten and drunk, and he was in a contented mood, he went to lie down at the end of the heap of grain. Then she came quietly and uncovered herself at his feet, and lay down. 8 At midnight the man was startled and turned over, and there, lying at his feet, was a woman!

Lord, whose kindness has not forsaken the living or the dead!' Naomi also said to her, 'The man is a relative of ours, one of our nearest kin.' 21 Then Ruth **the Moabite** said, 'He even said to me, "Stay close by my servants, until they have finished all my harvest."' 22 Naomi said to Ruth, her daughter-in-law, 'It is better, my daughter, that you go out with his young women, otherwise you might be bothered in another field.' 23 So she stayed close to the young women of Boaz, gleaning until the end of the barley and wheat harvests; and she lived with her mother-in-law.

Chapter 3

3 Naomi her mother-in-law said to her, 'My daughter, I need to seek some security for you, so that it may be well with you. 2 Now here is our kinsman Boaz, with whose young women you have been working. See, he is winnowing barley tonight at the threshing-floor. 3 Now wash and anoint yourself, and put on your best clothes and go down to the threshing-floor; but do not make yourself known to the man until he has finished eating and drinking. 4 When he lies down, observe the place where he lies; then, go and uncover his feet and lie down; and he will tell you what to do.' 5 She said to her, 'All that you tell me I will do.'

6 So she went down to the threshing-floor and did just as her mother-in-law had instructed her. 7 When Boaz had eaten and drunk, and he was in a contented mood, he went to lie down at the end of the heap of grain. Then she came quietly and uncovered his feet, and lay down. 8 At midnight the man was startled and turned over, and there, lying at his feet, was a woman! 9 He said,

9He said, 'Who are you?' And she answered, 'I am Ruth, your servant; spread your cloak over your servant, for you are next-of-kin.' 10He said, 'May you be blessed by the Lord, my daughter; this last instance of your kindness is better than the first; you have not gone after young men, whether poor or rich. 11And now, my daughter, do not be afraid; I will do for you all that you ask, for all the assembly of my people know that you are a worthy woman.

13Remain this night, and in the morning, then, as the Lord lives, I will act as next-of-kin for you. Lie down until the morning.'

14 So she lay at his feet until morning, but got up before one person could recognize another; for he said, 'It must not be known that the woman came to the threshing-floor.' 15Then he said, 'Bring the cloak you are wearing and hold it out.' So she held it, and he measured out six measures of barley, and put it on her back; then he went into the city. 16She came to her mother-in-law, who said, 'How did things go with you, my daughter?' Then she told her all that the man had done for her, 17saying, 'He gave me these six measures of barley, for he said, "Do not go back to your mother-in-law empty-handed."' 18She replied, 'Wait, my daughter, until you learn how the matter turns out, for the man will not rest, but will settle the matter today.'

Act 4: 4:2, 3, 9–12

42Then Boaz took ten men of the elders of the city, and said, 'Sit down here'; so

'Who are you?' And she answered, 'I am Ruth, your servant; spread your cloak over your servant, for you are next-of-kin.' 10He said, 'May you be blessed by the Lord, my daughter; this last instance of your **loyalty** is better than the first; you have not gone after young men, whether poor or rich. 11And now, my daughter, do not be afraid; I will do for you all that you ask, for all the assembly of my people know that you are a worthy woman. **12But now, though it is true that I am a near kinsman, there is another kinsman more closely related than I.** 13Remain this night, and in the morning, **if he will act as next-of-kin for you, good; let him do so. If he is not willing to act as next-of-kin for you,** then, as the Lord lives, I will act as next-of-kin for you. Lie down until the morning.'

14 So she lay at his feet until morning, but got up before one person could recognize another; for he said, 'It must not be known that the woman came to the threshing-floor.' 15Then he said, 'Bring the cloak you are wearing and hold it out.' So she held it, and he measured out six measures of barley, and put it on her back; then he went into the city. 16She came to her mother-in-law, who said, 'How did things go with you, my daughter?' Then she told her all that the man had done for her, 17saying, 'He gave me these six measures of barley, for he said, "Do not go back to your mother-in-law empty-handed."' 18She replied, 'Wait, my daughter, until you learn how the matter turns out, for the man will not rest, but will settle the matter today.'

Chapter 4

4No sooner had Boaz gone up to the gate and sat down there than

they sat down. 3He then said, 'Naomi, who has come back from the fields of Moab, is selling the field that belonged to our kinsman Elimelech.

the next-of-kin, of whom Boaz had spoken, came passing by. So Boaz said, 'Come over, friend; sit down here.' And he went over and sat down. 2Then Boaz took ten men of the elders of the city, and said, 'Sit down here'; so they sat down. 3He then said **to the next-of-kin,** 'Naomi, who has come back from the **country** of Moab, is selling the **parcel** of land that belonged to our kinsman Elimelech. **4So I thought I would tell you of it, and say: Buy it in the presence of those sitting here, and in the presence of the elders of my people. If you will redeem it, redeem it; but if you will not, tell me, so that I may know; for there is no one prior to you to redeem it, and I come after you.' So he said, 'I will redeem it.' 5Then Boaz said, 'The day you acquire the field from the hand of Naomi, you are also acquiring Ruth the Moabite, the widow of the dead man, to maintain the dead man's name on his inheritance.' 6At this, the next-of-kin said, 'I cannot redeem it for myself without damaging my own inheritance. Take my right of redemption yourself, for I cannot redeem it.'**

7 Now this was the custom in former times in Israel concerning redeeming and exchanging: to confirm a transaction, one party took off a sandal and gave it to the other; this was the manner of attesting in Israel. 8So when the next-of-kin said to Boaz, 'Acquire it for yourself,' he took off his sandal. 9Then Boaz said to the elders and all the people, 'Today you are witnesses that I have **acquired** from the hand of

9Then Boaz said to the elders and all the people, 'Today you are witnesses that I have purchased from the hand of Naomi all that belonged to Elimelech and all that belonged to Chilion and Mahlon. 10I have also purchased Ruth, the wife of Mahlon, to be my wife, to maintain the dead man's name on his inheritance, in order that the name of the dead may not be cut off from his kindred and from the gate of his native place; today you are witnesses.' 11Then all the people who were at the gate, along with the elders, said, 'We are witnesses. May the Lord make the woman who is coming into your house like Rachel and Leah, who together built up the house of Israel. May you produce children in Ephrathah and bestow a name in Bethlehem; 12and, through the children that the Lord will give you by this young woman, may your house be like the house of Perez, whom Tamar bore to Judah.'

Act 5: 4:13–17a13

So Boaz took Ruth and she became his woman. When they came together, the Lord made her conceive, and she bore a son. 14Then the women said to Naomi, 'Blessed be the Lord, who has not left you this day without next-of-kin; and may his name be renowned in Israel! 15He shall be to you a restorer of life and a nourisher of your old age; for your daughter-in-law who loves you, who is more to you than seven sons, has borne him.' 16Then Naomi took the child and laid him in her bosom, and became his nurse. 17The women of the neighborhood gave him a name, saying, 'A son has been born to Naomi.' They named him Obed.

Naomi all that belonged to Elimelech and all that belonged to Chilion and Mahlon. 10I have also **acquired** Ruth **the Moabite**, the wife of Mahlon, to be my wife, to maintain the dead man's name on his inheritance, in order that the name of the dead may not be cut off from his kindred and from the gate of his native place; today you are witnesses.' 11Then all the people who were at the gate, along with the elders, said, 'We are witnesses. May the Lord make the woman who is coming into your house like Rachel and Leah, who together built up the house of Israel. May you produce children in Ephrathah and bestow a name in Bethlehem; 12and, through the children that the Lord will give you by this young woman, may your house be like the house of Perez, whom Tamar bore to Judah.'

13 So Boaz took Ruth and she became his **wife**. When they came together, the Lord made her conceive, and she bore a son. 14Then the women said to Naomi, 'Blessed be the Lord, who has not left you this day without next-of-kin; and may his name be renowned in Israel! 15He shall be to you a restorer of life and a nourisher of your old age; for your daughter-in-law who loves you, who is more to you than seven sons, has borne him.' 16Then Naomi took the child and laid him in her bosom, and became his nurse. 17The women of the neighborhood gave him a name, saying, 'A son has been born to Naomi.' They named him Obed; **he became the father of Jesse, the father of David.**

18 Now these are the descendants of Perez: Perez became the father of Hezron, 19Hezron of Ram, Ram of Amminadab, 20Amminadab

of Nahshon, Nahshon of Salmon, 21Salmon of Boaz, Boaz of Obed, 22Obed of Jesse, and Jesse of David.

Contrasting the Naomi Story Performance Tradition and the Book of Ruth

There are several noticeable differences between our reconstruction of the Naomi Story and the literary remake in the book of Ruth.

1. The contextualization "in the days of judging the judges" (1:1) is a necessary part of the book of Ruth, often translated as a time signifier, eventually leading to the genealogy of David in 4:18–22. In the Naomi Story, the opening serves a very different purpose. In the Naomi Story, the opening context is not primarily a time but a condition. The awkward phrase that opens the Naomi Story points to a topsy turvy time, upside down, and abnormal. A time when judges were judged. There is a general consensus that the genealogy at the end of the book (4:17b–22) is a later addition to the story,[5] although the mention of David in 4:17b does form a balance to the mention of Bethlehem in the beginning of the story.

2. The point of view in 1:2, 3, and 5 has, in the book of Ruth, assumed Elimelech as the main character. A simple restructuring of the affected sentences easily places Naomi back on center stage making these three statements consistent to the point of view normative in chapters 1–3.

3. Act Four in the Naomi Story is the most speculative part of the reconstruction. The current rendering of 4:1–12 is remarkable in that it deviates from the female orientation generally found through chapters 1–3, offering instead a male perspective on the transaction at the city gate. Chapter 4:1–12 also evidences the heaviest amount of sixth century redaction, demonstrating a significantly higher percentage of complex syntactical structure including complex subordinate clauses and nouns with attribute, when compared to the rest of the book. These two observations may indicate that it was not part of the original Naomi Story. Nevertheless, there are connectors in Act Four,

---

5. Eissfeldt, *The Old Testament*, 480; Fohrer, *Introduction of the Old Testament*, 251; Gunneweg, *Understanding the Old Testament*, 164.

integrating 4:1–12 to the rest of the story. Three options for the reconstruction of Act Four are presented below.

- The first option is to remove 4:1–12 from the Naomi Story. A natural transition occurs between 3:18 and 4:13 allowing the story to
proceed to a conclusion following Naomi's foreshadowing statement in 3:18. Removing the city gate scene preserves the female
orientation found throughout the rest of the story and provides
greater syntactical consistency throughout the story. With the
removal of the city gate scene, the complication represented by a
kinsman more qualified than Boaz,[6] Mr. So-and-So, is removed,
and so, too, his awkward introduction in 3:12. It may be that the
awkwardly placed statement in the book of Ruth appearing in 2:1
gives evidence of the secondary addition of 3:12; 4:1–12. The identification of Boaz as the kinsman (2:1) makes perfect sense in the
Naomi Story tradition, but in the book of Ruth is a bit misleading,
at least in its present location.[7] Conversely, the addition of 3:12 and
4:1–12 well serves the proposed "project" of the book of Ruth. The
levirate system failed and Ruth demonstrated loyalty (חסד) apart
from the law. In a sense, 3:12 and 4:1–12 provide double confirmation. Their removal makes the gender oriented project of the Naomi Story quite clear, and the insertion of these sections partially
transforms the story to focus on the role of Torah in providing
righteousness, a concern more appropriate to the book of Ruth.

- The second option, and the one we recommend, is to truncate Act
Four, consisting of 4:2, 3, 9–12. This configuration, while making Boaz the main actor, preserves Naomi's presence through the
"field" that suddenly appears in 4:3. Naomi and Ruth are present in
Act Four as pawns in the economic dealings of the males. The contrast to the previous character development of the females in Acts
1–3 is dramatic. Act Four serves as illustration of the complaint
made in 1:9. Although Naomi's "field" appears quite abruptly in
4:3 and provides the supposed impetus for the proceedings at the
city gate, the strategic, and unusual use of "field" in 1:1, 2, 6, 22;

6. Stephen Bertman has considered a symmetrical design in the literary version of
Ruth that may well support our contention that the written version is an overlay of an
oral tradition. Bertman, "Symmetrical Design in the Book of Ruth," 165–68.

7. A similar observation is made by Russell Hendel, although he suggests it is chapter
3 that can be omitted not chapter 4. Hendel, "Ruth," 256.

2:6, and the near homonym used in the name given to the deity in 1:21, suggest that the field, and the act developing around the field, may be authentic to the Naomi Story.

Although awkward in its present construction,[8] the choral refrain in 4:11–12 (all those at the gate) offers a blessing on Boaz and Ruth. While given the appearance of spontaneity, the blessing of 4:11–12 is finely constructed and includes information not available to the townspeople. The choral blessing concludes by comparing Ruth to Tamar, certainly bringing to mind the story of Genesis 38. The comparison only makes sense to those aware of the threshing floor scene (of which the towns people were still in the dark). The blessing is for the benefit of and actually addressed to the audience, giving justification to Naomi's behind the scenes manipulations by invoking a comparison to Tamar.

- The third option is to consider Act 4 composed as all of 4:1–12. This configuration adds Mr. So-and-So to the drama and so requires restoring his introduction in 3:12 as well. While this arrangement of Act Four presents an even heavier male perspective, when compared to the rest of the Naomi Story, it may have a dramatic purpose. Mr. So-and-So is the personification of the male economic interests to which female security, the project of the drama, was subjected. Disdain for this male economic privilege is expressed in no uncertain terms. Mr. So-and-So is not even granted a proper name. In his mind, Naomi and Ruth are only economic benefits or liabilities. They have value only as they benefit him. This is unacceptable to the story teller, who responds by denying a name—denying personhood—to the representative of this economic arrangement. The somewhat irregular introduction of the levirate arrangement in this configuration of Act Four further implicates the failure of current social mores. If authentic to Act Four, it seems as if the storyteller is leaving no stone unturned in eliminating all possible excuses for the threat and insecurity experienced by women in ancient Israel. The "system" is failing and women must take matters into their own hands to secure their own future.[9]

8. The LXX separates the choral response from the townspeople: "We are witnesses" from the following choral blessing.

9. It is certainly possible that the Naomi Story contained material that was edited out of the book of Ruth—the add-ons need not all be written. Perhaps, the Naomi Story

The female perspective resumes in Act 5, at 4:13, and this section, 4:13–17a, also provides a satisfying conclusion to the story line, whether it resumes from 3:18 or 4:12.

4. The repeating identification of Ruth "the Moabitess" (1:22; 2:2, 6; 21; 4:5, 10) serves a function in the book of Ruth that is superfluous and out of context in the Naomi Story.[10] The removal of the repeating label serves to clarify and focus the project of the performance tradition and the addition of the repeating label effectively serves the altered purposes of the book of Ruth. Other terms to designate Ruth also seem to have rhetorical functions in both the Naomi Story and the book of Ruth. Ruth is called נכריה (foreign woman—a term often associated with dangerous sexual connotations—see Proverbs, Ezra, and Nehemiah) and אשת המת (wife of the dead[11]) but not גר (alien immigrant with legal rights).[12] The labels used seem to be of most interest to a female audience.

5. A thin veneer can be observed in the book of Ruth, overlaying the Naomi Story, effectively altering the perspective and theme of the story. Concern with female security, so effectively expressed in the Naomi Story, is, in the book of Ruth, overshadowed by an interest in communal definition, establishing boundaries, primarily ethnically based, between insiders and outsiders. Most obviously, the genealogy of 4:18–22 gives expression to those with ethnically based national interests. But, those ethnic and national interests can also be observed underlying the introduction of Boaz in 2:3–5 (particularly Boaz's question about Ruth: "to whom does this young woman belong?" in 2:5); the Boaz speech of 2:11–13; the dialogue between Boaz and Mr. So-and-So of 4:1–6; the concern with lineage in 4:7–12[13]; and perhaps

included the city gate scene but performed quite differently with the culminating sandal ritual told from a female perspective (see Deut 25:7–10) consistent with the previous three scenes.

10. Dorothea Harvey has observed that in at least 2:2 and 2:21, the title "Moabitess" appears "where the plot does not demand the title." Harvey, "The Book of Ruth," 133. Ellen Davis suggests that the very phrase in 1:4 (נשים מאביות) suggests surprise reinforced by the repetition. Davis, "Beginning with Ruth: An Essay on Translating," 17.

11. Perhaps implying certain legal rights: Deut 25:5 the only other usage of this term in the Hebrew Bible. Interestingly, Naomi is not called "wife of the dead."

12. Siquans, "Foreignness and Poverty in the Book of Ruth: a Legal Way for a Poor Foreign Woman to Be Integrated into Israel," 447.

13. Of this passage, Trible is quite explicit in her assessment: "A man's concerns have

even in the way the story is set up in 1:1–5. These passages may indeed reflect the remaking of the story, moving it from the domain of the female performer to the domain of the male scribe.

subsumed the woman Ruth." Trible, "Ruth," 147. Yet, the incomplete transference to the male domain is evidenced by the resumption of the female voices in 4:13–17 in which this male concern for sons is subsumed by the worth of Ruth (4:15).

6

The Naomi Story Script[1]

The Naomi Story resides in a tradition of performance, of which, the following is only one possible reconstruction. We present this reconstruction, attempting to remain faithful to the nuances of the Story preserved in the book of Ruth, yet mindful that a performance tradition admits variety in presentation. This is not the only way the Naomi Story can be enacted.

In the Performance Notes that follow, we will use a standard format for theatrical scripts. This allows us to provide stage directions to help visualize a possible performance of the Naomi Story, or in this case, The EVERYWOMAN Play. In the play script that follows with each section of Performance Notes, we have allowed for four actors and an interactive audience. The actor who plays Orpah returns to the audience once Orpah leaves. This way, she can help the narrator manage the spectators when necessary. The key actor, drawing on a storyteller tradition, is the Narrator. She not only directs the performance by controlling the temporal and spatial aspects, but is also the most accomplished of the performers, taking on the male roles at critical moments. And so our performance begins.

Our storyteller knows her audience. These are her neighbors, friends, and even those with whom she may not be so friendly. They are her community, forming what is known as a closed audience which is also assumed in our scripted EVERYWOMAN play.[2]

1. Text based on NRSV.
2. See chapter three for a fuller discussion of "closed audience."

Introduction 1:1–6

¹ In the days of the judging of the judges, there was a famine in the land, and a certain woman of Bethlehem in Judah went to live in the fields of Moab, she and her husband and two sons. ²The name of the woman was Naomi and the name of her husband Elimelech, and the names of her two sons were Mahlon and Chilion; they were Ephrathites from Bethlehem in Judah. They went into the fields of Moab and remained there. ³But Naomi's husband, Elimelech, died, and she was left with her two sons. ⁴These took Moabite wives; the name of the one was Orpah and the name of the other Ruth. When they had lived there about ten years, ⁵both Mahlon and Chilion also died, so that the woman was left without her two sons and her husband.

⁶Then she started to return with her daughters-in-law from the fields of Moab, for she had heard in the fields of Moab that the LORD had considered his people and given them food.

Performance Notes

The Narrator steps forward. She pauses and looks out across the spectators, establishing a visual connection between the stage and the audience. She takes the time to scan the audience and make eye contact with several people. With a gesture of open arms, she begins to speak. These initial words of the introduction are critical for the Narrator to establish the storyteller's connection with the audience. It is in this initial exchange that the act of telling links human to human in a live spatial relationship, or stage-audience pattern, which essentially governs the theatrical process.[3] What she delivers in this opening sequence is most often referred to as exposition, given circumstances, or, as we will call it here, the precipitating context.[4] It is information that the audience needs, tying together elements of the past and present, and pointing them toward a future. It is through the precipitating context that the audience begins to develop a sense of the potential action and energetic forces that will animate the characters. The Narrator anticipates the specific points of connection with the audience, using tone, pace, and rhythm of speech to create a shared experience. The

3. Beckerman, *Dynamics of Drama*, 42.
4. Ibid., 69–70.

Narrator speaks with the confidence that her audience hears what they are supposed to hear.

Narrator

In the days of the judging of the judges, there was a famine in the land, and a certain woman of the House of Bread in Judah went to live in the fields of (she coughs, as if the very word Moab sticks in her throat) . . . Moab, she and her husband and two sons. The name of the woman was Pleasantness, and the name of her husband, My God is King, and the names of her two sons were Obliterated and Eliminated . . . and these two took wives from the land of many-tongued whores. I mean from (cough, cough) Moab; the name of one was Cloud and the other was Satisfy . . .

(Perhaps she smiles gently, or holds eye contact with a spectator briefly, as a way of acknowledging they are in this story together. She takes her time, crossing slowly from one side of the space to the other, savoring the complex mix of humor, pathos, and tension as the spectators conjure images of leaving a house of bread for a place where bread and water were denied, among other word plays we discuss in Notes below. She builds rhythmically on the simple structure of naming, identifying, providing a clear sense of time and segmentation,[5] or of what happened and when—they went, they died, she was left with—using simple hand gestures to imaginatively place each event before the spectators. Imagine our Narrator as you have seen characters like the Stage Manager in Thornton Wilder's famous *Our Town*, a play done with absolute minimal props and scenery, the world being created and evoked from the voice and gestures of the Stage Manager who shows us where Mrs. Gibbs' garden was, where the railroad tracks divided the haves from the have-nots, etc. Our Narrator takes an extended pause after telling the spectators that both sons have died.)

Obliterated and Eliminated also died, so that the woman was left without her two sons and her husband. (Pause)

(This pause tells the spectators that we are nearing the end of this prologue and about to enter the action of the play. Perhaps with a single gesture of raising the right arm, followed by sweeping the left arm across the space,

5. Ibid., 38.

thereby erasing the Moabite territory and setting the stage for their return to the House of Bread, she declares.)

Then she started to return with her daughters-in-law from the fields of the land of arrogance, idolatry, and gross ingratitude—I mean (cough, cough) Moab, for she had heard that the LORD had considered his people and given them food. But let's just stop right here for minute shall we? I feel kind of silly making all these little side references to (cough, cough)—I can hardly bring myself to say it . . . Moab. What was Naomi thinking? Come on. I mean what do you expect from a land named after a guy who was born in a cave to his daddy and his sister after she seduces him with wine and a little dirty dancing??? And the Greeks think Oedipus had it rough. Wait a minute, wait a minute . . . that's not the same thing that happens in our story. What Ruth does is different. I mean Moab, come on, that's worse than being from Cleveland right? *(Insert your favorite bad city here with caution!)* Anyway, back to our story.

(The Narrator circles the space, indicating travel and the passage of time. She may even circle the audience depending on the configuration, simulating the journey we are about to experience.)

Critical Notes

1:1 The book of Ruth begins, "in the days of the judging of the judges." Although acknowledged by Jack Sasson as a literal translation, he claims it is "too precise."[6] Perhaps not. As we will see in the remaining introductory set-up, the storyteller establishes an upside down world. Unlike Sasson, we do not try to establish a precise time for the story (as Rabbinic commentators do by identifying Boaz with the Ibzan of Bethlehem in Judg 12:8–10).[7] Rather than describing a particular point of time in the past, our contention is that the storyteller is describing a condition, engaged in setting a backdrop for the story where things are not as they should be. Things are upside down, a situation where judges are judged.

1:1 Moabite territory. In the MT, the place to where Elimelech and his family migrated is, in Sasson's opinion, "for obscure reasons,"[8] referred to as שדי (*sedey*: masculine plural construct: 1:2, 6a, 22; 2:6) or שדה (*sedeh*:

6. Sasson, *Ruth,* 15.

7. Midrash Rabbah, *Ruth,* 47.

8. Sasson, *Ruth,* 16.

masculine singular construct—1:6b; 4:3).[9] Literally "field" or "fields," Sasson translates as "territory" understanding that more than the literal agricultural areas are implied.[10] Perhaps there is further irony intended by the storyteller. Elimelech and family have left a "House of Bread" (Bethlehem) to migrate to Moabite "fields" (places where food is grown). One source of food has been left for another. And the masculine plural construct (*sedey*) sounds very similar to an appellation for God (Almighty—שׁדי: *shadey*) used in 1:20–21, as well as the plural term for (female) breasts (*shedey*). Would an audience hearing the story have sensed a play on words? Did the use of the term to describe the Moabite locale have a comedic, double entendre function? And, if that audience was all female would the double entendre have had a very personal and intimate affect?

1:1 Famine in the land—a certain woman left Bethlehem (house of bread) to travel to Moab. The narrator leaves the woman's identity a mystery (to this point) so that the audience has no option but to concentrate on the places involved in the background setup. Moab (a notorious place of danger where bread and water were denied, Deut 23:3–4) is preferred over the House of Bread.

Had the opening read "Elimelech of Bethlehem, together with his wife and his two sons went to sojourn in Moab . . ." the audience's focus of attention would have changed. The emphasis would have shifted from place to person—and it's much too soon for that. The places Bethlehem and Moab form the broadest backdrop to which the other details (names of characters, precipitating context) are added. All the other contextual details of the story find their meaning in an Alice-in-Wonderland like upside down imagined reality. The story is set in a breadless House of Bread, exchanged for a place where safety and bread are found—a place of danger where previously bread was denied. Bread or Bethlehem (House of Bread) are mentioned six times in this opening chapter. The place and the condition both seem to be in play. By whom and under what circumstances can bread be found in the House of Bread?

9. 4QRuth[a] appears to read the masculine singular "field of Moab" in 1:1, 2, 6, while 4QRuth[b] agrees with the MT and reads the plural construct. Joüon, "4QRuth[a], 4QRuth[b]," 188–89.

10. Sasson, *Ruth*, 16.

Moab

The opening scene takes place in Moab and the storyteller (in both the oral and even more the written version) goes to great lengths to make sure that Ruth is remembered as a Moabitess. It's not enough that Elimelech took Naomi to a foreign county in search of relief from the famine in Bethlehem. He took his family to Moab, a region and people notorious for a feminine threat directed toward the wandering Israelites (Num 25:1–5) and ever since consistently spoken of pejoratively within biblical literature.[11]

In this upside down landscape a double entendre may have been introduced. The certain man in verse one journeyed to the "fields of Moab" (1:1, 2, 6 [2x], 22; 2:6; 4:3) and most definitely not the territory[12] or country[13] of Moab. But there is an irregularity here. On five occasions a masculine plural construct (1:1, 2, 6a, 22; 2:6) appears (שדי) in place of the expected שדות or masculine singular construct (שדה). Attempted explanations for this irregularity range from: an old poetic form[14] to "scribal indecision,"[15] to the form presenting as "difficult to decide and immaterial as far as meaning is concerned."[16] Far from immaterial or unintentional, this unusual construction sets up an opposition between the fields of Moab and the Almighty (שדי) of Israel, both of which are very similar to the construct form of "female breast" (שדי). Where will bread be found, and is God Almighty reliable to provide what is needed? Certainly, this is the focus of 6b. Naomi, in the field (שדה) of Moab, has heard that the LORD has given bread to his people.

1:2 Having established an upside down imagined reality in 1:1, the audience is now prepared to meet the characters of the story—equally topsy-turvy.[17] First is Elimelech (God-is-King) followed by Naomi (Pleasant)

---

11. LaCocque, *The Feminine Unconventional*, 85.

12. Bush, *Ruth / Esther*, 57.

13. NRSV.

14. Campbell, *Ruth*, 50.

15. Sasson, *Ruth*, 16.

16. Bush, *Ruth / Esther*, 58.

17. Watson describes delayed identification of characters as a technique that heightens suspense and creates interest. Watson, *Classical Hebrew Poetry*, 336–37. We agree that heightened suspense is certainly at work in the Ruth opening—but in addition, the delayed identification of Elimelech focuses the attention of the reader / listener on the precipitating context of the drama and prepares us to appreciate Elimelech as a minor character in what is about to unfold.

and their two sons Mahlon (Obliterated) and Chilion (Eliminated). God-is-King quickly dies followed ten years later by both, Obliterated and Eliminated, leaving Pleasant and her two daughters-in-law (Orpah—"Little Cloud" or "Back [of neck]" and Ruth—"Satisfy") to fend for themselves.[18] God-is-King has proven unable to care for Naomi either now or in the future and the system of male inheritance, in which Naomi should have been able to find refuge, is equal to the aptly named deceased sons.

1:5 After establishing the fact of Elimelech's death and that of his two sons, the narrator tells us "the woman" is left bereaved. It isn't Naomi's plight with which we are concerned—but that of "the woman." The story-teller refers to Naomi in this fashion in order to emphasize the distinguishing characteristic that will propel the plot. Naomi is not, the widow, the Bethlehemite, the Judaite, the mother, or the sojourner. She is the woman.[19] Lénart de Regt suggests that "emotional impact is lost when one translates 'Naomi' (as in NIV, GNB, CEV) rather than 'the woman.'"[20] Perhaps this focus on "the woman" as typical of all women is reinforced by the singular form of verbs in 1:6 where a plural verbal form would be expected ("they returned," "they heard" as in LXX).[21] A similar focus on character (this time Ruth) as archetype may be evident in 3:14, and again in 4:13.

1:5 ילדיה. Naomi's sons are referred to as "her children" in place of the expected "her sons" (בינים). Certainly this is intentional and foreshadows a resolution as Naomi, bereft of her children in 1:5 will clutch a "child" (ילד) to her bosom (breast?) in 4:16.

1:6b The LORD (YHWH). Names are important in the Naomi Story. The personal name of God, YHWH, appears three times in Ruth: 1:6b; 1:21a; and 4:13. Only in 4:13, the narrated resolution to the drama, is YHWH actually present in the story.

18. De Regt notes that since Ruth is Mahlon's widow, we should expect either the order of the brother's names to be reversed (as he suggests for 1:2, 5) or the recognition of a chiastic pattern concluding with "Orpah and Ruth." De Regt, *Participants in Old Testament Texts and the Translator,* 85.

19. Lois Durbin sees here a type. Naomi is, "without name, without face, universal in her dereliction." Durbin, "Fullness and Emptiness, Fertility and Loss," 132.

20. De Regt, *Participants in Old Testament Texts and the Translator,* 14.

21. Interestingly, this archetypal function has been attributed to Ruth by some modern commentators. Hawkins, "Ruth Amid the Gentiles," 84.

Act One 1:7–22

Scene 1: Naomi destitute—The Project of the Play (1:9)

7So she set out from the place where she had been living, she and her two daughters-in-law, and they went on their way to go back to the land of Judah. 8But Naomi said to her two daughters-in-law, "Go back each of you to your mother's house. May the LORD deal kindly with you, as you have dealt with the dead and with me. 9The LORD grant that you may find security, each of you in the house of your husband." Then she kissed them, and they wept aloud. 10They said to her, "No, we will return with you to your people." 11But Naomi said, "Turn back, my daughters, why will you go with me? Do I still have sons in my womb that they may become your husbands? 12Turn back, my daughters, go your way, for I am too old to have a husband. Even if I thought there was hope for me, even if I should have a husband tonight and bear sons, 13would you then wait until they were grown? Would you then refrain from marrying? No, my daughters, it has been far more bitter for me than for you, because the hand of the LORD has turned against me." 14Then they wept aloud again. Orpah kissed her mother-in-law, but Ruth clung to her. 15So she said, "See, your sister-in-law has gone back to her people and to her gods; return after your sister-in-law." 16But Ruth said, "Do not press me to leave you or to turn back from following you! Where you go, I will go; Where you spend the night, I will spend the night; your people shall be my people, and your God my God. 17Where you die, I will die—there will I be buried. May the LORD do thus and so to me, and more as well, if even death parts me from you!" 18When Naomi saw that she was determined to go with her, she said no more to her.

Script: Adjacency Pairs

1:8–10

A. **Naomi**: Go back each of you to your mother's house. May the LORD deal kindly with you, as you have dealt with the dead and with me. 9The LORD grant that you may find security, each of you in the house of your husband.

B. **They** (two daughters-in-law): No, we will return with you to your people.

1:11–14

A. **Naomi**: Turn back, my daughters, why will you go with me? Do I still have sons in my womb that they may become your husbands? [12]Turn back, my daughters, go your way, for I am too old to have a husband. Even if I thought there was hope for me, even if I should have a husband tonight and bear sons, [13]would you then wait until they were grown? Would you then refrain from marrying? No, my daughters, it has been far more bitter for me than for you, because the hand of the LORD has turned against me.

B. **Verbal Silence Narrative Reply**: Then they lifted up their voices and wept again.

1:15–17

A. **Naomi**: See, the widow of your dead husband's brother has gone back to her people and to her gods; return after the widow of your dead husband's brother.

B. **Ruth**: Do not press me to leave you or to turn back from following you! Where you go, I will go; Where you spend the night, I will spend the night; your people shall be my people, and your God my God. [17]Where you die, I will die—there will I be buried. May the LORD do thus and so to me, and more as well, if even death parts me from you!

1:19–21

A. **The women**: Is this Naomi?

B. **She (Naomi)**: Call me no longer Naomi, call me Mara, for the Almighty has dealt bitterly with me. [21]I went away full, but the LORD has brought me back empty; why call me Naomi when the LORD has dealt harshly with me, and the Almighty has brought calamity upon me?

Performance Notes

As we noted at the end of our prologue (1:1–6), the Narrator circles the space, indicating travel and the passage of time. She may even circle the audience depending on the configuration, simulating the journey we are about to experience, and setting the stage for the entrance of Naomi, Ruth, and Orpah. The Narrator, through a deft delivery of exposition, including a bit of repetition, has generated an image of Naomi that establishes her as a destitute and isolated woman, the widow and survivor of the deaths of three men. She has essentially, created the presence of this character we are about to meet, or performatively speaking, she has created the need for this character to step forward and speak. And so begins Act One.

(In the interaction to follow, the project of the drama is introduced and, through the characters of Orpah and Ruth, two possible realities with which the audience may identify. The Narrator steps to the side of the acting space as she says,)

Narrator
But Naomi said to her two daughters-in-law.

(Three women enter: first, Naomi, followed by Ruth and hesitantly by Orpah. They each carry a small bundle of possessions. Orpah's hesitance helps to foreshadow her dilemma of wanting to stay with Naomi, but also wanting to return home. She looks several times in the opposite direction, the direction she will ultimately choose. Ruth, however, enters almost on Naomi's heels, making it physically clear that she has no intention of abandoning Naomi. Naomi notices these two different behaviors, summing up the situation before she speaks. What follows is the layout of Act 1 scene 1 as a play script with suggested stage directions. As in the prologue, the directions include possible behaviors that point to the project of the Naomi Story and the goals and objectives of the characters. Built into these suggestions are the dramatic elements of tension, conflict, and the rising and falling action that leads to the final resolution.)

Naomi
(Naomi gestures that the two women should stop. She holds Ruth at bay with this gesture, leaving some distance between them. After making eye contact with both women, she speaks, beginning with a command.)

Go back each of you to your mother's house. This is very important. Your mother's house. Not your father's house, or brother's house, or your uncle's house, but your mother's house. Know what I'm saying here? (When used elsewhere in the Hebrew Bible, the "mother's house" is a place of female power and sometimes specifically female sexual power.) At least there, if you recall, you can take care of your own needs (wink, wink, nudge, nudge). May the LORD deal kindly with you, as you have dealt with the dead and me. The LORD grant that you may one day find security, each of you in the house of your husband. But until then, go back to your mother's house. (She turns to the audience). Nod if you understand.

(Ruth and Orpah rush to Naomi's side. Naomi kisses them, they weep aloud. As they weep, Naomi leans heavily into Ruth, silently communicating a need for support without the use of words. In this way, Naomi pursues her project, which will ultimately include Ruth.)

Ruth and Orpah

(Proclaiming together.)

No, we will return with you to your people.

Naomi

(Naomi once again commands the daughters to turn back, using a series of questions that seem to blend a keen sense of irony with sarcasm in order to paint the picture of her predicament. She commands them twice to turn back, using repetition of phrasing to build the tension. There is nothing fake, or inauthentic about Naomi's performance. Her sense of bitterness and desolation is sincere, but she is also preparing the way for her journey to include Ruth.)

Turn back, my daughters, why will you go with me? Do I still have sons in my womb that they may become your husbands? Turn back my daughters, go your way, for I am too old to have a husband. Even if I thought there was hope for me, even if I should have a husband tonight and bear sons, would you then wait until they were grown? Would you then refrain from marrying? No, my daughters, it has been far more bitter for me than for you, because the hand of the LORD has turned against me.

(Ruth and Orpah are silent. Then, they all weep aloud again. Orpah kisses Naomi while Ruth clings to Naomi. Orpah turns and exits the stage slowly. She stops and turns briefly for one more glance at Naomi and Ruth. Orpah's gaze passes briefly over the spectators, giving them a clear look at the sorrow and resignation she feels at leaving.)

Naomi

(Naomi confronts Ruth. Once again commanding that she leave. Ruth continues to cling to Naomi, Naomi does not try to escape her grasp.)

See, your sister-in-law has gone back to her people and to her gods; return after your sister-in-law.

Ruth

(Ruth suddenly commands Naomi to stop pressing her to leave. She follows this with a clear declaration of allegiance to Naomi. Ruth gathers the small bundles of belongings the women have with them, making it clear that she will journey on with Naomi.)

Do not press me to leave you or to turn back from following you! Where you go, I will go; where you spend the night, I will spend the night; your people shall be my people and your God my God. Where you die, there will I be buried. May the LORD do thus and so to me, and more as well, if even death parts me from you!

Naomi

(Silence) (Naomi does not speak, but it is clear from her body language that she is satisfied with this outcome.)

Critical Notes

1:7 This verse appears redundant, repeating the information already given in 1:6. Repetition has a specific function in the Naomi Story. Verse 6 brings the Introduction to a close and verse 7 opens Act One. Here, and elsewhere (see 1:18 for example), repetition serves to signal an Act or Scene change.

1:8 "Deal kindly" (חסד) appears three times in in the Naomi Story (1:8; 2:20; 3:10). In 1:8 the term appears as part of Naomi's farewell blessing. She recognizes that her daughters-in-law have "dealt kindly" toward her and her dead sons and so asks that the LORD reciprocate and "deal kindly" toward them. In 2:20 it appears that Naomi's prayer has been answered, although certainly not in the manner she expected. In Boaz's treatment of Ruth, Naomi recognizes the "kindness" of the LORD. But, as acknowledged by Boaz, the ultimate "kindness" is extended by Ruth in 3:10 when she offers sexual kindness to Boaz.

1:8 Naomi references the "mother's house" instead of the usual "father's house." The term is used elsewhere only in Gen 24:28; Prov 31:21, 27 (her household); and Song of Songs 3:4; 8:2. LaCocque is of the opinion, "That the books of Ruth and Song of Songs were both written by women explains the choice of expression."[22] We agree with LaCocque's assessment, except we assign female composition to the Naomi Story usurped by a male (probably) scribe in the composition of the book of Ruth. The Naomi Story was performed by and for women.

1:9 This verse introduces the project of the drama. Naomi wishes that "security" (מנוחה) be found for both herself, and more, her daughters-in-law. The search is repeated in 3:1. The search for female security is the project of the story, directing the plot to its resolution in 4:17. Where will security be found?

1:10–13 Naomi's soliloquy has been described as "devastating in its mordant self-deprecation" bordering on "sarcasm."[23] Perhaps, but if used in the performance as an explanation of the project initiated in 1:9, Naomi's statement isn't sarcasm directed at Orpah and Ruth, but at the audience, implicitly asking them to consider the validity of the predicament Naomi represents.

1:12 Naomi states, "I am too old to have a husband"[24] (זקנתי מהיות לאיש). Literally "I am too old to belong to a man." While certainly, on the surface, the intent of the statement is to declare that Naomi is past child bearing age—the way the statement is phrased brings to mind the economy of child bearing in a manner pertinent to the project introduced in 1:9— finding security in the house of a husband—and reinforced by the rhetorical question posed by Naomi to Orpah and Ruth in 1:13, as translated by Sasson "would you restrain yourself so as not to be[long] to a man?"[25] (תעגנה לאיש). The verb עגן appears only here in the Hebrew Bible and, in LaCocque's opinion, signifies a "woman abandoned by her husband, but not divorced."[26] LaCocque's rendition focuses our attention even more on the quest for security and the dismal prospects faced by "the woman" and her daughters. Where will a woman, unattached to a male household (not belonging to a man), find security. Notice that a similar disposition is expressed by Boaz in 2:5: "Whose maiden is this?" (i.e. "To whom does this girl belong?").

22. LaCocque, *Ruth*, 44.
23. Sasson, *Ruth*, 24.
24. RSV.
25. Sasson, *Ruth*, 25.
26. LaCocque, *Ruth*, 49.

1:12–13 A grammatical abnormality appears here in the repeated use of לֹהֶן (3rd fem plural: "they" referring to the hypothetical and yet un-born "sons") when לֹהֶם (3rd mas plural) is expected. This construction has received a fair amount of comment with a number of different proposed explanations.[27] One proposal suggests that this construction represents an Aramaism that is then used to help date the literary construction.[28] Gary Rendsburg has effectively countered the argument that this represents an Aramasim in Ruth and instead points out that "gender neutralization of 2 pl and 3 pl independent pronouns and pronominal suffixes was a character-istic feature of spoken Hebrew in Biblical times."[29] In fact, this use of לֹהֶן is, for Rendsburg, evidence of the presence of a "spoken dialect" appearing in a written composition. His analysis gives support to the application of Con-versation Analysis conducted by Frank Polak and others. We suggest that between spoken and written, a third dialect, that of "performed" speech be considered. This grammatical construction reflects the oral substrate (the Naomi Story) of the book of Ruth.

1:14 Without extraneous comment, the Naomi Story combines emo-tion, character development, and action to propel the audience into ac-tive engagement with the project of the play. A choice is presented to the audience. Will they become Orpah or Ruth? What path will the audience choose by which to obtain security—the safe and familiar, but perhaps un-satisfying (remember Orpah is the "Little Cloud") pursuit of "belonging to a man," or the bold potential embodied by Ruth and her devotion to the woman, Naomi. That this choice is presented to the audience is reinforced by Naomi's odd use of term for Orpah in 1:15.

1:14 A powerful term is used to describe the Naomi—Ruth relation-ship. Ruth "clings" (דבק) to Naomi. Elsewhere, "cling" is used to describe the scales on a crocodile (Job 41:9) and often used to describe devotion to God (Deut 4:4; Josh 22:5) or sometimes the closeness of lovers (Gen 2:24; 1 Kgs 11:2). Used here to describe Ruth's devotion to Naomi, the term is lat-er used to describe Ruth's closeness to the gleaners in Boaz's field (2:8, 21). Ruth's dedication to Naomi is going to be realized through her dedication

27. See, for instance, the comments by Campbell, *Ruth*, 68–69; and Sasson, *Ruth*, 25.

28. Gordis, "Love, Marriage, and Business," 243–46.

29. Rendsburg, *Diglossia in Ancient Hebrew*, 53. Rendsburg accepts a pre-exilic date for the Ruth composition, allowing additional glosses that may have been added centu-ries later. Rendsburg, *Diglossia in Ancient Hebrew*, 164.

beginning in the "fields" (remembering the word play constructed around this term) of Boaz.

1:15 Naomi refers to Orpah as Ruth's יבמתך. To translate as "sister-in-law," while fitting the plot of the story, is an odd use of the term and perhaps misses a sense of foreshadowing that the storyteller intended. In other usages (Gen 38:8 and Deut 25:5–10) יבמה designates "a widow in relation to her husband's brother," the יבם is the surviving brother—"the redeemer" who will provide safety and security, a family, for the widow of the dead brother. What then does Naomi mean when she informs Ruth of this legal bound with Orpah? Sasson, considering the usage found in a text recovered from Tell Iltani, opts for a sister-in-law relationship unburdened by the levirate complications discussed in both Genesis 38 and Deuteronomy 25[30] while LaCocque argues persuasively that the levirate relationship is intended and, more, that the Naomi storyteller intends a parallel to Genesis 38.[31]

If we are correct in identifying the project of the story as voiced by Naomi in 1:9 (find a home each of you in the house of your husband), then the use of this word to describe the relationship between Ruth and Orpah is loaded with meaning and by no means incidental. The יבם brings to mind not just kin relationships but a system of security based upon kinship bonds. And if we are correct that the performance was primarily by and for women—then the significance is multiplied. What would a group of women listening to this performance in eighth-sixth-BCE rural Judah have heard when this word was spoken? Would they have sensed responsibility and solidarity—a need to provide "redemption" for each other that went beyond legal requirements imposed upon males? Would the use of the term describing the relationship between two women rather than a man and a woman have occasioned a sense of regret or disappointment, knowing, after all, that the legal conditions of the levirate custom were designed to protect a line of male inheritance, and only incidentally to provide security for a bereaved woman? Would Naomi's use of the word be freeing to the female audience? Would it have suggested hope in a sisterhood that went far deeper than the machinations of the legal system? Perhaps Naomi's statement to Ruth had all these effects on the female audience. Perhaps this one word was one more step on a bridge carrying the audience from the

---

30. Sasson, *Ruth*, 29.

31. LaCocque, *Ruth*, 51.

lived world to the imagined world of the performance, and promising a gift that upon return to the lived world would change their everyday existence.

1:16–17 Ruth's soliloquy is an expression of devotion unparalleled in the Hebrew Bible. The phrase באשר תליני אלין translated in RSV as "where you lodge I will lodge" deserves closer attention. Generally, it is considered that Ruth, by this pronouncement, is agreeing to accompany Naomi on her journey to Bethlehem and so the emphasis is on the place where they will stay the night. But the storyteller's use of the verb "lodge" (לון), used also in 3:13, suggests something quite different. The verb does not emphasize place but condition or situation. That is, Ruth is agreeing to risk "security in the house of a husband" in order to join Naomi's quest. Once again, the storyteller is focusing the audience's attention on the central project of the play—what kind of life, what amount of security can be expected by joining Naomi?

As on other occasions, the storyteller will come back to this strategically placed verb—לון (lie down, spend the night, lodge, dwell). In 3:13, Boaz tells Ruth to "remain [ליני] this night." Ruth's commitment to an uncertain future with Naomi, to share her *lodging* (lifestyle), is now brought to the audience's attention by Boaz's invitation to spend the night. Ruth will "lie down until the morning" (3:13) and, in so doing, a *lodging* will be secured.

1:17 "may the LORD do so to me and more . . ." the end of Ruth's soliloquy invokes an imprecation that implicates YHWH in creating the conditions of distress that currently surround Naomi. In 1:13 Naomi indicts YHWH as an adversary. By throwing her lot in with Naomi, Ruth accepts the risk of similar divine mistreatment and, in fact, invites that mistreatment should she break her bond with Naomi. We can imagine Ruth gesturing to the staging around her—the scene of tragedy, death, and weeping and now lifting her eyes upward, invoking YHWH to do the same and more should she be dissuaded from her chosen path. Female solidarity is an important theme of the Story.

Scene 2: Return to Bethlehem

¹⁹So the two of them went on until they came to Bethlehem. When they came to Bethlehem, the whole town was stirred because of them; and the women said, "Is this Naomi?" ²⁰She said to them, "Call me no longer Naomi, call me Mara, for the Almighty has dealt bitterly with me. ²¹I

went away full, but the LORD has brought me back empty; why call me Naomi when the LORD has dealt harshly with me, and the Almighty has brought calamity upon me?" ²²So Naomi returned together with Ruth, her daughter-in-law, who came back with her from the fields of Moab. They came to Bethlehem at the beginning of the barley harvest.

Script: Adjacency Pairs

1:19–21

A. Women of Bethlehem (Chorus): Is this Naomi?

B. Naomi—Dispreferred Response Call me no longer Naomi, Call me Mara, for the Almighty has dealt bitterly with me. I went away full, but the LORD has brought me back empty; why call me Naomi when the LORD has dealt harshly with me, and the Almighty has brought calamity upon me?

Performance Notes

As the Act 1 Scene 1 ends, Naomi and Ruth circle the stage twice to indicate their journey to Bethlehem. As they do so, the Narrator steps forward, watches their journey for a moment, then looks out and speaks directly to the audience about their journey. The Narrator steps down and becomes part of the audience, who know this story well, allowing her to become one of them as she facilitates the audience becoming characters in the story. As she says, "the whole town was stirred" because of their arrival, the Narrator gestures to the crowd to join her and to become the stirred up crowd. They join in, all eyes focused on the stage, as we hear "Is this Pleasantness," repeating across the crowd.

Naomi and Ruth complete their journey around the stage, stopping near center and facing the audience, who have now become the townspeople of Bethlehem.

Naomi

(Naomi holds up her hands to silence the crowd. She waits until the murmuring stops. Her voice is choked by the bitterness she feels, and she is confident this will move the spectators. She speaks forcefully, but does not yell or shout. Ruth stands resolutely by her side, gazing out at the crowd of strangers.)

Call me no longer Pleasantness! Call me Bitterness! For the Breasted One (Almighty) has dealt bitterly with me. I went away full, but the LORD has brought me back empty. Why call me Pleasantness when the LORD has dealt harshly with me, and the Breasted One has brought calamity upon me? Famine, death, widowhood, and now forced to beg a man for mercy! Is this how the Breasted One treats women? Is this our lot in life?

(When Naomi finishes speaking, the Narrator returns to the stage from the crowd. Her final words provide us with a new set of given circumstances in terms of time, place and action, "They came to the House of Bread at the beginning of the barley harvest.")

Critical Notes

1:19-20 The women of Bethlehem greet Naomi upon her return. The women function as the chorus both, here and later in the story (4:14–15).

1:19 The town was "stirred" (ותהם). Sasson translates this verb "hummed,"[32] indicating the undifferentiated humming or buzz that surrounded the couple as they entered the Bethlehem stage.

In the first interchange with the chorus—the chorus announces Naomi's name and provides the platform for Naomi to request a name change based upon a change in her circumstances. She tells the chorus—Do not call me Naomi (pleasant) call me Mara (bitter) and the rationale:

> For the Almighty has dealt very bitterly with me. I went away full
> and the LORD has brought me back empty. Why call me Naomi,
> when the LORD has afflicted me and the Almighty has brought
> calamity upon me?

This interchange with the chorus provides the audience with a partial definition to the problem that will guide the action of the plot. Is the LORD just and can the Almighty be depended upon? Nehama Aschkenasy believes this interchange represents Naomi's recognition that her predicament is "a consequence of a sin—not sin committed directly by her but a sin in which she participated as part of her family."[33] But is this so? The sin

32. Sasson, *Ruth*, 32.

33. Ascheknasy, "From Aristotale to Bakhtin: The Comedic and the Carnivalesque in a Biblical Tale," 271. See also Moore, "Ruth the Moabite and the Blessing of Foreigners,"

to which Aschkenasy must refer to is leaving Bethlehem during a time of famine, as established in the introduction to the performance in 1:1. But there is no indication of sin here and Naomi's address to the chorus admits no wrong doing—at least on her part.

If anything, Naomi's address is a complaint evoked by the unjust treatment she has received from the deity—alternately identified as "Almighty" (שדי Shaddai—"Breasted") and "LORD" (יהוה—YHWH). This is the first time the "Almighty" label appears in Ruth.[34] The deity, earlier referred to as LORD (1:9, 17) now takes on the appellation Almighty. The alternating use of Almighty and LORD in Naomi's address to the chorus is significant.[35] "Almighty," is the "Provider" (literally "Breasted"—see Gen 49:25), the one who gives security and offspring, while "LORD" is the personal name of the God of Israel. Naomi's complaint functions as an accusation. The LORD has failed to provide for Naomi. The divine Breast of Israel has failed Naomi, leaving her bitter and empty. Another breast (שד) is needed. In chapter 3, at Naomi's instruction, Ruth will offer her breast to Boaz and will return to Naomi from her nocturnal visit to the threshing floor with an apron bulging (3:15). Emptiness is going to be filled and security will be provided. The Divine Provider will work (or be replaced) through a human female breast. Naomi's empty womb (1:11) will be satisfied with a baby (4:16).

Once again the double entendre with "fields of Moab" is evident. The Breast of Israel (שדי) has attacked Naomi (1:21) leading Naomi to return from the fields (שדי) of Moab in favor of the House of Bread (Bethlehem) just at the beginning of the barley harvest.

1:21 ויהוה ענה בי "YHWH is against me." Sasson recognizes the judicial possibilities in the phrase with the sense that YHWH is "testifying" against Naomi. But he also suggests that the unusual use of ענה may be an intentional pun, a wordplay with נעמי (Naomi).[36] The word choice here conveys Naomi's pain on several levels. "We feel not only her sense of legal impotence but also her sense of emotional betrayal, and yes, even her sense of theological abandonment."[37]

209; Angel, "A Midrashic View of Ruth Amidst a Sea of Ambiguity," 91–99.

34. שדי minus the אל (God) preface is found elsewhere in Num 24:4, 16 (Balaam oracles); Ps 68:15; 91:1; Isa 13:6; Ezek 1:24; and throughout Job. The Psalms praise שדי for his provision while Job (like Naomi) protests mistreatment from שדי.

35. LaCocque, *Ruth*, 57.

36. Sasson, *Ruth*, 35–36.

37. Moore, "Two Textual Anomalies in Ruth," 236.

Far from acknowledging sin for which punishment is deserved, Naomi's address to the chorus in 1:20–21 is an indictment of Israel's God and a challenge to the social institutions and mores intended to legitimize the expression of divine justice from the LORD and Almighty. It's hard to believe that this first address to the chorus by Naomi would not have had a profound impact on a female audience, considering the role of their own breasts (their status as females) in the social system so deftly manipulated by Naomi and Ruth.

Act Two—Ruth in the Fields: 2:1–23

Now Naomi had a kinsman on her husband's side, a respected worthy man of the family of Elimelech, whose name was Boaz. ²And Ruth said to Naomi, "Let me go to the field and glean among the ears of grain, behind someone in whose sight I may find favor." She said to her, "Go, my daughter." ³So she went. She came and gleaned in the field behind the reapers. As it happened, she came to the part of the field belonging to Boaz, who was of the family of Elimelech.

⁴Just then Boaz came from Bethlehem. He said to the reapers, "The LORD be with you." They answered, "The LORD bless you." ⁵Then Boaz said to his servant who was in charge of the reapers, "To whom does this young woman belong?" ⁶The servant who was in charge of the reapers answered, "She is Ruth who came back with Naomi from the fields of Moab. ⁷She said, 'Please, let me glean and gather among the sheaves behind the reapers.' So she came, and she has been on her feet from early this morning until now, without resting even for a moment." ⁸Then Boaz said to Ruth, "Now listen, my daughter, do not go to glean in another field or leave this one, but keep close to my young women. ⁹Keep your eyes on the field that is being reaped, and follow behind them. I have ordered the young men not to bother you. If you get thirsty, go to the vessels and drink from what the young men have drawn." ¹⁰Then she fell prostrate, with her face to the ground, and said to him, "Why have I found favor in your sight, that you should take notice of me, when I am a foreigner?" ¹¹But Boaz answered her, "All that you have done for your mother-in-law since the death of your husband has been fully told me, and how you left your father and mother and your native land and came to a people that you did not know before. ¹²May the LORD reward you for your deeds, and may you have a full reward from the LORD, the God of Israel, under whose wings you have come

for refuge!" [13]Then she said, "May I continue to find favor in your sight, my lord, for you have comforted me and spoken kindly to your servant, even though I am not one of your servants." [14]At mealtime Boaz said to her, "Come here, and eat some of this bread, and dip your morsel in the sour wine." So she sat beside the reapers, and he heaped up for her some parched grain. She ate until she was satisfied, and she had some left over. [15]When she got up to glean, Boaz instructed his young men, "Let her glean even among the standing sheaves, and do not reproach her. [16]You must also pull out some handfuls for her from the bundles, and leave them for her to glean, and do not rebuke her."

[17]So she gleaned in the field until evening. Then she beat out what she had gleaned, and it was about an ephah of barley. [18]She picked it up and came into the town, and her mother-in-law saw how much she had gleaned. Then she took out and gave her what was left over after she herself had been satisfied. [19]Her mother-in-law said to her, "Where did you glean today? And where have you worked? Blessed be the man who took notice of you." So she told her mother-in-law with whom she had worked, and said, "The name of the man with whom I worked today is Boaz." [20]Then Naomi said to her daughter-in-law, "Blessed be he by the LORD, whose kindness has not forsaken the living or the dead!" Naomi also said to her, "The man is a relative of ours, one of our nearest kin."

[21]Then Ruth said, "He even said to me, 'Stay close by my servants, until they have finished all my harvest.'" [22]Naomi said to Ruth, her daughter-in-law, "It is better, my daughter, that you go out with his young women, otherwise you might be bothered in another field." [23]So she stayed close to the young women of Boaz, gleaning until the end of the barley and wheat harvests; and she lived with her mother-in-law.

Script: Adjacency Pairs

2:2

A. Ruth the Moabitess: Let me go to the field and glean among the ears of grain, behind someone in whose sight I may find favor.

B. She (Naomi): Go, my daughter.

2:4

A. Boaz: The LORD be with you.

B. They (the reapers): The LORD bless you.

A. Boaz: To whom does this young woman belong?

B. The servant in charge of the reapers: She is the Moabite who came back with Naomi from the country of Moab. 7She said, 'Please, let me glean and gather among the sheaves behind the reapers.' So she came, and she has been on her feet from early this morning until now, without resting even for a moment.

A. Boaz: Now listen, my daughter, do not go to glean in another field or leave this one, but keep close to my young women. 9Keep your eyes on the field that is being reaped, and follow behind them. I have ordered the young men not to bother you. If you get thirsty, go to the vessels and drink from what the young men have drawn.

B. She (Ruth): Why have I found favor in your sight, that you should take notice of me, when I am a foreigner?

A. Boaz: All that you have done for your mother-in-law since the death of your husband has been fully told me, and how you left your father and mother and your native land and came to a people that you did not know before. 12May the LORD reward you for your deeds, and may you have a full reward from the LORD, the God of Israel, under whose wings you have come for refuge!

B. She (Ruth): May I continue to find favor in your sight, my lord, for you have comforted me and spoken kindly to your servant, even though I am not one of your servants."

A. Boaz: Come here, and eat some of this bread, and dip your morsel in the sour wine.

B. Verbal silence. Narrated preferred response

A. **Boaz**: Let her glean even among the standing sheaves, and do not reproach her. [16]You must also pull out some handfuls for her from the bundles, and leave them for her to glean, and do not rebuke her.

B. **Verbal silence**. Implied narrated preferred response

2:19

A. **Her mother-in-law**: Where did you glean today? And where have you worked? Blessed be the man who took notice of you.

B. **Narrated preferred response followed by Ruth**: The man's name with whom I worked today is Boaz.

2:20–21

A. **Naomi**: "Blessed be he by the LORD, whose kindness has not forsaken the living or the dead!" Naomi also said to her, "The man is a relative of ours, one of our nearest kin."

B. **Ruth the Moabitess**: He even said to me, "Stay close by my servants, until they have finished all my harvest."

2:22

A. **Naomi**: It is better, my daughter, that you go out with his young women, otherwise you might be bothered in another field.

B. **Narrated preferred response**

Performance Notes

The Narrator pauses as Naomi and Ruth move to the side of the stage. Her pause is another indicator of the passage of time. When she speaks, "Now Pleasantness had a kinsman on her husband's side, a respected worthy man, of the family of God is King, whose name was Strength," she sets the stage for the next set of characters, in particular the character of Boaz, affecting a male voice and stance as she conjures him into being. In fact, it is our Narrator who will play Boaz and his servant, deftly moving between characters, a woman inhabiting these male characters to the delight of her audience.

Through a gesture from our Narrator, who has just impersonated Boaz, our focus shifts momentarily to Naomi and Ruth as Ruth, now filled with the confidence Naomi anticipated, suggests that she go work in the fields, and find favor in some man's eyes. Naomi quickly gives her approval, and our Narrator immediately picks up the pace of the plot and in a playful moment with the audience, smiles, saying,

Narrator

(As she delivers this line, the Narrator assumes the voice and body of Boaz, entering a female "Drag" or "Camp[38]" that the female spectators respond to immediately as co-conspirators in the performance. Boaz is played as the classic Emperor with New Clothes—bombastic, arrogant, and completely unaware of his metaphoric nakedness. As the footnote below explains, this is a performance strategy for the Narrator, allowing her to critique certain notions of maleness, using classic comic techniques of exaggeration.)

As it happened, she came to a part of the field belonging to Strength, who was a family member of God is King. (Pause) JUST THEN, (the Narrator says with emphasis,) Strength arrived from the House of Bread.

(The Narrator must now display an almost virtuoso level of performance skill, moving between multiple male characters (Boaz and his Servant) and then interacting with Ruth. These character changes can be accomplished efficiently with a single gesture and posture, along with a simple voice inflection for each character. We have included suggestions for these physical choices in the following section of script. The spectators, familiar with the story and eager to participate, become interactive participants following the lead of the Narrator.)

Boaz

(A slightly bent older middle aged man, obviously impressed with his own sense of self-importance, stands with feet spread wide. He speaks loudly, as if he wants to be sure all can hear him. He uses the consonants of words for emphasis. He looks out over the audience and speaks to them as if they are the reapers, inviting them to respond.)

The LORD be with you.

---

38. Robertson. "The Kind of Comedy That Imitates Me," 57. "Camp, however, offers feminists a model for critiques of sex and genderroles. But I suggest that camp as astructural activity has an affinity with feminist discussions of gender construction, performance, and enactment; and that, as such, we can examine a form of camp as a feminist practice. In taking on camp for women, I reclaim a female form of aestheticism, related to female masquerade, that articulates and subverts the image- and culture-making processes to which women have traditionally been given access."

Spectators/Reapers

The LORD bless you.

Boaz

(Still maintaining the stance and voice of Boaz, the Narrator looks at an imaginary Servant standing next to her. She looks over at Ruth. The following exchange is about raising one's status by lowering the status of another, or status reversal, which are classic patterns of exchange in many comedic forms.)

To whom does this young woman belong? (He arrogantly speaks for all to hear).

Servant

(The Narrator steps to her left, and quickly transforms into the Servant. She straightens up, feet close together, hands clasped in front of her. With a slight bow to Boaz, and with a slightly effeminate and sarcastic voice, she speaks. He defers to Boaz, but also shows just a hint of contempt for his bombastic boss.)

She is Satisfy who came back with Pleasantness from Moab where food is grown. She pleaded with me, *Please, let me glean and gather among the sheaves behind the reapers.* So she came and has been on her feet from early this morning until now, without resting even for a moment.

(Ruth quickly approaches the Narrator, who immediately transforms back into Boaz, perhaps even "adjusting himself," as men are want to do, as Ruth approaches him.)

Boaz

Now listen my daughter, do not glean in another field or leave this one, but keep close to my young women. Keep your eyes on the field that is being reaped, and follow behind them. I have ordered the young men not to bother you. If you get thirsty, go the vessels and drink from what the young men have drawn. (We hear a murmur in the crowd at the unusual command for a woman to drink from what the young men have drawn). (Boaz speaks to the crowd). That's right, you heard me. I said, if you get thirsty, go to the vessels and drink from what the young men have drawn!

Ruth

(Falls prostrate before Narrator/Boaz. She is at his feet, which she will later "cover." This move is clearly a form of sarcasm on Ruth's part, taking her cue from Boaz's over-the-top behavior and topping that!)

Why have I found favor in your sight, that you should take notice of me, when I am a foreigner?

Boaz

(Standing over Ruth, peering down on her prostrated form. Boaz is clearly excited by this, but tries to maintain the decorum of his imagined pious and self-important status. He doesn't have a clue Ruth is mocking him.)

All that you have done for your mother-in-law since the death of your husband has been fully told me, and how you left your father and mother and your native land and came to a people that you did not know before. (Narrator/Boaz stretches her arms out over Ruth's body in a blessing). May the LORD reward you for your deeds, and may you have a full reward from the LORD, the God of Israel, under whose wings you have come for refuge.

Ruth

(Ruth stands with head bowed and takes Boaz's hands. After she speaks, she turns away from Boaz to return to the fields. Ruth circles the stage to the left, while Boaz, in his wide-footed stance, circles to the right.)

May I continue to find favor in your sight, my lord, for you have comforted me and spoken kindly to your servant, even though I am not one of your servants.

Narrator

(As Narrator/Boaz and Ruth circle the stage, the Narrator speaks. The two meet, and we know that a little time has passed.)

At mealtime, Boaz said to her . . .

Boaz

Come here, (Ruth approaches him). Eat of this bread, and dip your morsel in the sour wine.

(He opens his arms before him, a gesture meant to indicate a table of food, but also a gesture that presents his body to Ruth. Ruth kneels and begins to eat.)

PART 2

Spectators/Reapers

(The spectators, very familiar with the story, begin to murmur and laugh at this flirtation. Ruth looks out over the spectators, aware of what is happening, but plays along. Ruth stands and returns to reaping. In the spirit of subversion, her reaping continues as flirtation, metaphorically speaking. A performance for Boaz that plays right into his arrogance and bloated self-image. It is a strategy. The Narrator/Boaz rises to speak.)

Boaz

(Addresses the Spectators/Reapers. It is clear from their reaction that they know the old man is smitten. Boaz is performing for Ruth, using voice and body to impress her with his power, strength, and generosity. The Narrator/Boaz looks furtively at Ruth as he speaks.)

Let her glean even among the standing sheaves, and do not reproach her. You must also pull out some handfuls for her from the bundles, and leave them for her to glean, and do not rebuke her.

Narrator

(The Narrator drops out of the Boaz posture and speaks to the spectators. As she does so, Ruth travels around the stage gleaning and picking up the results of her labor, until she meets up with Naomi.)

So Satisfied gleaned until evening. Then she beat out what she had gleaned, picked it up, and came into town where she met Pleasantness.

Naomi

(Crosses to meet Ruth)

Where did you glean today? And where have you worked? Blessed be the man who took notice of you.

Ruth

(Ruth pauses briefly before answering. She ignores Naomi's first question (although repeated twice) and gets right to the heart of the issue. The place is unimportant—the man who owns the field is what matters.)

The name of the man with whom I worked today is Strength.

Naomi

(Naomi smiles at her daughter-in-law and at the spectators as well.)

Blessed be he by the LORD, whose kindness has not forsaken the living or the dead! (Naomi pauses). The man is a relative of ours, one of our nearest kin. (They exit.)

Critical Notes

2:1 An editorial statement that serves as narrative backdrop, setting the stage for the next scene.

2:2 Ruth asks that Naomi permit her to glean in the fields of "him in whose sight I shall find favor." Finding favor is going to lead the audience to a resolution of the project of the play. In 2:10, Ruth, through an interrogative, asserts that she has found favor with Boaz and reaffirms that status in 2:13. Over the next two chapters, the reaping will take place among the sheaves of wheat and barley. Jon Berquist understands Ruth's request as "Ruth's announced intentions to seduce some man."[39] But this is perhaps going too far. Although compliant with Naomi's instruction, the plan to use Ruth's sexuality seems to be Naomi's alone.

2:7 Todd Linafelt has described this verse as "undoubtedly the most difficult Hebrew in the whole book."[40] Translating the phrase, "without resting even for a moment"[41] (זה שבתה הבית מעט), Sasson offers "she must have spent little time at home" although he still considers his translation not "entirely satisfactory."[42] Daniel Lys suggests; "This [the field] is her residence, the house hardly so."[43] Could the absence of a "house" for Ruth in this awkward phrase be designed to resurface the central project of the Story (1:9) the search for a "house"? And if the "field" is implied or indicated demonstrably by the storyteller while speaking, the association with the fields of Moab, the Breasted One of Israel, and the search for security is unmistakable. Michael Carasik offers that the confused phrase (זה שבתה הבית מעט) is here offered by an embarrassed overseer explaining to Boaz a case of "sexual harassment" experienced by Ruth, prompting Boaz's response of 2:8–9.[44] Should Carasik be correct, the phrase certainly does emphasize the role that sexuality will play in the unfolding drama. Jonathan Grossman

---

39. Berquist, "Role Dedifferentiation in the Book of Ruth," 29.

40. Linefelt, *Ruth*, 31.

41. Also RSV.

42. Sasson, *Ruth*, 48.

43. Lys, "Residence ou repos? Notule sur Ruth ii 7," 501.

44. Carasik, "Ruth 2:7," 493–94.

is of the opinion that the overseer's speech was intended as a request for Boaz to impose restrictions on Ruth. A request to which Boaz responds by granting even more freedom to Ruth while imposing restrictions on the workmen.[45]

2:8 The address by Boaz to Ruth is saturated with expressions of social power. Boaz refers to Ruth as "my daughter" and tells her not to glean in another field or to "leave this one."[46] The phrase "leave this one" (לא תעבורי מזה) could also be rendered "do not transgress this command"[47] as עבר is typically used in context of a divine or royal command. The first interchange between Boaz and Ruth firmly establishes a social hierarchy. Sasson suggests the following as the sense of the verse: "Is it understood, daughter, that you ought not to glean in another field? [Furthermore,] you are not to transgress this [command], but must keep close to my girls here!"[48] Perhaps, this expression of power is also be resident behind the use of לוא which is often used to emphasize a negative command.[49] Undoubtedly, the interchange is designed to communicate Boaz's understanding of social power and position, sarcastically inflated by the female storyteller.

2:9 When thirsty, Ruth, the Moabitess, is to drink water from that drawn by the young men. Quite a reversal of Deut 23:2–4.

2:10 The expression of social power and station is continued in Ruth's exaggerated and perhaps sarcastic response to Boaz. Just like the terms embedded in Boaz's command are often used to express royalty or deity, so too Ruth's prostration (ותפל על-פניה ותשתחו ארצה) is generally reserved as an act of respect given to the king or deity. Performed in the presence of Boaz, it would be an exaggerated, and perhaps sarcastic, acknowledgement of male social power, presented even more effectively if received as genuine by Boaz. Ruth's reply to Boaz contains a word play almost musical or whimsical in its delivery: להכירני ואנכי נכריה "Why [How can it be] you notice the unnoticeable [foreigner or family-less]"!

2:11 And it's almost as if Boaz did not hear her! He continues from verse 9 without missing a beat. Boaz describes Ruth in glowing terms that bring to mind the patriarch Abraham (Gen 12:1–3) and invokes YHWH's, the God of Israel, blessing on her, under whose wings she has taken refuge.

---

45. Grossman, "'Gleaning Among the Ears'—'Gathering among the Sheaves,'" 716.

46. RSV.

47. Sasson, *Ruth*, 50. See also Shepherd, "Violence in the Fields?," 444–61.

48. Sasson, *Ruth*, 50.

49. *GKC*, 518b.

Little does Boaz know that the God of Israel will indeed "spread" his wings over Ruth, but not in the way Boaz envisioned!

In a manner reminiscent of Naomi's speech in 1:20–21, in which she alternates references to YHWH and Almighty, Boaz invokes YHWH and the God of Israel in 2:11–12. "God of Israel" appears only here in Ruth and it is significant that the title is used in a metaphoric picture that will undo the damage done by the Almighty. The irony is unmistakable. The *God of Israel* will spread his wings over a *Moabitess*.

2:13 At the conclusion of the dialogue, Ruth seems to accept, or at least bring to mind (teasingly?) a social reality. In Boaz's eyes, Ruth has gone from "young girl" (נערה) in 2:5, to "Moabite girl" (נערה מואבית) in 2:6; to "my daughter" (2:8 בתי), to foreigner (2:10 נכריה), to finally maidservant" (שפח) in 2:13, even though she is not maidservant to Boaz. This whole passage revolves around the male prerogative to define the female. It will meet an unexpected conclusion in the question asked by Boaz in Act Three (3:9).

2:13 דברת על־לב translated, "console" or "comfort," not the expected אל־לב. The phrase appears nine times in the Hebrew Bible, generally with the meaning to "console" (Gen 50:21; Isa 40:2) but can also mean to "seduce" (Gen 34:3; Judg 19:3; Hos 2:16). Even if the meaning here is to comfort or console, a subtext is not far from the surface particularly when spoken by Ruth who will later seduce the seducer.

2:14 תשבע He "passed" it to her, or he "tended" her. This is the only time this root is used in the Hebrew Bible. Is there a bit of a tease shared by Boaz and Ruth? LaCocque believes the action described by the verb is "already a marital act."[50] Certainly, the setting is unusual and may have raised eyebrows as it blurred social boundaries. Ruth has invaded the male sphere—eating with the harvesters, and apparently not with the other gleaners.

2:14 Ruth ate, was satisfied, and had some left over. LaCocque draws our attention to a similar description in 2 Chron 31:10.[51] In contrast to the Chronicles description of blessing heaped upon those ritually and ethnically pure, Ruth, the Moabitess, without any pretense of ritual cleanness, shares the bounty.

---

50. LaCocque, *Ruth*, 75.

51. Ibid., 75.

2:17 Ruth gleaned an ephah of barley. Estimated by Campbell to be somewhere between 29–47 lbs.[52] By all accounts an impressive amount! Should we see here an intentionally exaggerated—almost farcical—amount? Is this exaggerated amount also expressed in the dialogue of 2:19? The identity of Boaz is left to the end of Ruth's response to Naomi, the focus, rather, placed on the amount of grain and the identity of the co-workers.

2:18b "she also brought out and gave her what food she had left over after being satisfied." אשר־הותרה Ruth shares with Naomi from the surplus. Sasson sees here a contrast to 1:5, the bereavement that functioned as the conflict propelling the action of the drama.[53] Certainly it offers a visual contrast to Naomi's statement of 1:21.

2:19 "Blessed be the man who took notice of you." The verb, "took notice" (מכירך), based on the root נכר is also used in 2:10, in Ruth's statement to Boaz where she admits that Boaz took notice of a foreigner (נכריה).

2:19 In response to Naomi's question, Ruth withholds the identity of the field owner until the very last. It becomes clear that the pivotal bit of information in the dialogue is Boaz's identity. This last part of Ruth's response is what will now propel the action even further.

2:20 "whose [LORD's] kindness has not forsaken the living or the dead!"[54] The phrase has occasioned a great deal of comment, considering it unusual to extend the kindness of the LORD to the dead.[55] Perhaps Naomi is acknowledging that YHWH has followed the lead set by Ruth and Orpah. In 1:8, Naomi expresses gratitude to the Moabite girls for the "kindness" they have shown to the dead and now YHWH is doing the same.[56]

Naomi blesses YHWH because he has not withheld (עזב "withhold," NRSV—forsaken) his kindness from the living or the dead. It is very likely that the term also functions as an inverted pun on the name Boaz (בעז).

L. J. de Regt considers 2:20–22 a "climactic point in the text, indicated by the repetition of full references to the participants."[57] Rhetorical devises, such as repetition, slow the action so that the event, dialogue, or narration

---

52. Campbell, *Ruth*, 104.

53. Sasson, *Ruth*, 58.

54. NRSV.

55. See the discussion in Sasson, *Ruth*, 60.

56. A connection is also noted by L.J. de Regt, between 1:8 and 2:20 evident through the speaker identification used in each passage. De Regt, *Participants in Old Testament Texts and the Translator*, 61–62.

57. Ibid., 61.

does not "go by too fast."[58] In the oral presentation of the Naomi Story we might well think of this repetition of speaker identification between the speech of 2:20a and 2:20b as indicating a prolonged pause. The pause is suggestive of a plan beginning to form by which Naomi will make use of Boaz as a near relative. The pause allows the audience to follow Naomi's lead and anticipate what might come next.

2:23 Ruth is said to have gleaned until the end of the barley and wheat harvests. In 1:22 Naomi and Ruth return to Bethlehem at the beginning of the barley harvest. In 2:17 Ruth returns home with an overflow of barley. And in 3:2, Boaz is winnowing barley. So why the mention of wheat in 2:23, especially since, "wheat ripens later than barley and, according to the Gezer Manual, was harvested during the sixth agricultural season."[59] LaCocque sees the mention of wheat and barley as an effort to bring to mind Passover (celebrating a return to the Promised Land) and Pentecost (celebrating the gift of Torah). At this point in the story, Naomi has *returned* but has yet to experience the *gift* of security.[60] While this certainly makes wonderful symbolism, we are not convinced by LaCocque's suggestion. Had this been the intention of the storyteller, it would have made more sense to have Boaz winnowing wheat in 3:2. Yet, given the storyteller's overall attention to detail, we do think there is some significance behind the mention of both wheat and barley in 2:23, particularly since the Bethlehem region doesn't seem to be particularly well suited to wheat production.[61] Could this be another of the Nomi Storyteller's wordplays? The word used for wheat (חטים) is very similar in sound to the infrequently used "sinful" (חטאים). What exactly is Ruth harvesting? The storyteller has already introduced the question of morality and divine justice (1:21; 2:12, 20), so perhaps the theme surfaces here again at the end of the Act 2 in preparation for the unorthodox measures to follow in Act 3.

Sasson offers an explanation for the mention of wheat that also promotes the plot of the story. In chapter three, Naomi instructs Ruth in the threshing floor scene during the threshing of the barley. The encounter between Ruth and Boaz on the threshing floor motivates Boaz to act quickly, perhaps immediately—the next day. In the long version of Act 4, Boaz's action preempts any action taken by Mr. So-and-So, who was presumably

58. Longacre, "A Spectrum and Profile Approach to Discourse Analysis," 349.

59. Borowski, *Agriculture in Iron Age Israel*, 88.

60. LaCocque, *Ruth*, 80.

61. Borowski, *Agriculture in the Iron Age*, 89.

waiting until the end of the wheat harvest to advance a claim on the field and so purchase the field at a more reasonable price. In 4:1–10 Boaz preempts any action by Mr. So-and-So by surprisingly stating his intention to buy Ruth and so dissuade Mr. So-and-So from the field. The mention of wheat in 2:23 allows this surprise action.[62] What is less convincing is Sasson's suggestion that the mention of wheat harvest frames the entire action of the drama. That is, the purchase of Ruth (4:9–10) occurred immediately, but the marriage of 4:13 occurred after the wheat harvest.

Act Three—The Threshing Floor: 3:1–18

3Naomi her mother-in-law said to her, "My daughter, I need to seek some security for you, so that it may be well with you. 2Now here is our kinsman Boaz, with whose young women you have been working. See, he is winnowing barley tonight at the threshing floor. 3Now wash and anoint yourself, and put on your best clothes and go down to the threshing floor; but do not make yourself known to the man until he has finished eating and drinking. 4When he lies down, observe the place where he lies; then, go and uncover his feet and lie down; and he will tell you what to do." 5She said to her, "All that you tell me I will do."

6So she went down to the threshing floor and did just as her mother-in-law had instructed her. 7When Boaz had eaten and drunk, and he was in a contented mood, he went to lie down at the end of the heap of grain. Then she came stealthily and uncovered herself at his feet, and lay down. 8At midnight the man was startled, and turned over, and there, lying at his feet, was a woman! 9He said, "Who are you?" And she answered, "I am Ruth, your servant; spread your cloak over your servant, for you are next-of-kin." 10He said, "May you be blessed by the LORD, my daughter; this last instance of your loyalty is better than the first; you have not gone after young men, whether poor or rich. 11And now, my daughter, do not be afraid, I will do for you all that you ask, for all the assembly of my people know that you are a worthy woman. 13Remain this night, and in the morning, as the LORD lives, I will act as next-of-kin for you. Lie down until the morning."

14So she lay at his feet until morning, but got up before one person could recognize another; for he said, "It must not be known that the woman came to the threshing floor." 15Then he said, "Bring the cloak you are wearing and hold it out." So she held it, and he measured out six measures of

62. Sasson, *Ruth*, 130.

barley, and put it on her back; then he went into the city. [16]She came to her mother-in-law, who said, "How did things go with you, my daughter?" Then she told her all that the man had done for her, [17]saying, "He gave me these six measures of barley, for he said, 'Do not go back to your mother-in-law empty-handed.'" [18]She replied, "Wait, my daughter, until you learn how the matter turns out, for the man will not rest, but will settle the matter today."

Script: Adjacency Pairs

3:1–5

A. Naomi: My daughter, I need to seek some security for you, so that it may be well with you. Now here is our kinsman Boaz, with whose young women you have been working. See, he is winnowing barley tonight at the threshing floor. "Now wash and anoint yourself, and put on your best clothes and go down to the threshing floor; but do not make yourself known to the man until he has finished eating and drinking. When he lies down, observe the place where he lies; then, go and uncover his feet and lie down; and he will tell you what to do.

B. She (Ruth): All that you tell me I will do

3:9

A. He (the man [Boaz]): Who are you?

B. She (Ruth): I am Ruth, your servant; spread your cloak over your servant, for you are next-of-kin.

3:10–13

A. He (Boaz): May you be blessed by the LORD, my daughter; this last instance of your loyalty is better than the first; you have not gone after young men, whether poor or rich. And now, my daughter, do not be afraid, I will do for you all that you ask, for all the assembly of my people know that you are a worthy woman. But now, though it is true that I am a near kinsman, there is another kinsman more closely related than I. Remain this night, and in the morning, if he will act as next-of-kin for you, good; let him do it. If he is not willing to act as next-of-kin for you, then, as the LORD lives, I will act as next-of-kin for you. Lie down until the morning.

B. Narrated preferred response

3:14–15

A. He (Boaz): It must not be known that the woman came to the threshing floor.

A^1. He (Boaz): Bring the cloak you are wearing and hold it out.

3:16–17

A. Mother-in-law (she [Naomi]): How did things go with you, my daughter?[63]

B. She (Ruth): He gave me these six measures of barley, for he said, 'Do not go back to your mother-in-law empty-handed.'

3:18

A. She (Naomi): Wait, my daughter, until you learn how the matter turns out, for the man will not rest, but will settle the matter today.

B. Implied preferred response as a transition leading to final act.

Performance Notes

Narrator/Boaz

(At the end of Act Two, as Naomi and Ruth leave the stage, the Narrator goes down among the spectators. She clears a space to function as the threshing floor, moving the spectators around to surround it. Naomi and Ruth enter the stage.)

Naomi

My daughter, I need to seek some security for you, so that it may be well with you. (Naomi points to Narrator/Boaz down among the spectators, working on the threshing floor). Here is our kinsman, Strength, with whose young women you have been working. See, he is winnowing barley tonight

---

63. JPS translates: How is it with you . . . ? Davis and Parker translate Naomi's question: "Who are you now, my daughter?" Davis and Parker, *Who are You, My Daughter?*, 19.

on the threshing floor; but do not make yourself known to the man until he has finished eating and drinking. When he lies down, observe the place here he lies; then, go and uncover his feet and lie down; and he will tell you what to do.

Ruth

(Exits the stage to enter the threshing floor among the spectators. She follows the directions of the Narrator. This choreographed exchange creates the tension of the forbidden, a live sex act, comically rendered by the two female performers. The spectators now surround the action.)

All that you tell me I will do.

Narrator/Boaz

So she went to the threshing floor and did just as her mother-in-law had instructed her. When Strength had eaten and drunk, he went to lie down at the end of the heap of grain. Then, Satisfied came stealthily and uncovered herself at his feet, and lay down.

(What follows is an extended pantomime, or dance that is choreographed for maximum comic effect. If the Narrator and the actor portraying Ruth possess the physical skill, it can be raised to the level of a gymnastic exchange, all taking place under a blanket! The Narrator assumes the physical presence of Boaz and lies down next to Ruth. Ruth stands up, straddles Boaz, and is about to "cover his feet." Startled, the Narrator/Boaz jumps up, toppling Ruth who lands on her backside, and stands over her.)

Who are you?

Ruth

I am Satisfied, your servant; spread your cloak over your servant, for you are next-of-kin.

(The pantomime begins again. Using the ubiquitous rule of three, a comic technique rooted in the belief that repeating something three times, with the third time being a variation that has the element of surprise, our threshing floor scene proceeds. One application of the rule of three would be to have Ruth pop her head out from under the blanket twice, showing the spectators a weary and uninterested face—an expression that mocks Boaz's virility. The third time this happens, it is Boaz who pops out from under the blanket, looking like he just conquered the world!)

Narrator/Boaz

May you be blessed by the LORD, my daughter; this last instance of your loyalty is better than the first; you have not gone after young men, whether rich or poor. And now, my daughter, do not be afraid, I will do for you all that you ask, for all the assembly of my people know that you are a worthy woman. Remain this night, and in the morning, as the LORD lives, I will act as next-of-kin for you. Lie down until the morning.

Narrator

(Narrator transforms in and out of the physical character of Boaz. She speaks to the spectators/reapers, as Ruth follows her directions.)

So she lay at his feet until morning, but got up before one person could recognize another; for he said, "It must not be known that the woman came to the threshing floor." Then he said, "Bring the cloak you are wearing and hold it out." So she held it, and he measured out six measures of barley, and put it on her back; then he went into the city.

Ruth

(Ruth pantomimes the spreading of the blanket and then hoists it on her back for her journey back to her mother-in-law. She returns to the stage as Naomi approaches her.)

Naomi

How did things go with you, my daughter?

Ruth

(With a flourish she pantomimes opening the blanket to reveal the bounty she has brought from Boaz.)

He gave me these six measures of barley, saying "do not go back to your mother-in-law empty-handed."

Naomi

(Pauses, reaches out to run her hands through the barley and raise them to her face, breathing in the smell of this food. She smiles at Ruth and at the spectators as well.)

Wait, my daughter, until you learn how the matter turns out, for the man will not rest, but will settle the matter today.

Critical Notes

3:1 The opening dialogue in this scene reiterates the main project of the drama (1:9). Naomi seeks a future security (מנוח) for Ruth that it may be well with her.

3:2 מדעתנו ("our relative") is a rare term. Campbell refers to this as a "unique feminine noun form"[64] of ידע ("to know"). Campbell suggests that the referent is an abstract group "one of our circle of redeemers."[65]

3:2 Boaz winnowing barley. Earlier, Ruth has gleaned barley and wheat (2:17, 23). Barley has already been woven into the prefiguring of a resolution in the form of Ruth's bulging apron filled with an ephah of barley (2:17). Campbell suggests here "gates"[66] instead of "barley" aware that barley ripens prior to wheat and seems out of sync with the notation of wheat and barley in 2:23. We find Campbell's explanation unnecessary and unconvincing, suggesting instead that the storyteller, in 3:2, has moved the audience to the conclusion of harvest and that the discrepancy is in 2:23 (see above). Naomi is moving the audience "fast-forward" from the scene in 2:23. Ruth has been living with Naomi, gleaning barley with the young girls in Boaz's employ. Some few weeks have transpired (harvest probably less than a month from 1:22 to 3:2), allowing Boaz to become familiar with and recognize Ruth even in uncertain light—a condition vital in what is about to transpire.

3:3 Naomi's instructions for Ruth's preparations are clear. Boaz will be at the threshing floor, winnowing barley with other men of the city. The winnowing will be concluded with a party, involving eating and drinking, until alcohol induced sleep overtakes the partiers. Naomi intends Ruth to creep into the party, prepared for a sexual encounter (see Ezek 16: 8–12), that she will initiate with Boaz.

"Go down to the threshing floor." Naomi's instructions are given to Ruth and so are expected in a 2fs but we find the verb in 1s ("I will go down") and a similar 1s "lie down" (שכבתי) in 3:4 where a 2fs is clearly the intent. Are these instances of the grammatical irregularities appearing in dialogue embedded in narrative[67] or an expression of intensity?[68] If we

64. Campbell, *Ruth*, 117.

65. Ibid., 117.

66. Ibid., 117–18.

67. Rendsburg, *Diglossia in Ancient Hebrew*, 53.

68. LaCocque, *Ruth*, 90.

keep in mind the female solidarity already established in the Naomi Story between a female audience, the Naomi character, and soon, in Act 4, the Ruth character, then this verbal construction is powerful. A first person rendition brings the audience into the story making Ruth's actions the group's actions.

3:6 "his heart was merry" Boaz is described as buzzed if not drunk. Or, as Campbell more delicately puts it, Boaz was "mellower-than-usual"[69] or, as Sasson describes: "Ruth was to wait until Boaz was filled with the proper spirit and thus brought to the proper frame of mind."[70]

3:7 "She came stealthily" the word describing Ruth's approach (בלט) is used only three times in the Hebrew Bible, here and twice in Samuel in reference to David.[71] Used here, the sense is that Ruth "came softly"— "secretly." The convenient connection to the genealogy added in 4:18–22 and helping to form the book of Ruth is unmistakable.

3:7 ותגל The normal translation is "she uncovered" with the following "his feet" (מרגלתיו) functioning as the direct object (although the sign of the direct object את is absent). Alternately the phrase ותגל מרגלתיו can be translated "she uncovered *herself* at his feet" with מרגלתיו indicating the place of the action (as with all other instances of the use of the word in the Hebrew Bible), not the object.[72] Boaz, or his feet (genitalia), is therefore not the object of the uncovering (already assumed in the instructions of 3:4), but the place where Ruth uncovers—herself -making very plain Ruth's sexual initiative and her subsequent request in 3:9 for Boaz to cover her. The "covering" by the wings of God contained in Boaz's blessing in 2:12 is now made concrete in the sexual intimacy Ruth initiates under the cloak Boaz has spread over them both.[73]

This reversal of fortunes, in which the patriarch becomes the pawn, implies a reversal of social power that must have elicited a variety of responses from the female audience. Shock, knowing agreement, satisfaction; could all these be present in the audience response?

---

69. Campbell, *Ruth*, 122.

70. Sasson, *Ruth*, 69.

71. Polen, "Dark Ladies and Redemptive Compassion," 71.

72. Van Wolde, "Intertextuality," 444.

73. Thomas Mann comments, "Those who included Ruth in the canons of both Judaism and Christianity were not as puritanical as the compilers of the *Revised Common Lectionary* who omitted the 'sex scene' in ch.3." Mann, "Ruth 4," 178. Mann might find the same critique of Theodoret. See Mitchell, "Ruth at Antioch," 212.

In the verses that follow, Boaz's activities are expressed in a series of four finite verbal forms. The series forms a nice balance to the instructions given by Naomi to Ruth in 3:4.

3:8 "The man was startled" (ויחרד האיש). The phrase can also be translated: The man "was terrified" or "shuttered with fear." Perhaps this extreme reaction is, like the exchange in 2:8–10, intended for dramatic effect or to provide comic relief.[74] This, strong and self-confident, Boaz is terrified of the sexual advances of the Moabite girl! Certainly, Boaz is reacting to more than a sudden cool draft![75]

"And turned over" (וילפת). Perhaps better "he was grasped or seized." Boaz suddenly awakens in a fright and is "seized by forces beyond his control. Given the double entendres that fill the chapter, one also should not overlook the possible sexual connotations of shuddering and involuntary physical reactions."[76] Midrash Rabbah suggests something a bit more gentle. "She clung to him like ivy, and he began to finger her hair. 'Spirits have no hair,' he thought, so he said, 'Who art thou?'"[77]

Boaz has enjoyed the day. He has eaten his fill and has drunk enough to be "happy." The day's activities, a full stomach, and alcohol are having their effect. Boaz finds his way to a soft place on the pile of grain, presumably somewhat removed from others, but still near in proximity to the other party goers, and falls asleep. He awakes in a fright to discover a woman (notice the question: Who are you?" is framed using the feminine pronoun מי־את) has initiated a sexual encounter with him.

3:9 In answer to Boaz's question: Who are you? Ruth responds, identifying herself as "handmaid" (אמה), in careful distinction from the "maidservant" (שפח) of 2:13. Although the terms are used interchangeably in biblical narrative, a distinction seems to be warranted in the Naomi Story.[78] It may be that Sasson is correct in suggesting that אמה connotes a potential mate in a way that שפח does not.[79] It is no doubt significant that Ruth does not use any of the other identifiers that have been attached to her throughout the story. She is not daughter, Moabitess, foreigner, or maidservant. She is Ruth, an unattatched, upwardly mobile, female.

---

74. Sasson, *Ruth*, 75.

75. Joüon, *Ruth*, 71–72.

76. Linafelt, *Ruth*, 53–54.

77. Midrash Rabbah, *Ruth*, 74.

78. Contra Campbell, *Ruth*, 123.

79. Sasson, *Ruth*, 81.

3:9 "spread your robe over your handmaid" Ruth's request to Boaz is direct and blunt. She asks (tells) him to include her in his family (see Deut 23:1; Ezek 16:8). "Your robe" (כנפך) undoubtedly another of the storyteller's wordplays bringing to mind the "wings of YHWH" 2:12 (כנפיו). Boaz's own words are coming back to mind and his prayer is being answered—just not at all how he imagined! In this action, Boaz represents YHWH. Naomi's complaint against YHWH in 2:20 will be resolved through the plan now being implemented on the threshing floor. Both divine and human justice are being secured through Naomi's ingenuity.[80]

In this verse Boaz is identified as "redeemer" (גאל). Boaz is elsewhere identified by others as the "kinsman" (2:1, 3:2—מדע) and redeemer (גאל) in 2:20. In 3:12 he self identifies as redeemer (גאל). Naomi first uses the redeemer term upon learning that Ruth has attracted the attention of Boaz and his largesse (2: 20) but not in 3:2 during her instructions to Ruth regarding the proposed midnight rendezvous. Sasson's take on 3:9 is that Ruth brought up the topic of "redeemer" to Boaz on her own, independent of Naomi's instruction and so did not calculate that there was another who could function in that role ahead of Boaz.[81] Meek, believes Ruth's statement to Boaz an intentional overstatement on her part, identifying Boaz as the "next-of-kin" even though Naomi only called Boaz a near relative or "next after the next-of-kin" in 2:20.[82] Whosever idea it was, Naomi's or Ruth's, the frame of Ruth's request and Boaz's response are pivotal to the drama. This drama is about finding security in the house of a husband and sometimes women need to take things into their own hands, even if manipulating the social system is required! The use of the term "redeemer" takes the plot from a strictly interpersonal and family affair, interjecting social institutions and economic norms for review as they contribute to either resolve or complicate the problem driving the story.

The Naomi Storyteller cloaks the scene in ambiguity and inference. Ruth's actions are an invitation to either sexual intercourse, marriage, or both. By her actions, Ruth has initiated sexual intercourse and by her words; inviting Boaz to spread his "wing / skirt" (bringing to mind Boaz's own words in 2:12) over her and identifying him as her "redeemer" (גאל), she has invited Boaz to an enduring relationship, in which sexuality will

80. Maré, Coetzee, and Minnaar, "The Concept of יראת יהוה as Wisdom Motif in the Book of Ruth," 188.

81. Sasson, *Ruth*, 83.

82. Meek, "Translating the Hebrew Bible," 333.

have its home.[83] "Thus, it is not just that the reader must decide what to make of Ruth's ambiguous invitation, but that Boaz must as well."[84]

3:11 "You have not gone after young men, whether rich or poor." Boaz has no misgivings identifying what Ruth is up to and his reaction is quick—"Thank God!" In Boaz's estimation, this present expression of Ruth's "kindness" (חסד) is greater than the first, presumably Ruth's care for Naomi as mentioned in 2:11. The ability of Ruth to seek a suitor other than Boaz—to go after the young men—will prove to be an important detail later in the Long Version of the story (4:5). Ruth was under no legal obligation to limit her choice of husband. A clear departure from the levirate custom described in Deuteronomy 25 or the Tamar story of Genesis 38.

The irony of the next several phrases is powerful. Boaz tells Ruth to "not fear" even though he is the one trembling. Then Boaz promises to do "all you ask" thinking that he is acting on his own accord when all the while his reactions have been carefully anticipated and planned by Naomi.

Boaz uses the phrase "my daughter" twice in conversation with Ruth. He refers to Ruth as "my daughter" introducing into the story once again an element of unequal social power. Yet, now, quite unlike the somewhat pompous address in 2:8, in which Boaz is firmly in control, here on the threshing floor that control has slipped away. It should be pointed out as well that the first time Ruth is referred to as "my daughter" (1:12) is by Naomi expressing the futility that will greet Ruth in any attempts to find a husband should she accompany Naomi back to Bethlehem. Throughout the story, Boaz has been very conscious of social status—in a sense he is the foil personifying the problem that Naomi and Ruth seek to overcome. Just as the problem is about to be conquered—so, too, Boaz will be conquered.

The whole town knows you are a woman of worth. A new descriptive for Ruth has been added: "woman of worth" (אשת חיל). It is no accident that this description finds a parallel in 2:1 where Boaz is described as a "man of great worth" (איש גבור חיל). A sense of equality has been recognized and it may be that this gives to Boaz a sense of freedom to marry Ruth. Ruth's sexuality has rendered her Boaz's equal.

3:12 Ruth has achieved social equality with Boaz (he has become a trembling fright and she is a respected socialite) and now it's time for the social customs themselves to be conquered in order to assure Naomi and Ruth a future.

83. Fewell and Gunn, *Compromising Redemption*, 129.
84. Linafelt, *Ruth*, 55.

3:13 Boaz's revelation that there is a "redeemer" more closely related to Ruth than he complicates the plot and adds suspense, yet does not dissuade either Boaz or Ruth from spending the rest of the night together. This part of the Boaz dialogue was probably not part of the Naomi Story and is only required in presenting the Long Version of Act 4.

3:13 The verse begins and ends with Boaz instructing Ruth to stay the night. The prospect of spending the night with Ruth certainly seems to be on Boaz's mind—and the storyteller's too. For the next verse repeats this bit of information one more time.[85]

3:14 So she lay at his feet until morning. The phrase brings the story back to Naomi's instruction of 3:4.

3:14 "Let it not be known that *the woman* came to the threshing floor." Boaz's use of "*the woman*" appears strange in the context of this dialogue. Some have considered that the statement is intended to convey Boaz's internal thoughts rather than represent direct address to Ruth.[86] The statement is prefaced by ויאמר a finite form, that elsewhere in Ruth frames a direct quotation.[87] In Ruth, the infinitive לאמר is used to introduce an indirect quotation of the disclosure of inner thoughts (4:4).[88] Consequently, we should most probably understand 3:14 as a direct address and the use of האשה (the woman) is intentional.[89] Why then this awkward occurrence here? Since Boaz is speaking to Ruth in direct address, wouldn't the feminine pronoun (את—you) function better? Given the storyteller's penchant for wordplays and semantic connections, we are drawn to similarly surprising uses of "the woman" in 1:5 and 4:11. In setting up the project of the play, Naomi, as *the woman*, represents all women—the female. Similarly, in 3:14 it is now Ruth's turn to embody *the woman*. On the threshing floor she represents an intrusion of female power and influence in a male dominated

---

85. Perhaps the repetition here does indicate the secondary nature of the disclosure in 3:13 of a near kinsman.

86. Hubbard, *Ruth*, 220. See also Niehoff, "Do Biblical Characters Talk to Themselves?," 577–92.

87. Hatav, "(Free) Direct Discourse in Biblical Hebrew," 7. L. de Regt is also of the opinion that proper names are not required at the beginning of direct speech. De Regt, *Participants in Old Testament Texts and the Translator*, 19.

88. Cynthia Miller is correct to remind us however that the author is free to vary typical usage. Miller, *The Representation of Speech in Biblical Hebrew Narrative*, 427.

89. See also the discussion provided by Frank Polak on speaker and addressee in Polak, "Speaker, Addressee, and Positioning: Dialogue Structure and Pragmatics in Biblical Narrative," 360–62. Also, de Regt, *Participants in Old Testament Texts and the Translator*.

world. And finally in 4:11 *the woman* will be the agent of prosperity and continuity. If presented in a performance, it must be remembered that the dialogue also includes the audience. It may be useful to consider Boaz's statement directed to the audience, bringing the audience into the drama of the play, and so the reference to Ruth as *the woman* is quite natural and effective.

Some commentators believe Naomi's instruction need not conclude with a sexual encounter. It is true that this formulation is not the usual way to express sexual intercourse (as we find in 4:13), but as Sasson describes Ruth's activity in 3:14, "whatever its precise nature, it should be reminded that her activity was sufficiently physical to awaken a man deep in slumber."[90]

Boaz's final instructions in 3:14 further the sense of irony in the threshing floor scene. This is the third time we are told Boaz directs Ruth to spend the night with him. This time, however, the storyteller provides a rationale that seems less than convincing. Boaz appears to be concerned for Ruth's respectability and so makes sure that she leaves the threshing floor before it is light enough for anyone to identify her. But hasn't Ruth already proven her stealth? She had no trouble sneaking into the threshing floor, successfully found Boaz, and made her intentions quite plain to him. Did she really need to spend the night with him? Couldn't she have just as easily snuck out the way she snuck in? And could they have burdened Ruth with a load of barley (3:17) and she still make her way noiselessly away from the threshing floor?

Campbell recognizes the ambiguities woven into the threshing floor scene and writes; "It is not prudery which compels the conclusion there was no sexual intercourse at the threshing floor; it is the utter irrelevance of such a speculation."[91] But is it irrelevant? The project of the drama is about women finding security in the "house of a husband" (1:9; 3:1). Sexuality, and the social power of sexuality is at the heart of the drama and so the threshing floor is a crucial scene. Yet, we see something here more than "the wily ways of a woman to get her man."[92] Even this assessment, reveals an androcentric point of view and power bias that is foreign to the Naomi Story. Ruth is not an opportunistic gold digger. Neither is the story about Boaz. Midrash Rabbah describes the night on the threshing floor: "All that night his evil inclination contended with him saying, 'You are un-

90. Sasson, *Ruth*, 93.
91. Campbell, *Ruth*, 138.
92. Meek, "Translating the Hebrew Bible," 333.

married and seek a wife, and she is unmarried and seeks a husband. Arise and have intercourse with her, and make her your wife.'"[93] Midrash Rabbah understands the sexual power resident in the scene but persists in assuming the sexual power resides with the male. Naomi and Ruth are subverting a male biased legal and economic system in order to accomplish a legitimate goal. They are exercising female sexual power in a fashion that reduces the powerful Boaz to a quaking fright.

3:15 Ruth returns with her apron bulging full of six measures of barley. Sasson offers a rough estimate of about 30lbs of barley filling Ruth's apron, slightly more than she was able to glean in 2:17.[94] Ruth's night with Boaz has visible results! She returns home burdened with seed. Would anyone who noticed a woman leaving the threshing floor at dawn with a payment of grain not conclude her to be a prostitute? Indeed, this is how Mays considers the gift.[95] But, if anything, the actual nature of the gift stands in contrast to "what people might have thought." The gift is, if not given to Naomi, given with Naomi in mind.

3:16–18 This Act closes as did the previous in chapter 2. Ruth returns to Naomi with a load of barley. Ruth is once again referred to as "my daughter" just as did Boaz in 3:10.

3:16 Naomi asks of Ruth "how did you fare" literally—"who are you?" (מי־את). The exact same question asked by Boaz in 3:9. Yet, Naomi knows full well that it is Ruth approaching her. Sasson speculates that the question might have the intent of "Whose [wife/woman] are you?"[96] In other words, Naomi is asking if the plan was successful, is Ruth now Boaz's wife. There is a connection or better a contrast made between Boaz and Naomi—both ask of Ruth the same question and both refer to her as "my daughter." One interlocutor, Boaz, is in the dark and the other, Naomi, is in the know.

3:17 Ruth claims that Boaz instructed her not to go back to her mother-in-law empty handed—when the dialogue between Ruth and Boaz contains no such statement. Perhaps, this also is a parallel to an earlier exchange in which Ruth adds an instruction from Boaz in 2:21 to glean in his fields until the end of harvest—an addition to what Boaz is actually reported to have said in 2:8–9. Also, Boaz tells Ruth to stay close to the young *girls* while Ruth reports Boaz said to stay close to the young *men*. Are these

93. Midrash Rabbah, *Ruth*, 81.

94. Sasson, *Ruth*, 97.

95. May, "Ruth's Visit to the High Place at Bethlehem," 77.

96. Sasson, *Ruth*, 100.

discrepancies between dialogue and reported dialogue significant? Do they give Ruth an active role? If so, she becomes more than simply a messenger, but is responsible for composing at least part of the reported message. There is no doubt that the command not to return "empty" handed brings to mind Naomi's statement of 1:21. In 1:21 she went out full and returned empty. In Act 3 Ruth, on Naomi's behalf, went out empty and returned full.

It is perhaps symbolic that Ruth hands the seed to Naomi. The threshing floor episode is for the benefit of Naomi. Once Ruth procures the "seed" she fades into the background in a manner very similar to the conclusion of the drama in 4:16–17. Linafelt still senses the female solidarity resident in the scene. "The fact that this narrative development mirrors the actual course of many women's lives in the ancient world—and even one supposes, today—in which procreation is thought to be the only worthwhile goal, makes it all the more poignant and disturbing."[97]

3:16–18 These verses comprise the last dialogue from either Naomi or Ruth. They have set a plan into action. Now they must wait and learn how the matter will turn out.

Act 4 returns the drama to the daylight and public sphere. Despite the seeming clairvoyance of the elders and townspeople in 4:12, only Boaz and the audience are aware of the events of Act 3. The social conventions that helped produce the project of the Naomi Story are now in focus again—this time, however, having been influenced by the night on the threshing floor.

Act Four—The City Gate—4:2, 3, 9–12

Then Boaz took ten men of the elders of the city, went up to the city gate, and said, "Sit down here"; so they sat down. ³He then said, "Naomi, who has come back from the fields of Moab, is selling the field that belonged to our kinsman Elimelech. ⁹Then Boaz said to the elders and all the people, "Today you are witnesses that I have purchased from the hand of Naomi all that belonged to Elimelech and all that belonged to Chilion and Mahlon. ¹⁰I have also purchased Ruth, the wife of Mahlon, to be my wife, to maintain the dead man's name on his inheritance, in order that the name of the dead may not be cut off from his kindred and from the gate of his native place; today you are witnesses." ¹¹Then all the people who were at the gate, along with the elders, said, "We are witnesses. May YHWH make the woman who is coming into your house like Rachel and Leah, who together

97. Linafelt, *Ruth*, 61.

built up the house of Israel. May you produce children in Ephrathah and bestow a name in Bethlehem; [12]and, through the children that YHWH will give you by this young woman, may your house be like the house of Perez, whom Tamar bore to Judah."

Script: Adjacency Pairs

4:2–3

A. Boaz: Sit down here

B. Narrated preferred response—the elders do as requested.

4:9–12

A. Boaz: "Today you are witnesses that I have acquired from the hand of Naomi all that belonged to Elimelech and all that belonged to Chilion and Mahlon. [10]I have also acquired Ruth, the wife of Mahlon, to be my wife, to maintain the dead man's name on his inheritance, in order that the name of the dead may not be cut off from his kindred and from the gate of his native place; today you are witnesses."

B. The elders and all the people said: Preferred Response—"We are witnesses." Then all the people who were at the gate said, "May the LORD make the woman, who is coming into your house, like Rachel and Leah, who together built up the house of Israel. May you prosper in Eph'rathah and be renowned in Bethlehem; and may your house be like the house of Perez, whom Tamar bore to Judah, because of the children that the LORD will give you by this young woman."

Performance Notes

Narrator

(As Naomi and Ruth exit the stage, the Narrator resolves the Boaz posture and leaves the threshing floor area to return to the stage. She indicates to the spectators that they can return to their original positions. She also counts off ten of the spectators from the first row and indicates that they should follow her onto the stage. Now, along with the Narrator, these ten female spectators will become the ten male elders, each being encouraged to assume a male identity as they arrive on stage. As she travels back on to the stage, she says,)

Then Boaz took ten men of the elders of the city, and went up to the city gate.

Narrator/Boaz

(The Narrator once again assumes the persona of Boaz. She does this as the ten spectators also transform themselves into men, passing among them, shaking hands, slapping several on the back, and gathering as elder men do, feeling the strength and power of their maleness and their position as elders.)

Sit down here! (Narrator/Boaz pauses as they sit). Pleasantness, who has come back from the fields of Moab, is selling the field that belonged to our kinsmen, God-is-King.

The Ten Elders

(The elders murmur and mumble amongst themselves in response to Boaz's statement.)

Narrator/Boaz

(Silences the elders with a gesture. He then looks over the elders and takes in the rest of the spectators as well. He speaks with great authority, swelling with pride as his words progress to the final pronouncement.)

Today you are witnesses that I have purchased from the hand of Pleasantness all that belonged to God-is-King and all that belonged to Eliminated and Obliterated. I have also purchased Satisfied, the wife of Obliterated, to be my wife, to maintain the dead man's name on his inheritance, in order that the name of the dead may not be cut off from his kindred and from the gate of his native place; today you are witnesses!

The Ten Elders

(Rise quickly from their seated positions and begin to congratulate Narrator/Boaz as they return to the audience. Simultaneously, the spectators are encouraged by Narrator/Boaz and the Elders to chime in with congratulations, allowing for the ten elders to return to the audience. Once they are in place, Narrator/Boaz resolves back into the female Narrator.)

Narrator

(Raises her arms in a gesture that sweeps over the entire audience.)

Then all the people who were at the gate, along with the elders, said, (Narrator gestures for the audience to join her in saying the following:) We are witnesses. May YWHW make the woman who is coming into your house like Sheep and Tired Cow, who together built up the house of Israel!

(All the women, spectators and Narrator, laugh, and perhaps even cheer, at this moment of shared identity. This is followed by a silence, the silence of communal knowing. The Narrator then speaks alone.)

May you produce children in Ephrathah and bestow a name in Bethlehem; and through the children that the LORD will give you by this young woman, may your house be like the house of Perez, whom Tamar bore to Judah.

Critical Notes

4:2 In a fashion unusual in Ruth, there is perfect agreement—repetition between command and response in 4:1 and 2. Both Mr. So-and-So (if indeed authentic to the Naomi Story) and the ten elders do exactly as Boaz commands. Is this obedience in contrast to the slightly deviant manner by which Ruth consistently responds to commands throughout the book? Or, is the narrator simply setting the scene in concise, abbreviated language; allowing the play to carry on with the following dialogue? Boaz, and the ten elders take their places in the market area just outside the city gate. It is a public venue, people are bustling by while venders are busy hawking their produce and wares.

4:3 Boaz refers to Elimelech as "our brother." It is enough that Boaz is asserting a kin relationship between himself (and Mr. So-and-So if authentic to the scene). The term need not be pressed to imply that they were in fact real brothers.

"Naomi, who returned from the fields of Moab, is selling [literally: sold] the field that belonged to our brother Elimelech." But see verses 5 and 9 (in the Long Version) in which the field seems to be still in Naomi's possession. This is a very sudden and unexpected appearance in the story. This land possession does not figure into the story previously. Rudolf resolves the issue by revocalizing the MT to a feminine participle "Naomi is one selling" the field.[98] Campbell prefers to keep the perfect and sees the action

98. Rudolph, *Das Buch Ruth, Das Hohe Lied, Die Klagellieder*, 59.

as simply not completed by the time Boaz speaks.[99] Lipinski resolves the issue by understanding the verb מכר as to "hand over" or "deliver" not "to sell" and sees Naomi as positioned to release the land to the goʾel.[100] Robert Gordis suggested that Naomi indeed did return to Bethlehem destitute, but was in line to receive at the next jubilee a field that had belonged to her deceased husband. Unable to wait until the property returned to her possession, she was in a position to sell her future claim to the land.[101]

All of these solutions seem to miss the point. Why was the field not mentioned earlier? After ten years absence does the widow of the property holder have any legal stake in the property? Some have suggested that Naomi did not know of the land and it was Boaz who, armed with knowledge of Elemelech's field, used it in his bargaining with Mr. So-and-So.[102] Sasson suggests that Naomi had no legal standing in the council of elders and so needed a representative in order to lay claim to the land. When Boaz assumed the role of spokesperson or representative it became possible for the matter of land ownership to be addressed. The land could be sold with proceeds going to Naomi and should Naomi ever have a male heir, he would have the right to repossess Elemelech's field (Lev 25:25). Knowing that an heir was highly unlikely, Mr. So-and-So had no objection at all to possess the land—he could only gain.[103]

Rather than looking for legal precedent in an effort to find out what actually transpired, we should ask questions designed to expose the dramatic effect of this twist in the plot. To be sure, all this would not be lost on a female audience. If the drama was presented for women by women, the impact of the sudden insertion of a field (שדה), would not be lost. And the parallel to the "fields of Moab" in the set up to the drama should not be overlooked either. The concern driving the women—security—is now and clearly presented as secondary to the economic concerns of the male representatives in Bethlehem. Mr. So-and-So is motivated by economic benefit and so is no help to Naomi or Ruth. And Boaz acts only after spending the night with Ruth and has, presumably, fallen hopelessly in love with Ruth. Money and love drive the discussion. The male discussion in the city gate has taken the mask from any altruistic claims they might make. In either

99. Campbell, *Ruth*, 143–44.

100. Lipínski, "Le marriage de Ruth," 126.

101. Gordis, "Love, Marriage and Business in the Book of Ruth," 252.

102. Rowley, *The Servant of the Lord and Other Essays on the Old Testament*, 183.

103. Sasson, *Ruth*, 114–15.

case, the needs of the women are a distant second to the interests of the men. The best the women can do is manipulate things behind the scenes—something which, at least in this story, is done expertly and laudably.

"The one returned from Moab." Sasson thinks this phrase is added for legal identification purposes.[104] We prefer to look for rhetorical dramatic functions in the phrase. Both Naomi and Ruth have been silenced—neither are allowed to speak in this scene. They are present through the description of others. Their identities depend on the reconstruction of other people. Is it significant that Naomi is not the one who "grew up here in Bethlehem" and if she had, presumably members of her birth family were still in the area or certainly in the memory of those present. Naomi is cast in terms of the "other" and Ruth is not mentioned at all.

4:9–10 Boaz describes his purchase formally to the town witnesses. There are two purchases:

1. All that belonged to Elemelek and all that belonged to Chilion and Mahlon—purchased from Naomi.

2. Ruth—presumably also purchased from Naomi

The first mentioned is "all that belonged." Up to this point, only the field was considered for sale, and it appeared as unexpectedly in the story as does the mention of "all that belongs." Sasson believes this simply unclutters the tale by removing the need for an itemization of movable and immovable property.[105] But this seems out of character with the Naomi Storyteller who is very intentional and shrewd in word usage. Should this story be told by women for women, could Boaz's declaration have additional significance? Boaz's statement only makes sense if additional property was known to be in Naomi's possession. Naomi offered a field for sale but ended loosing claim to everything. Could there have been another field? What about a house in which Naomi and Ruth had been living? Did that become Boaz's also? That Boaz's inclusive pronouncement is tantamount to financial care for Naomi seems unlikely, for in the conclusion to the story, it is the son born to Ruth (interestingly not to Boaz) in 4: 15 that is the hope for Naomi's future security. So, could it be that Boaz is, in actuality, expressing what women considered an example of male greed. Under the pretense of fulfilling social obligations, the males, in fact, usurped women's rights.

104. Ibid., 115.
105. Ibid., 149.

Were Naomi present in the background while this transaction was taking place, would her facial expression have been one of surprise and shock or satisfaction and contentment when Boaz announced his defacto ownership of everything that had belonged to Naomi?

The second purchase, also from the hand of Naomi, is Ruth. Ruth is described as the widow of Mahlon. The purchase has two functions: 1) that Ruth would be his wife and, 2) to perpetuate the name of the dead. The motivation publicly expressed by Boaz, here, in the presence of witnesses is quite different than that expressed privately by Boaz on the threshing floor. Here, at the city gate, Ruth is a means to achieving male economic ambitions. Phyllis Trible clearly describes how different this address is from the threshing floor scene. "In a private conversation with Ruth, Boaz made her welfare the sole object of his concern, but in a public discussion with men he makes Ruth the means for achieving a male purpose."[106] The difference in tone between the speech on the threshing floor and the speech at the city gate, is unmistakable, but is probably an overstep to say that Ruth's welfare was Boaz's only concern on the threshing floor. He does seem to have had other things on his mind!

Although these two transactions will bring to a positive conclusion the project of the drama described in 1:9, neither Naomi or Ruth are allowed to verbalize their own satisfaction.

4:11–12. Verse 11 is contains a variant of some dramatic significance.

> MT: And all the people at the gate with the elders said," We are witnesses. May the LORD make the woman entering your home like Rachael and Leah" . . .

> LXX: And all the people said, "We are witnesses." And the elders said, "May the Lord make the woman entering your home like Rachael and Leah" . . .

Does the LXX represent a Hebrew *vorlage* preferable to the reading preserved in the MT? The variant does not affect the understanding of the general meaning of the passage (Ruth 4:11–12) but does impact the dramatic delivery of the passage. Alexander Rofé concludes that the reading preserved in the LXX is secondary, emerging from the land of Israel in the Hebrew *Vorlage* of the LXX prior to translation and consistent with late Second Temple midrash.[107] Rofé believes that the LXX rendering, split-

---

106. Trible, *God and the Rhetoric of Sexuality*, 192.

107. Rofé, "Ruth 4:11 LXX," 136. Yet, Rofé allows that the *vorlage* to the LXX and

ting the speech of 4:11 between the people and the elders, "improves the narrative by adding vitality and poignancy, in a word, dramatization."[108] We, however, follow the MT, considering the whole speech by the elders and townspeople a choral response to Boaz, directed to the audience. The blessing concludes with a reference to Tamar (Gen 38). The parallel to Ruth is quite obvious to the audience, knowing what occurred on the threshing floor, but is out of place coming from the townspeople, who, supposedly, were unaware of what happened the night before.

In terms of dramatic development, verses 11–12 signal the entrance of the chorus. The elders, sitting at the gate and all the people affirm Boaz's statement by a simple reply: We are witnesses!" followed by a threefold blessing directed at: the bride (as part of the groom's household), the groom, and their offspring. Parker has noticed parallels between the blessing in Ruth 4 and a similar blessing in Ugaritic literature pronounced at the marriage of King Keret and Lady Hurriya[109] and Linafelt has described the balanced and symmetrical form of the Ruth 4 blessing. The point is that, despite the dramatic context, the blessing has no semblance of spontaneity. It is constructed quite carefully, not something that you would expect from a random crowd—both the elders and the observers from the town.

4:11 "may the woman" Ruth is identified as: האשה translated as either "wife" or "woman." The term is used in parallel to the הנערה (young woman) at the end of verse 12 and so is perhaps understood best as "woman" both here and in 4:13. Linafelt sees in this reference a denigrating of Ruth, being reduced to "the role of child-producer, that she has been summarily re-defined as no more than a womb."[110] We agree with Linafelt that the terminology is important but perhaps not as denigrating as Linafelt believes. Throughout the story, the terms by which Ruth is described are carefully chosen, so we should expect the same here. Who is being blessed by the town? Without doubt Ruth's femaleness is being emphasized in contrast to other possible identities (Moabitess, daughter [possible here of Naomi], maiden) used throughout the story and that femaleness does seem to include her ability to have children. But, could it be that the blessing of the

---

the reading preserved in the MT may point to a time when "the biblical books were still copied in quite a free fashion, apparently before the Hasmonean period." Ibid., 138.

108. Ibid., 132.

109. Parker, "The Marriage Blessing in Israelite and Ugaritic Literature," 28–29; Linafelt, *Ruth*, 73.

110. Ibid., 75.

woman, here, in 4:11 is a fitting conclusion to the dilemma of "the woman" introduced in 1:5? In chapter one, Naomi is *the woman*, bereft of husband and children, without security and representing the potential plight of all women. Ruth was "the woman" who entered the realm of the men (3:14). Now, in chapter four, Ruth, is *the woman*, blessed with security in the house of a husband and anticipating the prospect of children, representing, in the universe of this drama, the hope of all women.

In the course of the blessing, parallels are established, securing Ruth in the constellation of memorable Israelite women: Rachel, Leah, and Tamar.

4:11 ועשה־חיל "so that you may prosper" probably in the sense: "may you have many children"[111] but also a bit of an ironic twist. Boaz was earlier described as "prosperous" (2:1) but now Boaz's prosperity will be dependent upon Ruth and her ability to conceive. The blessing confers prosperity upon Boaz, but, in an ironic twist, that blessing is dependent upon "the woman." The woman sought security in the house of a husband, but now the house of the husband is dependent upon the woman. The house of Boaz will be dependent on Ruth just like the house of Israel was dependent upon Rachel and Leah. The house of Israel is probably the house of Jacob but cannot be separated from the ancestors of the twelve tribes: the children of Rachel and Leah (and Bilhah and Zilpah at the initiative of Rachel and Leah). More, Boaz's house will also be like the house of Perez, son of Tamar, conceived by a woman robbed of family security, who also acted unconventionally to secure her future and the future of the house of her deceased husband (Gen 38). While the comparison between Ruth and Tamar makes perfect sense to the reader or the listener (possessing insider's knowledge of the threshing floor incident) able to connect all of the women: Rachel, Leah, Tamar, and Ruth as "brides-in-the-dark,"[112] it is strangely out of place in the mouth of the crowd pronouncing the blessing. Out of place, and even more poignant when we are informed in 4:8 that Perez is the ancestor of Boaz. Boaz is doubly dependent upon brave and inventive women. Perez would not have been born had Tamar not risked everything to expose the dilemma faced by all women confronted with the fallacies of a male oriented social system as expressed by Judah's callous and self-centered behavior. Now, Boaz's own house will only be blessed after the enactment of the bold and equally un-conventional plan conceived by Naomi and executed by Ruth.

---

111. Labuschagne, "The Crux in Ruth 4 11," 366.

112. Black, "Ruth in the Dark," 34.

Did the crowd know Boaz's ancestry? If they did, it seems unlikely that this association would have popped to mind in immediate response to the transaction at the city gate. No. The blessing is carefully constructed for the audience. Despite what might appear at the city gate, with only males acting and perhaps only males present, there is no doubt that it is the women who make things happen. This blessing is a strong encouragement for female initiative, in the face of pressures toward passivity. The blessing finds its fullest impact among those who know of the threshing floor incident and so are able to appreciate the strength of Rachel, Leah, Tamar, and Ruth, "the woman."

4:11b "make a name" קרא־שם occurs only here in the Hebrew Bible and may well foreshadow the naming episode of 4:17. Sasson is certainly correct that "making a name" is tantamount to establishing a reputation in Bethlehem and may well serve as a pointer to the Davidic dynasty.[113] 4:11b–12 has been considered a secondary addition to the story with the mention of Perez functioning as a bridge to the genealogy of 4:18.[114] If indeed this is so, the addition is skillfully woven, for the concluding phrase, "the young woman" (הנערה)[115] functions as a balance to the opening reference to Ruth in 4:11.

Act Five: Grand Finale 4:13–17a

So Boaz took Ruth and she became his wife; and he went in to her, and the LORD gave her conception, and she bore a son. [14]Then the women said to Naomi, "Blessed be the LORD, who has not left you this day without next of kin; and may his name be renowned in Israel! [15]He shall be to you a restorer of life and a nourisher of your old age; for your daughter-in-law who loves you, who is more to you than seven sons, has borne him." [16]Then Naomi took the child and laid him in her bosom, and became his nurse. [17]And the women of the neighborhood gave him a name, saying, "A son has been born to Naomi." They named him Obed.

---

113. Sasson, *Ruth*, 156.

114. Parker, "The Marriage Blessing in Israelite and Ugaritic Literature," 30.

115. Any effort to see here an age difference between Boaz and Ruth seems forced and unnecessary.

Script: Adjacency Pairs

4:14–15

A. The women: Blessed be the LORD, who has not left you this day without next-of-kin; and may his name be renowned in Israel! 15He shall be to you a restorer of life and a nourisher of your old age; for your daughter-in-law who loves you, who is more to you than seven sons, has borne him.

B. Narrated preferred response

4:17

A. The women of the neighborhood: A son has been born to Naomi.

Performance Notes

Narrator

(The Narrator circles the stage one more time, indicating the passage of some time. As she does so, Ruth enters at one side of the stage and Naomi at the other. Ruth holds her arms linked below her belly indicating that she is with child. The Narrator emphasizes, "the LORD gave her conception" for this one phrase provides justification for all Naomi's actions. On the line, "she bore a son," Ruth raises her arms up as if she is cradling the child. Once the Narrator has completed the circle, she speaks.)

So Boaz took Ruth and she became his wife; and went in to her, and the LORD gave her conception, and she bore a son. Then the women said to Naomi,

Narrator

(Lifts her arms to indicate that the spectators should join her. Ruth and Naomi move center stage to be near the Narrator.)

Blessed be the LORD, who has not left you this day without next of kin; and may his name be renowned in Israel! He shall be to you a restorer of life and a nourisher of your old age; for your daughter-in-law who loves you, who is more to you than seven sons, has borne him.

(Naomi gently takes the child from Ruth's arms and cradles him to her breast. The Narrator speaks the final words.)

A son has been born to Pleasantness. His name is Servant.

(End)

4:13 changes the scene one last time. The male orientation of 4:1–12 is retained (Ruth appears only in the passive voice) but the transitional nature of this setup to scene five is clear. In an amazingly concise and fast paced sequence, Boaz and Ruth marry, have sex, Ruth conceives and gives birth to a son. The terseness of the verse is unusual within the story as is the editorial insertion "the LORD gave her conception." The comment proves the validity of the blessing in 4:12b, but more, serves as the only appearance of the LORD in the story. Hubbard argues that the comment here serves as an inclusio to the reference in 1:6b[116] but this does not seem quite accurate. In 1:6b the LORD is reported to have acted as is the case in 1:21, but 4:13 is different. In 1:6b and 21, a character in the story (Naomi) reports on her perception of the LORD's activity. Here we have a direct insertion of the LORD into the story and into the wedding bed of Ruth and Boaz by the omniscient narrator. One has to wonder: why here? Where was YHWH when Ruth was gleaning in the fields? Where was He when Naomi was developing her plan for Ruth and Boaz, and why was He absent from the threshing floor? In 4:13, Ruth and Boaz are made respectable by following conventions that imply male dominance: Boaz took Ruth and went in to her. Is divine favor found only in a man's world?[117] And YHWH's intervention is unusually direct: "The LORD gave to her conception."[118] Eve claims that the LORD helped her (Gen 4:1), and Hannah was "remembered" by the LORD (1 Sam 1:19) but only here does YHWH give a pregnancy. Boaz doesn't cause the conception—the LORD does. There is no indication that Ruth is barren and so in need of divine intervention. Neither does the unusual phrase: "The LORD gave to her conception" seem to be a stock way of saying she became pregnant. Rabbi Simeon b. Lakish suggests that "the Holy One, blessed be He, shaped a womb for her."[119] YHWH's action here, in 4:13, comes very close to the activity described of the Holy Spirit in Mat 1:20. Certainly this direct and unusual action on YHWH's part is in answer to the accusation made by Naomi in 1:21 and the plight that directs the

116. Hubbard, *Ruth*, 267.

117. Is it by accident that YHWH is also absent from Gen 38 when Tamar acts to resolve her dilemma and only present as witness in Genesis 37 when Tamar is placed in such a precarious position?

118.. Linafelt, *Ruth*, 77.

119. *Midrash Rabbah, Ruth*, 91.

story from 1:9, as recognized by the chorus of neighborhood women in 4:14–15.

4:14–17 Once again (see 1:19) it is the women who play the role of the chorus. While the audience is fully aware of the whole drama leading to the birth of the boy, the women are not. They know only that Naomi was destitute but loved by Ruth who has now produced a son through her marriage with Boaz. That son will be Naomi's future.

Sasson points out that the Obed birth narrative 4:13–17 is woven from two types—one emphasizing the goel function (vs 14–15) and the other emphasizing the son status (vs 16–17).[120] In this fashion, the storyteller ties together loose ends, if a bit awkwardly. The child will be able to remain Naomi's goel and so remain the child of Ruth, (interestingly neither Ruth nor Boaz are present even by name in these verses; Ruth has once again become Naomi's "daughter-in-law) while also becoming Naomi's "son" and so fulfilling Boaz's pledge to maintain the line of Mahlon.[121]

An obvious difficulty arises in the contradiction formed by placing Obed in Naomi's and so Mahlon's family in 4:17, while at the same time placing Obed in Boaz's family tree in 4:18–22.

4:16 Naomi took the boy (הילד) forming a concluding framing to 1:5. The loss is now restored. She placed the child on her lap and became his nurse. Hoffner sees this act as a practice of legal adoption.[122] Sasson disagrees and notes the apparent intentionally ambivalent language used by the storyteller. We do not know if Naomi placed the baby at her breast (שדה not used in 4:16) or for what reason she claims the infant. Sasson puts forward an hypotheses, suggesting that this verse is intended to call to mind a quasi-divine ancestry attributed to David through Naomi's actions, an act normally associated with royal or divine personages.[123] Sasson himself believes this ending to the story is "less than satisfying."[124] Perhaps another alternative can be offered.

Ruth 4:16–17a is the final time the chorus appears in the story and is undoubtedly the grand finale. Naomi puts the child on her lap, with the "women of the neighborhood" looking on, presumably looking over her

---

120. Sasson, *Ruth*, 159–60.

121. The awkwardness of this double function has led some to conclude two sons born. See Brichto, "Kin, Cult, Land, and Afterlife," 22–23.

122. Hoffner, "Birth and Name-Giving in Hittite Texts," 201.

123. Sasson, *Ruth*, 238–40.

124. Ibid., 240.

shoulder and vying for a glimpse of the baby, and who, as a group, proclaim Naomi's motherhood and name the boy, Obed. Naomi, "the woman"
(1:5), has returned center stage. What could be a more powerful way to
complete the story: Naomi the center of attention, now seated, surrounded
by admiring onlookers, and holding the child that completes her quest for
security. In an unusual manner it is the women only (there isn't a man to
be seen) who finally name the child. And that child is quite appropriately
named: Servant. While some modern commentators prefer to see Obed a
shortened form of Obadiah,[125] Josephus was of the opinion that the child
was "to be brought up in order to be subservient" to Naomi as the chorus
of women celebrate (4:15).[126] Josephus was right about the subservient role
the child played, but we need not look into the future to find that service to
Naomi. The chorus anticipates a role that we as audience know has already
been established, born in Naomi's mind long before the child's conception;
the male has become the servant in the female quest for security.

---

125. Some see Obed as a short form of Obediah: Servant of YHWH. See Hubbard,
Ruth, 277.

126. Josephus, *Antiquities* 5.9.4.

APPENDIX

Act Four – Long Version

Although we believe that Act Four of the Naomi Story was a truncated version of Ruth chapter four (4: 2, 3, 9–12), there are reasons to include vss.1, 4–8 in the original story (see chapter five). The following is the Long Version of Act Four.

Act Four: Mr. So-and-So 4:1–12[1]

No sooner had Boaz gone up to the gate and sat down there than the next-of-kin, of whom Boaz had spoken, came passing by. So Boaz said, 'Come over, Mr. So-and-So; sit down here.' And he went over and sat down. Then Boaz took ten men of the elders of the city, and said, 'Sit down here'; so they sat down. He then said to the next-of-kin, 'Naomi, who has come back from the fields of Moab, is selling the field that belonged to our kinsman Elimelech. So I thought I would tell you of it, and say: Buy it in the presence of those sitting here, and in the presence of the elders of my people. If you will redeem it, redeem it; but if you will not, tell me, so that I may know; for there is no one prior to you to redeem it, and I come after you.' So he said, 'I will redeem it.' Then Boaz said, 'The day you buy the field from the hand of Naomi, you are also buying Ruth, the widow of the dead man, to maintain the dead man's name on his inheritance.' At this, the next-of-kin

---

1. Text based on NRSV.

said, 'I cannot redeem it for myself without damaging my own inheritance. Take my right of redemption yourself, for I cannot redeem it.'

Now this was the custom in former times in Israel concerning redeeming and exchanging: to confirm a transaction, one party took off a sandal and gave it to the other; this was the manner of attesting in Israel. So when the next-of-kin said to Boaz, 'Buy it for yourself,' he took off his sandal. Then Boaz said to the elders and all the people, 'Today you are witnesses that I have purchased from the hand of Naomi all that belonged to Elimelech and all that belonged to Chilion and Mahlon. I have also purchased Ruth, the wife of Mahlon, to be my wife, to maintain the dead man's name on his inheritance, in order that the name of the dead may not be cut off from his kindred and from the gate of his native place; today you are witnesses.' Then all the people who were at the gate, along with the elders, said, 'We are witnesses. May the LORD make the woman who is coming into your house like Rachel and Leah, who together built up the house of Israel. May you prosper in Ephrathah and bestow a name in Bethlehem; and, through the children that the LORD will give you by this young woman, may your house be like the house of Perez, whom Tamar bore to Judah.'

Script: Adjacency Pairs

4:1

A. Boaz: Come over, Mr. So-and-So; sit down here.

B. Narrated preferred response

4:2

A. He (Boaz): Sit down here

B. Narrated preferred response

4:3–4

A. He (Boaz): Naomi, who has come back from the fields of Moab, is selling the field that belonged to our kinsman Elimelech. So I thought I would tell you of it, and say: Buy it in the presence of those sitting here, and in the presence of the elders of my people. If you will redeem it, redeem it;

but if you will not, tell me, so that I may know; for there is no one prior to you to redeem it, and I come after you.

B. He (Mr. So-and-So): I will redeem it

4:5–6

A. Boaz: The day you buy the field from the hand of Naomi, you are also buying Ruth, the widow of the dead man, to maintain the dead man's name on his inheritance.

B. Mr. So-and-So: I cannot redeem it for myself without damaging my own inheritance. Take my right of redemption yourself, for I cannot redeem it.

4:8–10

A. Mr. So-and-So: Acquire it for yourself

Followed by the preferred narrated response of the sandal

B /A. Boaz: Today you are witnesses that I have purchased from the hand of Naomi all that belonged to Elimelech and all that belonged to Chilion and Mahlon. I have also purchased Ruth, the wife of Mahlon, to be my wife, to maintain the dead man's name on his inheritance, in order that the name of the dead may not be cut off from his kindred and from the gate of his native place; today you are witnesses.

The preferred response of Boaz becomes the request directed at elders and so the Boaz speech functions as both response and request.

4:11–12

B1. Then all the people who were at the gate, along with the elders: We are witnesses. May the LORD make the woman who is coming into your house like Rachel and Leah, who together built up the house of Israel. May you prosper in Ephrathah and bestow a name in Bethlehem; and, through the children that the LORD will give you by this young woman, may your house be like the house of Perez, whom Tamar bore to Judah.

Performance Notes:[2]

Narrator

(As Naomi and Ruth exit the stage, the Narrator resolves the Boaz posture and leaves the threshing floor area to return to the stage. She indicates to the spectators that they can return to their original positions. She also counts off ten of the spectators from the first row and indicates that they should follow her onto the stage. Now, along with the Narrator, these ten female spectators will become the ten male elders, each being encouraged to assume a male identity as they arrive on stage. The actress who previously played Orpah assumes the role of Mr. So-and-So. As the Narrator/Storyteller travels back on to the stage, she says,)

No sooner had Boaz gone up to the gate and sat down there than the next-of-kin, of whom Boaz had spoken, came passing by. Then Boaz took ten men of the elders of the city,

Narrator/Boaz

(Takes hold of Mr. So-and-So, played by the actress who previously played Orpah. She has also assumed a male posture, though a bit younger than the old man our Narrator gives us as Boaz.)

Mr. So-and-So, sit down here. All of you sit down here for a minute.

(The Narrator does this as Mr. So-and-So and the ten spectators transform themselves into men, passing among them, shaking hands, slapping several on the back, and gathering as elder men do, feeling the strength and power of their maleness and their position as elders.)

Sit down here! (Narrator/Boaz pauses as they sit. She addresses Mr. So-and-So directly). Well, Mr. So-and-So, Pleasantness, who has come back from the field of that place whose name I cannot bring myself to speak, is selling the field that belonged to our kinsmen, God-is-King. Being the honest, forthright, and God-fearing man that I am, I thought I would tell you of it, and say, "Buy it in the presence of those sitting here, and in the presence of the elders of my people. If you will redeem it, redeem it; but if

---

2. We begin as we do in Chapter Six where we develop the entire performance script.

you will not, tell me, so that I may know; for there is no one prior to you to redeem it, and I come after you."

Mr. So-and-So
(Mr. So-and-So stands, scratches himself several times, and thinks about this offer. The longer he takes, the more agitated Boaz becomes.)
I will redeem it.

Boaz
Well, I think you should know that the day you buy that field from the hand of Pleasantness, you are also buying her daughter-in-law, the widow of the dead, in order to restore the name of the dead to his inheritance. You might want to give this a little more consideration before you jump right into bed, er, I mean, jump right into marriage with a widow *with obligations*.

(The Elders, who have been watching this exchange very closely, have a very vocal response to this: ooohs and aahs are accompanied by other derogatory comments.)

Mr. So-and-So
Wait, wait, just wait a minute! Don't rush me. You're getting me all confused . . .. (pause) On second thought, I really can't redeem it for myself. I don't want to mess up my own inheritance. You take it Boaz. Take my right of redemption for yourself.

(Narrator/Boaz takes off his sandal, smiles broadly, and says to the elders and all the spectators gathered.)

You are witnesses this day that I have purchased from the hand of Pleasantness all that belonged to her husband and to Obliterated and Eliminated. Also Ruth, (The chorus of elders begins to make cat calls about Ruth, but Boaz raises his arms and voice to silence them). I said RUTH shall be my woman and perpetuate the name of the dead, that the name of the dead may not be cut off from among his brethren and from the gate of his native place; you are witnesses this day.

Chorus

(Roars with laughter at Boaz's triumph over Mr. So-and-So).

We are witnesses. May the LORD make the woman who is coming into your house like Rachel and Leah, who together built up the house of Israel. May you prosper in Ephrathah and bestow a name in Bethlehem; and, through the children that the LORD will give you by this young woman, may your house be like the house of Perez, whom Tamar bore to Judah.

Critical Notes:

4:1 sets the scene for Act Four (4:1–12) which is exclusively male in orientation. 4:13 uses a series of passive verbs denoting the action that is done to Ruth. The male power bias of the social conditions is clearly evident in chapter 4. Unlike the opening of the drama, however, we, as audience, are very aware of the female expressions of power that have gone on behind the scenes making chapter 4 more a front than would be otherwise known. Aharon Pollack is convinced that the scene at the city-gate was well orchestrated "the entire production was done only for the splendor of fine words, and the decision to be rendered by the president was known from the beginning" and that "this performance was concluded with excellent food and drink, in accord with established practice. And everything was at Boaz's expense."[3]

The action in 4:1 moves quickly. While Ruth returned home to speak with Naomi, presenting to her the gift of seed, Boaz goes up to the gate and remarkably, the next-of-kin, of whom Boaz spoke, just happened to be passing by. Timing seems to be important. The wait suggested by Naomi in 3:18 will not be long.

4:1 Translated in RSV "friend." Elsewhere translated, "Mr. So-and-So,"[4] capturing the whimsical sounding, פלני אלמני (Peloni Almoni). As in other instances, the Naomi Story teller uses a word play, this time a rhyming pair to refer to the next-of-kin standing in the way of the culmination of Naomi's plan. Sasson labels this devise a "farrago" (example: hodge-podge; helter-skelter).[5] It is no doubt significant that this character remains un-

3. Pollack, "Notes on Megillat Ruth – Chapter 4," 185.

4. Sasson, *Ruth*, 106.

5. Ibid., 106.

named except for this dismissive label. The naming of the parties involved in conversation and / or negotiations can have significance in constructed dialogue. The kinsman's lack of a name implies here both, Boaz's power position in the negotiations and the narrator's negative disposition toward the unnamed kinsman.[6] Mr. So-and-So represents a social system that was intended to provide economic security for an unattached woman. In this arrangement, the closest living relative to the deceased husband was to include the widow and her family into his household and thereby extend security and care for her. The city gate transaction of Ruth 4 is presented in terms of the levirate system described in Deut 25: 5–6. Sasson suggests that Mr. So-and-So remains unnamed in order to forestall unnecessary speculation concerning alternative possibilities to David's genealogical line.[7] There may be a more immediate reason, integral to the unfolding story. The plot of the story has been driven by the female characters' desire to "find security in the house of a husband." Publicly, the male characters in the story are playing their part and the system appears to be working. Privately, we, the audience, know this isn't the case. The system is broken. The powerful men are powerless and the welfare of needy women is not at all a priority in the way the system really works. Naomi and Ruth will find the security they sought, but not because of the social network – rather - in spite of it! Disregard for the social system is reflected in the namelessness of the primary character required for the implemented social care for the needy women.

4:4 And I say. . . .. (ואני אמרתי) Sasson thinks this unusual construction a legal form.[8] Campbell considers the perfect form of the verb to refer to a previous conversation and reconstructs a whole unseen dialogue between Boaz and Naomi taking place between the end of chapter 3 and the beginning of chapter 4.[9] There does seem to be an air of formality about the opening to Boaz's statement (perhaps consistent with his somewhat pompous public persona of Act 2) and that it need not indicate some sort of reference to a previous deliberation either with Naomi or simply his own thought processes. Perhaps impressed with his own self-importance, Boaz,

---

6. Polak, "Negotiations, Social Drama and Voices of Memory in Some Samuel Tales," 52.

7. Sasson, *Ruth*, 106.

8. Sasson, *Ruth*, 115.

9. Campbell, *Ruth*, 144.

thinking he is acting on his own initiative, is totally blind to the fact that he is acting out a plan of someone else's making!

4:4 "I would tell you of it" (RSV) אגלה אזנך literally – "let me uncover your ear." Certainly, an idiom that conveys the act of communicating previously unknown information. Is it another of the Naomi Story teller's wordplays? In 3:7, Ruth "uncovered" Boaz's *feet* (or better, herself at his *feet*) setting into motion the events that have led us to this moment when Boaz will now act the part of uncovering and so unwittingly bring Naomi's plan to a conclusion.

4:4 "Should he decide not to redeem it" (ואם לא יגאל) some emend to "you redeem"[10] with a number of manuscripts. The 3rd masculine singular construction is in keeping with the dramatic speech addressed to the elders and townspeople. The direction of the Boaz speech from Mr. So-and-So to the elders and back again has a dramatic flair to it, quite suitable for presentation.

4:5 The interchange in this verse provides a dramatic climax to the story. It is Boaz's trump card designed to dissuade Mr. So-and-So, but it is also key in exposing the way in which "the man's world" worked. Here the security of the bereaved women, the project of the story and the goal of the social custom of the levirate, is, in fact, seen as a detriment to the economic prosperity of the male transaction and enough to motivate Mr. So-and-So to back away from the deal – and all this in plain sight of the town elders – i.e. with the blessing of the powers that be. Many commentators have focused on the social custom referred to in this verse.[11] The RSV translates Mr. So-and-So as the subject of the verb – the day that you [Mr. So-and-So] buy the field from Naomi, you also buy Ruth, the Moabitess" (preserving the *qere*). The sense is that purchase of the field also involves purchase of Ruth and an obligation to raise up an heir for the deceased Elimelech. The insertion of "the Moabitess" is understood to present legal complications for Mr. So-and-So.[12] Sasson, however, translates: "Know that on that very day you are purchasing the field from Naomi, I am acquiring

---

10. Ibid., 139.

11. See the bibliography in Étan Levine, *The Aramaic Version of Ruth*, 100–101.

12. See Hubbard, *Ruth*, 243.

Ruth the Moabitess. . ."[13] and so preserves the 1st singular perfect (קניתי) the *ketiv* of the text. The sense of Sasson's translation is that Boaz is declaring his intention of marrying Ruth and so fathering an heir to Elimelech. Mr. So-and-So was initially interested in the field, thinking that there would be no heir, other than that sired by him, to lay claim to the field in the future. Boaz's revelation of his intent to "acquire" Ruth creates a new calculus for Mr. So-and-So, causing him to reconsider the cost of the field purchase. A child born to Ruth and Boaz would have legal claim to the field even if purchased by Mr. So-and-So.

Commentators have expressed disagreement over the use of קנה (to buy) with Ruth as an object. Can a wife be purchased? [14] It seems clear that in 4:9–10 a purchase of Ruth is considered but is separated – at least in Boaz's mind - from the purchase of the field. Objectifying Ruth as a commodity to be bought and sold seems, here, and in 4:10, no accident. The project of the drama involves a female objection to a male biased economic system. This city gate transaction casts Mr. So-and-So as the personification of that male biased system and is not complementary at all.

Sasson understands the transaction as a benefit paid to Naomi for both the field and the services of Ruth, who willingly bound herself to Naomi in 1:16–17.[15] The transaction is an exquisitely conceived plan on the part of Naomi to achieve security for both herself, through the financial gain, and for Ruth in the form of the marriage which assumes a more traditional and common expression in 4:13.

It should be noted that the application of the levirate custom to the city-gate scene has not met with universal agreement. Sasson[16] and others[17] have presented significant arguments disconnecting the city gate scene from the levirate custom. The application of the custom does seem to have the intended goal of making the threshing floor scene more respectable, untarnished by any sexual overtones. The sexual encounter on the threshing floor is, however, central to the whole point of the story. The public and economic transaction in 4:4–10 is shown to have a private and unseen dimension, functioning as the true motivation for Boaz's public display. More, the threshing floor encounter had to be kept secret until after the

---

13. Sasson, *Ruth*, 103.

14. Paul Humbert, "Art et lecon de l'histoire de Ruth," 248.

15. Sasson, *Ruth*, 125.

16. Ibid., 126–129.

17. Gordis, "Love, Marriage, and Business in the Book of Ruth," 246–252.

legal proceedings at the gate to protect the legal status of the future heir - a key part in Boaz's presentation of the economics of the transaction.

4:5 להקים שם־המת על־נחלתו "in order to restore the name of the dead to his inheritance."[18] Some commentators see this whole phrase a late addition to make the sense of the verse more in line with the levirate custom of Deut 25.[19] Sasson is of the opinion that the levirate custom is not applicable to Ruth but an addition to show that the real crux, the deciding factor in dissuading Mr. So-and-So from the field, was Boaz's intention to formally and legally proclaim the firstborn from his union with Ruth be declared Mahlon's heir.[20] If male, this firstborn would be legally positioned to reclaim the field belonging to Elimelech as rightful heir to Mahlon. Further, as Sasson postulates, financial support for Naomi and her "son" (born to Ruth and Boaz) could be an extended obligation imposed upon Mr. So-and-So and so the expense may have been substantially more than the original outlay for purchase of the field.[21] For Boaz, it's a winning scenario. By co-opting any action from Mr. So-and-So, Boaz retains use of the field, its possession falls to his heir (proxy to Mahlon), and he is free to marry Ruth. For both Boaz and Mr. So-and-So it's the economics of the transaction that prove persuasive.[22]

4:7–8 In an unusual move, the Ruth storyteller directly addresses the audience providing background information necessary to understand the next bit of the Ruth drama. The action is prefaced by: "It was previously in Israel" (וזאת לפנים בישראל). This phrase is used elsewhere to explain outmoded or forgotten practices (1 Sam 9:9). In explaining the ritual – the storyteller uses three rhyming abstract nouns (התמורה, הגאולה, התעודה) to describe the action. In broad terms, the ritual is clear. A shoe is exchanged thereby signifying the exchange of property or the completion of a transaction.[23] In its detail, we are less certain. Whose shoe is removed, by whom

18. RSV.

19. Wolfenson, "The Character, Contents, and Date of Ruth," 299.

20. Sasson, *Ruth*, 134.

21. Ibid., 140.

22. Beattie, "The Book of Ruth as Evidence for Israelite Legal Practices," 262. Sasson, *Ruth*, 138–139. Sasson, nevertheless, prefers to understand that Boaz is motivated by "no other reason but love" (140).

23. Josephus describes the scene, perhaps relying on Deut 25: 9 for additional detail, "so Boaz called the senate to witness, and bid the woman to lose his shoe and spit in his

and given to whom? Perhaps the use of the rhyming terms (התעודה rare in Biblical Hebrew) is the storyteller's way of adding a whimsical element to a solemn and formal scene. One commentator, offers that the shoe represented Ruth who was symbolically transferred in possession from Mr. So-and-So to Boaz.[24] Unlike Deut 25:5–10, the scene in Ruth 4 does not involve the women in question. In Ruth 4, the financially cautious Mr. So-and-So willingly loosed his own sandal and handed it to Boaz without any intervention from a distressed widow and seemingly without any hint of public humiliation. It appears that he is thereby relinquishing any social obligations or rights (גאלה) associated with the estate or beneficiaries and heirs of Elimelech. Those rights and privileges, particularly the purchase of Naomi's field, now fall to Boaz.

4:8 Mr. So-and-So has one last part to play. In verse 8 he is still referred to (for the last time) as the next-of-kin and in that role says to Boaz: "purchase for yourself." This ends Mr. So-and-So's social obligations and, by the way, his presence in the story.

---

face, according to the law." Josephus, *Antiquities of the Jews*, 5:9:4.

24. Carmichael, "A Ceremonial Crux: Removing a Man's Sandal as a Female Gesture of Contempt," 335–336.

Bibliography

Abbott, Andrew. "From Causes to Effects: Notes on Narrative Positivism." *Sociological Methods and Research* 20 (1992) 428–55.

Anderson, Robert, and Terry Giles. *The Samaritan Pentateuch: An Introduction to Its Origin, History, and Significance for Biblical Studies.* Resources for Biblical Studies 72. Atlanta: Society of Biblical Literature, 2012.

Angel, Hayyim. "A Midrashic View of Ruth Amidst a Sea of Ambiguity." *Jewish Bible Quarterly* 33 (2005) 91–99.

Ardener, Shirley and Edwin. *Perceiving Women.* New York: Halsted, 1978.

Aschkenasy, Nehama. "The Book of Ruth as Comedy: Classical and Modern Perspectives." In *Scrolls of Love: Ruth and the Song of Songs*, edited by Peter Hawkins et al., 31–43. New York: Fordham University Press, 2006.

———. "Reading Ruth through a Bakhtinian Lens: The Carnivalesque in a Biblical Tale." *JBL* 126 (2007) 437–53.

———. "From Aristotle to Bakhtin: The Comedic and the Carnivalesque in a Biblical Tale." In *Literary Construction of Identity in the Ancient World*, edited by Hanna Liss et al., 265–81. Winona Lake, IN: Eisenbrauns, 2010.

Assan-Dhote, Isabelle, and Jacqueline Moatti-Fine. *Ruth.* La Bible d'Alexandrie 8. Paris: Cerf, 2009.

Atkinson, J. M. "Two Devices for Generating Audience Approval: A Comparative Study of Public Discourse and Texts." In *Connectedness in Sentence, Discourse and Text*, edited by K. Ehlich et al., 199–236. Tilburg Studies in Language and Literature 4. Tilburg: Tilburg University, 1983.

Auld, A. Graeme. *Joshua, Judges, and Ruth.* Philadelphia: Westminster, 1984.

———. "Reading Kings on the Divided Monarchy: What Sort of Narrative?" In *Understanding the History of Ancient Israel*, edited by H. G. M. Williamson, 337–43. Oxford: Oxford University Press, 2007.

Bacon, Helen H. "The Chorus in Greek Life and Drama." *Arion: A Journal of Humanities and the Classics* 3.1 (1994–1995) 6–24.

Bal, Mieke. *Lethal Love: Feminist Literary Readings of Biblical Love Stories.* Indiana Studies in Biblical Literature. Bloomington: Indiana University Press, 1987.

Bar-Efrat, Shimon. *Narrative Art in the Bible.* Bible and Literature 17. Sheffield: Almond, 1989.

Barth, Fredrik. *Ethnic Groups and Boundaries: The Social Organization of Culture Difference.* Scandinavian University Books. Bergen: Universitetsforlaget, 1969.

Bauckham, Richard. *Is the Bible Male?: The Book of Ruth and the Biblical Narrative.* Grove Biblical Series 2. Cambridge: Grove, 1996.

———. "The Book of Ruth and the Possibility of a Feminist Canonical Hermeneutic." *Biblical Interpretation* 5 (1997) 29–45.

Beattie, D. R. G. "The Book of Ruth as Evidence for Israelite Legal Practice." *VT* 24 (1974) 251–67.

———. *Jewish Exegesis of the Book of Ruth.* JSOTSup 2. Sheffield: University of Sheffield University, 1977.

Beckerman, Bernard. *Dynamics of Drama: Theory and Method of Analysis.* New York: Knopf, 1970.

———. *Theatrical Presentation: Performance, Audience, and Act.* New York: Routledge, 1990.

Bellis, Alice Ogden. *Helpmates, Harlots, and Heroes: Women's Stories in the Hebrew Bible.* Louisville: Westminster John Knox, 2007.

Benford, Robert, and David Snow. "Framing Processes and Social Movements: An Overview and Assessment." *Annual Review of Sociology* 26 (2000) 611–39.

Ben Zvi, Ehud. "Introduction: Writings, Speeches, and the Prophetic Books—Setting an Agenda." In *Writings and Speech in Israelite and Ancient Near Eastern Prophecy,* edited by Ehud Ben Zvi et al., 1–29. SBL Symposium Series 10. Atlanta: Society of Biblical Literature, 2000.

Berger, Yitzhak. "Ruth and Inner-Biblical Allusion: The Case of 1 Samuel 25." *JBL* 128 (2009) 253–72.

Berman, Joshua. "Ancient Hermeneutics and the Legal Structure of the Book of Ruth." *ZAW* 119 (2007) 22–38.

Bernstein, Moshe. "Two Multivalent Readings in the Ruth Narrative." *JSOT* 50 (1991) 15–26.

Berquist, Jon. "Role Dedifferentiation in the Book of Ruth." *JSOT* 57 (1993) 23–37.

Bertman, Stephen. "The Symmetrical Structure of Ruth." *JBL* 84 (1965) 165–68.

Bird, Phyllis. "Images of Women in the Old Testament." In *Religion and Sexism: Images of Women in the Jewish and Christian Traditions,* edited by Rosemary Radford Ruether, 41–48. New York: Simon and Schuster, 1974.

Black, James. "Ruth in the Dark: Folktale, Law and Creative Ambiguity in the Old Testament." *Journal of Literature and Theology* 5 (1991) 20–36.

Bledstein, Adrien. "Female Companionships: If the Book of Ruth Were Written by a Woman . . ." In *A Feminist Companion to Ruth,* edited by Athalya Brenner, 116–33. Sheffield: Sheffield Academic, 1993.

Bohmbach, Karla. "Names and Naming in the Biblical World." In *Women in Scripture: A Dictionary of Named and Unnamed Women in the Hebrew Bible, the Apocryphal-Deuterocanonical Books, and the New Testament,* edited by Carol Meyers et al., 33–39. Grand Rapids: Eerdmans, 2001.

Borowski, Oded. *Agriculture in Iron Age Israel.* Winona Lake IN: Eisenbrauns, 1987.

Bos, Johanna. "Out of the Shadows: Genesis 38; Judges 4:17–22; Ruth 3." *Semeia* 42 (1988) 37–67.

Bovell, Carlos. "Symmetry, Ruth and Canon." *JSOT* 28 (2003) 175–91.

Bow, Beverly. "Sisterhood? Women's Relationships with Women in the Hebrew Bible." In *Life and Culture in the Ancient Near East*, edited by Richard Averbeck et al., 205–15. Bethesda MD: CDL, 2003.

Braulik, George. "The Book of Ruth as Intra-Biblical Critique on the Deuteronomic Law." *Acta Theologica* 19 (1999) 1–20.

Brenner, Athalya. *The Book of Ruth: Literary, Stylistic and Linguistic Studies.* Tel Aviv: Afik and Sifriyat Po'lam, 1988.

———. "Naomi and Ruth: Further Reflections," In *A Feminist Companion to Ruth*, edited by Athalya Brenner, 140–45. Sheffield: Sheffield Academic, 1993.

———. "Some Observations on the Figurations of Women in Wisdom Literature." In *Of Prophets' Visions and the Wisdom of Sages: Essays in Honour of R. Norman Whybray on his Seventieth Birthday*, edited by Heather McKay and David J. A. Clines, 192–208. JSOTSup 162. Sheffield: Sheffield Academic, 1993.

———. *The Intercourse of Knowledge: On Gendering Desire and 'Sexuality' in the Hebrew Bible.* Biblical Interpretation Series 26. Leiden: Brill, 1997.

Brenner, Athalya, and Fokkelien van Dijk-Hemmes, *On Gendering Texts: Female and Male Voices in the Hebrew Bible.* Biblical Interpretation Series 1: Leiden: Brill, 1993.

Brichto, Herbert. "Kin, Cult, Land, and Afterlife—A Biblical Complex." *HUCA* 44 (1973) 1–54.

Bush, Frederic. *Ruth / Esther.* Word Biblical Commentary 9. Dallas: Word, 1996.

———. "Ruth 4:17: A Semantic Wordplay." In *Go to the Land I Will Show You: Studies in Honor of Dwight W. Young*, edited by Joseph Coleson et al., 3–15. Winona Lake, IN: Eisenbrans, 1996.

Campbell, Edward. "The Hebrew Short Story: A Study of Ruth." In *A Light Unto My Path: Old Testament Studies in Honor of Jacob M. Myers*, edited by Howard Bream, 83–101. Philadelphia: Temple University Press, 1974.

———. *Ruth.* AB 7. Doubleday: New York, 1975.

———. "Ruth Revisited." In *On the Way to Nineveh: Studies in Honor of George M. Landes*, edited by Stephen Cook et al., 54–76. Atlanta: Scholars, 1999.

Carasik, Michael. "Ruth 2:7: Why the Overseer was Embarrassed." *ZAW* 107 (1995) 493–94.

Carmichael, Calum. "A Ceremonial Crux: Removing a Man's Sandal as a Female Gesture of Contempt." *JBL* 96 (1977) 321–36.

Carter, Charles. "A Discipline in Transition." In *Community, Identity, and Ideology: Social Science Approaches to the Hebrew Bible*, edited by Charles E. Carter and Carol L. Meyers, 3–36. Winona Lake, IN: Eisenbrauns, 1996.

da Silva, Aldina. "Ruth, plaidoyer en faveur de la femme." *Sciences Religieuses* 27 (1998) 251–61.

Davies, Ellen F. *Swallowing the Scroll: Textuality and the Dynamics of Discourse in Ezekiel's Prophecy.* JSOTSup 78. Bible and Literature Series 21. Sheffield: Almond, 1989.

———. "Beginning with Ruth: An Essay on Translating." In *Scrolls of Love: Ruth and the Song of Songs,* edited by Peter Hawkins et al., 9–19. New York: Fordham Uni-versity Press, 2006.

Davis, Ellen F., and Margaret Adams Parker. *Who Are You, My Daughter?: Reading Ruth through Image and Text.* Louisville: Westminster John Knox, 2003.

Davis, Joseph, ed. *Stories of Change: Narrative and Social Movements.* Albany: State University of New York Press, 2002.

de Fraine, Jan G. F. L. *Ruth, uit de Grondtekst vertaald en uigelegd, De Boeken van het Oude Testament (III).* Roermond: Romen, 1955.

DeMarinis, Marco, and Paul Dwyer. "Dramaturgy of the Spectator." *Drama Review* 31.2 (1987) 100–114.

Dearman, J. Andrew, and Sabelyn Pussman, "Putting Ruth in Her Place: Some Observations on Canonical Ordering and the History of the Book's Interpretation." *Horizons in Biblical Theology* 27 (2005) 59–86.

Derby, Josiah. "A Problem in the Book of Ruth." *Jewish Bible Quarterly* 22 (1994) 178–85.

Dijk-Hemmes, Fokkelien van. "Ruth: A Product of Women's Culture?" In *A Feminist Companion to Ruth*, edited by Athalya Brenner, 134–39. Sheffield: Sheffield Academic Press, 1993.

———. "Traces of Women's Texts in the Hebrew Bible." In *On Gendering Texts: Female and Male Voices in the Hebrew Bible,* edited by Athalya Brenner et al., 17–109. Biblical Interpretation Series 1. Leiden: Brill, 1993.

Doan, William, and Terry Giles. *Prophets, Performance and Power: Performance Criticism of the Hebrew Bible.* New York: T &T Clark International, 2005.

Donaldson, Laura. "The Sign of Orpah: Reading Ruth through Native Eyes." In *Ruth and Esther*, edited by Athalya Brenner, 130–44. Feminist Companion to the Bible. Sheffield: Sheffield Academic, 1999.

Douglas, Mary. "Responding to Ezra: The Priests and the Foreign Wives." *Biblical Interpretation* 10 (2002) 1–23.

Drew, Paul. "Conversation Analysis." In *Handbook of Language and Social Interaction*, edited by Kristine Fitch et al., 71–102. Mahwah, NJ: Erlbaum, 2005.

Durbin, Lois. "Fullness and Emptiness, Fertility and Loss." In *Reading Ruth: Contemporary Women Reclaim a Sacred Story*, edited by Judith Kates et al., 131–44. New York: Ballantine, 1994.

Eissfeldt, Otto. *The Old Testament: An Introduction.* Translated by P. R. Ackroyd. New York: Harper & Row, 1965.

Emirbayer, Mustafa. "Manifesto for a Relational Sociology." *American Journal of Sociology* 103 (1997) 281–317.

Eskenazi, Tamara. "Out of the Shadows: Biblical Women in the Postexilic Era." *JSOT* 54 (1992) 25–43.

Eskhult, Mats. "The Importance of Loanwords for Dating Biblical Hebrew Texts." In *Biblical Hebrew: Studies in Chronology and Typology*, edited by Ian Young, 8–23. JSOTSup 369. London: T&T Clark, 2003.

Ewick, Patricia, and Susan Silbey. "Narrating Social Structure: Stories of Resistance to Legal Authority." *American Journal of Sociology* 108 (2003) 1328–72.

Feder, Yitzhaq. "The Aniconic Tradition, Deuteronomy 4, and the Politics of Israelite Identity." *JBL* 132 (2013) 251–74.

Fewell, Dana Nolan, and David M. Gunn. *Compromising Redemption: Relating Characters in the Book of Ruth.* Literary Currents in Biblical Interpretation. Louisville: Westminster John Knox, 1990.

Fisch, Harold. "Ruth and the Structure of Covenant History." *VT* 32 (1982) 425–37.

Fischer, Irmtraud. "The Book of Ruth: A 'Feminist' Commentary on Torah?" In *Ruth and Esther*, edited by Athalya Brenner, 24–49. Feminist Companion to the Bible. Sheffield: Sheffield Academic, 1999.

———. *Rut.* Herders theologischer Kommentar zum Alten Testament. Freiburg: Herder, 2001.

Floyd, Michael H. "Write the Revelation!" In *Writings and Speech in Israelite and Ancient Near Eastern Prophecy*, edited by Ehud Ben Zvi et al., 103–43. SBL Symposium Series 10. Atlanta: Society of Biblical Literature, 2000.

Fohrer, Georg. *Introduction of the Old Testament*. Translated David Green. Nashville: Abingdon, 1968.

Friedmand, Debra, and Doug McAdam. "Collective Identity and Activism: Networks, Choices, and the Life of a Social Movement." In *Frontiers in Social Movment Theory*, edited by Aldon Morris et al., 156–73. New Haven: Yale University Press, 1992.

Fuchs, Esther. "The Literary Characterization of Mothers and Sexual Politics in the Hebrew Bible." In *Feminist Perspectives on Biblical Scholarship*, edited by Adela Yarbro Collins, 117–36. Society of Biblical Literature Centennial Publications. Atlanta: Scholars, 1985.

———. "Who is Hiding the Truth? Deceptive Women and Biblical Androcentrism." In *Feminist Perspectives on Biblical Scholarship*, edited by Adela Yarbro Collins, 137–44. Society of Biblical Literature Centennial Publications. Atlanta: Scholars, 1985.

Gamson, William. "How Storytelling Can Be Empowering." In *Culture in Mind: Toward a Sociology of Culture and Cognition*, edited by Karen Cerulo, 187–98. New York: Routledge, 2001.

Geoghegan, Jeffery. "Israelite Sheepshearing and David's Rise to Power." *Biblica* 87 (2006) 55–63.

Glanzman, George S. "The Origin and Date of the Book of Ruth." *CBQ* 21 (1959) 201–07.

Goffman, Erving. *Frame Analysis: An Essay on the Organization of Experience*. New York: Harper & Row, 1974.

Goldman, Michael. *On Drama: Boundaries of Genre, Borders of Self*. Ann Arbor: University of Michigan Press, 2000.

Goitein, S. D. "Women as Creators of Biblical Genres." *Prooftexts* 8 (1988) 1–33.

Gordis, Robert. "Love, Marriage, and Business in the book of Ruth." In *A Light unto My Path: Old Testament Studies in Honor of Jacob M. Myers*, edited by H. N. Bream et al., 241–64. Philadelphia: Temple University Press, 1974.

Goulder, M. "Ruth: A Homily on Deuteronomy 23–25?" In *Of Prophets, Visions and Wisdom of Sages: Essays in Honor of R. Norman Whybray on his Seventieth Birthday*, edited by Heather A. McKay and David J. A. Clines, 307–19. JSOTSup 162. Sheffield: Almond, 1993.

Gow, Murray. *The Book of Ruth: Its Structure, Theme and Purpose*. Leicester: Apollos, 1992.

Grant, Reg. "Literary Structure in the Book of Ruth." *Bibliotheca Sacra* 148 (1991) 424–41.

Grossman, Jonathan. "'Gleaning Among the Ears'—'Gathering among the Sheaves': Characterizing the Image of Supervising Boy (Ruth 2)." *JBL* 126 (2007) 703–16.

Gunkel, Hermann. "Ruth." In *Reden und Aufsätze*, 65–92. Göttingen: Vanderhoeck and Ruprecht, 1913.

———. *Genesis*. 3rd ed. Göttinger Handkommentar zum Alten Testament 1. Göttingen: Vanderhoeck & Ruprecht, 1910.

Gunneweg, A. H. J. *Understanding the Old Testament*. OTL. Philadelphia: Westminster, 1978.

Hamilton, M. W. "Who was a Jew? Jewish Ethnicity During the Achaemenid Period." *Restoration Quarterly* 37 (1995) 102–17.

Harm, Harry. "The Function of Double Entendre in Ruth 3." *Journal of Translation and Textlinquistics* 7 (1995) 19–27.

Harris, W. V. *Ancient Literacy*. Cambridge: Harvard University Press, 1991.

Harvey, Dorothea. "The Book of Ruth." In *Interpreter's Dictionary of the Bible*, edited by George Arthur Buttrick, 4:131–34. Nashville: Abingdon, 1962.

Hatav, Galia. "(Free) Direct Discourse in Biblical Hebrew." *Hebrew Studies* 7 (2000) 7–30.

Hawkins, Peter. "Ruth Amid the Gentiles." In *Scrolls of Love: Ruth and the Song of Songs*, edited by Peter Hawkins et al., 75–85. New York: Fordham University Press, 2006.

Heath, Malcolm. "Aristotelian Comedy." *Classical Quarterly* 39 (1989) 344–54.

Hendel, Russell. "Ruth: The Legal Code for the Laws of Kindness." *Jewish Biblical Quarterly* 36 (2008) 254–60.

Hoffner, Harry. "Birth and Name-Giving in Hittite Texts." *JNES* 27 (1968) 198–203.

Hornsby, Teresa. "Ezekiel Off-Broadway." *The Bible and Critical Theory* 2 (2006) 2.1–2.8

Hubbard, Robert L. *The Book of Ruth*. NIC 14. Grand Rapids: Eerdmans, 1988.

———. "*Ganzheitsdenken* in the Book of Ruth." In *Problems in Biblical Theology: Essays in Honor of Rolf Knierim*, edited Henry Sun et al., 192–209. Grand Rapids: Eerdmans, 1997.

Humbert, Paul. "Art et lecon de l'histoire de Ruth." *Revue de theologie et de philosophie* 26 (1938) 285–86.

Hunt, Scott, et al. "Identity Fields: Framing Processes and the Social Construction of Movement Identities." In *New Social Movements: From Ideology to Identity*, edited by Enrique Laraña et al., 185–208. Philadelphia: Temple University Press, 1994.

Hutchby, Ian, and Robin Wooffitt. *Conversation Analysis: Principles, Practices and Applications*. Malden, MA: Polity, 1998.

Irwin, Brian. "Removing Ruth: *Tiqqune Sopherim* in Ruth 3.3–4?" *Journal for the Study of the Old Testmant* 32 (2008) 331–38.

Jackson, Melissa. *Comedy and Feminist Interpretation of the Bible: A Subversive Collaboration*. Oxford: Oxford University Press, 2012.

Johnston, Hank. "Verification and Proof in Frame and Discourse Analysis." In *Methods of Social Movements Research*, edited by Bert Klandermans et al., 62–91. Minneapolis: University of Minnesota Press, 2002.

Joüon, Paul. *Ruth: commentaire philologique et exégétique*. Rome: Institut Biblique Pontifical, 1953.

———. "4QRuth[a], 4QRuth[b]." In *Qumran Cave 4: XI, Psalms to Chronicles, edited* by E. Ulrich et. al., 188–93. DJD 16. Oxford: Clarendon, 2000.

Kalmanofsky, Amy. *Dangerous Sisters of the Hebrew Bible*. Minneapolis: Fortress, 2014.

Kates, Judith. "Women at the Center." In *Reading Ruth*, edited by Judith Kates et al., 185–98. New York: Ballantine, 1996.

———. "Transfigured Night: Midrashic Reading of the Book of Ruth." In *Scrolls of Love: Ruth and the Song of Songs*, edited by Peter Hawkins et al., 47–58. New York: Fordham University Press, 2006.

Keita, Shadrac, and Janet Dyk, "The Scene at the Threshing Floor: Suggestive Readings and Intercultural Considerations on Ruth 3." *The Bible Translator* 57 (2006) 17–32.

Kelber, Werner. *The Oral and the Written Gospel: The Hermeneutics of Speaking and Writing in the Synoptic Tradition, Mark, Paul, and Q*. Bloomington: Indiana University Press, 1983.

———. "In the Beginning were the Words: The Apotheosis and Narrative Displacement of the Logos." *Journal of the American Academy of Religion* 58 (1990) 69–98.

———. "The Case of the Gospels: Memory's Desire and the Limits of Historical Criticism." *Oral Tradition* 17 (2002) 55–86.

Kloppenborg, John. *Q: the Earliest Gospel*. Louisville: Westminster John Knox, 2008.

Knauf, Ernst. "Ruth la Moabite." *VT* 44 (1994) 547–48.

Knoppers, Gary N. "Intermarriage, Social Complexity, and Ethnic Diversity in the Genealogy of Judah." *JBL* 120 (2001) 15–30.

———. *1 Chronicles* 1–9. AB 12. New York: Doubleday, 2004.

Korpel, Marjo. "Unit Division in the Book of Ruth." In *Delimitation Criticism: A New Tool in Biblical Scholarship*, edited Marjo Korpel et al., 130–47. Assen: Van Gorcum, 2000.

———. "Theodicy in the Book of Ruth." In *Theodicy in the World of the Bible*, edited by Antti Laato et al., 334–50. Leiden: Brill, 2003.

Labuschagne, C. "The Crux in Ruth 4 11." *ZAW* 79 (1967) 364–67.

LaCocque, André. *The Feminine Unconventional: Four Subversive Figures in Israel's Tradition*. Overtures to Biblical Theology. 1990. Reprinted, Eugene, OR: Wipf & Stock, 2005.

———. *Romance, She Wrote: A Hermeneutical Essay on Song of Songs*. 1998. Reprinted, Eugene, OR: Wipf & Stock, 2006.

———. *Ruth*. Translated K. C. Hanson. Continental Commentaries. Minneapolis: Fortress, 2004.

———. "Subverting the Biblical World: Sociology and Politics in the Book of Ruth." In *Scrolls of Love: Ruth and the Song of Songs*, edited Peter Hawkins et al., 20–30. New York: Fordham University Press, 2006.

Landy, Frances. "Ruth and the Romance of Realism, or Deconstructing History." *Journal of the American Academy of Religion* 62 (1994) 285–317.

Lange, Armin. "Literary Prophecy and Oracle Collection: A Comparison between Judah and Greece in Persian Times." In *Prophets, Prophecy, and Prophetic Texts in Second Temple Judaism*, edited by Michael Floyd et al., 248–75. New York: T&T Clark, 2006.

Lapsley, Jacqueline E. *Whispering the Word: Hearing Women's Stories in the Old Testament*. Louisville: Westminster / John Knox, 2005.

Larkin, Katrina J. A. *Ruth and Esther*. Sheffield: Sheffield Academic Press, 1996.

Lau, Peter H. W. *Identity and Ethics in the Book of Ruth: A Social-Identity Approach*. BZAW 416. Berlin: de Gruyter, 2011.

Lawrie, Douglas. "Narrative Logic and Legitimized Interposition in the Book of Ruth." *Ned Geref Teologiese Tydskrif* 40 (1999) 83–99.

Lemaire, Ria. *Passions et Positions. Contributions à une sémiotique du sujet dans la poésie lyrique médiéval en langues romanes*. Amsterdam: Rodopi, 1987.

Lenski, Gerhard. *Power and Privilege: A Theory of Social Stratification*. New York: McGraw-Hill, 1966.

Leuchter, Mark. "Gen 38 in Social and Historical Perspective." *JBL* 132 (2013) 209–27.

Levy, Shimon. *The Bible as Theatre*. Brighton: Sussex Academic Press, 2002.

Levine, Étan. *The Aramaic Version of Ruth*. Analecta Biblica 58. Rome: Pontifical Biblical Institute, 1973.

Licht, Jacob. *Storytelling in the Bible*. Second edition. Jerusalem: Magnes, 1986.

Lim, Timothy. "The Book of Ruth and its Literary Voice." In *Reflection and Refraction: Studies in Biblical Historiography in Honour of A. Graeme Auld*, edited by Robert Rezetko et al., 261–82. Leiden: Brill, 2007.

Linafelt, Tod, and Timothy Beal. *Ruth and Esther*. Berit Olam. Collegeville, MN: Liturgical, 1999.

Lipínski, E. "Le marriage de Ruth." *VT* 26 (1976) 124–27.

Lipschits, Oded, and Manfred Oeming, eds. *Judah and the Judeans in the Persian Period*. Winona Lake IN: Eisenbrauns, 2006.

Loader, James. "Yahweh's Wings and the Gods of Ruth." In *Wer ist wie du, HERR, unter den Göttern? Studien zur Theologie und Religionsgeschichte Israels: Für Otto Kaiser zum 70. Geburtstag*, edited by Ingo Kottsieper et. al., 389–401. Göttingen: Vandenhoeck & Riprecht, 1994.

———. "A Woman Praised by Women Is Better than a Woman Praised by Men." *Hervormde Teologiese Studies* 60 (2004) 687–701.

Longacre, R. E. "A Spectrum and Profile Approach to Discourse Analysis." *Text* 1 (1981) 337–59.

Lord, Albert B. *The Singer of Tales.* New York: Atheneum, 1968.

Löwisch, Ingeborg. "Genealogies, Gender, and the Politics of Memory: 1 Chronicles 1–9 and the Documentary film *Mein Leben Teil 2.*" In *Performing Memory in Biblical Narrative and Beyond*, edited by Athalya Brenner et al., 228–56. Bible in the Modern World 25. Sheffield: Sheffield Phoenix, 2009.

Luter, A. Boyd, and Richard Rigsby. "An Adjusted Symmetrical Structuring of Ruth." *Journal of the Evangelical Theological Society* 39 (1996) 15–28.

Lys, Daniel. "Residence ou repos? Notule sur Ruth ii 7." *VT* 31 (1981) 497–501.

Mann, Thomas. "Ruth 4." *Interpretation* 64 (2010) 178–80.

Maré, L., J. Coetzee, and W. Minnaar, "The Concept of יראת יהוה as Wisdom Motif in the Book of Ruth." *Journal for Semitics* 20 (2011) 176–91.

Margolis, Diane Rothbard. "Redefining the Situation: Negotiations on the Meaning of Women." *Social Problems* 32 (1985) 332–47.

Matthews, Victor H. *Judges and Ruth.* New Cambridge Bible Commentary. Cambridge: Cambridge University Press, 2004.

———. "The Determination of Social Identity in the Story of Ruth." *Biblical Theology Bulletin* 36 (2004) 49–54.

May, Herbert Gordon. "Ruth's Visit to the High Place at Bethlehem." *JRAS* (1939) 75–78.

McKay, Heather A. "Eve's Sisters Re-Cycled." In *Recycling Biblical Figures: Papers Read at Noster Colloquium in Amsterdam, 12–13 May 1997*, edited by Athalya Brenner et al., 169–91. Studies in Theology and Religion 1. Leiden: Deo, 1999.

Meek, Theophile J. "Translating the Hebrew Bible." *JBL* 79 (1960) 328–35.

Meinhold, A. "Theologische Schwerpunkte im Buch Ruth und ihr Schwergewicht für seine Datierung." *Theologische Zeitschrift* 32 (1976) 129–37.

Meyers, Carol. "'To Her Mother's House': Considering a Counterpart to the Israelite *Bet 'ab.*" In *The Bible and the Politics of Exegesis: Essays in Honor of Norman K. Gottwald on His Sixty-fifth Birthday*, edited David Jobling et. al., 304–07. Cleveland: Pilgrim, 1991.

———. "Returning Home: Ruth 1:8 and the Gendering of the Book of Ruth." In *A Feminist Companion to Ruth*, edited by Athalya Brenner, 85–114. Sheffield: Sheffield Academic, 1993.

———. "Family in Early Israel." In *Families in Ancient Israel*, edited by Leo Perdue, et. al., 1–27. Family, Religion, and Culture. Louisville: Westminster John Knox, 1997.

———. "Guilds and Gatherings: Women's Groups in Ancient Israel." In *Realia Dei: Essays in Archaeology and Biblical Interpretation in Honor of Edward F. Campbell, Jr. at His Retirement*, edited by Prescott Williams et al., 154–84. Scholars Press Homage Series 23. Atlanta: Scholars, 1999.

———. "Mother to Muse: An Archaeomusicological Study of Women's Performance In Ancient Israel." In *Recycling Biblical Figures: Studies in Theology and Religion*, edited by Athalya Brenner et al., 50–77. Studies in Theology and Religion 1. Leiden: Deo, 1999.

———. "Women of the Neighborhood (Ruth 4:17): Informal Female Networks in Ancient Israel." In *Ruth and Esther*, edited by Athalya Brenner, 110–27. The Feminist Companion to the Bible (Second Series). Sheffield: Sheffield Academic, 1999c.

———. "Everyday Life in Biblical Israel: Women's Social Networks." In *Life and Culture in the Ancient Near East*, edited by Richard Averbeck et al., 185–204. Bethesda, MD: CDL, 2003.

———. *Households and Holiness: The Religious Culture of Israelite Women*. Facets. Minneapolis: Fortress, 2005.

———. "Hierarchy or Heterarchy? Archaeology and the Theorizing of Israelite Society." In *Confronting the Past: Archaeological and Historical Essays on Ancient Israel in Honor of William G. Dever*, edited by Seymour Gittin, 245–54. Winona Lake, IN: Eisenbrauns, 2006.

Midrash Rabbah. *Ruth*. Translated Rabbi Dr. L. Rabinowitz. London: Soncino, 1983.

Miller, Cynthia. *The Representation of Speech in Biblical Hebrew Narrative: A Linguistic Analysis*. Atlanta: Scholars, 1996. [Reprinted with an Afterword. Winona Lake, IN: Eisenbrauns, 2003].

———. "Silence as a Response in Biblical Hebrew Narrative: Strategies of Speakers and Narrators." *Journal of Northwest Semitic Languages* 32 (2006) 23–43.

Miller, Robert D., II. *Oral Tradition in Ancient Israel*. Biblical Performance Criticism Series 4. Eugene, OR: Cascade Books, 2011.

Millett, Kate. *Sexual Politics*. New York: Ballantine, 1969.

Mitchell, Margaret. "Ruth at Antioch: An English Translation of Theodoret's *Quaestiones in Ruth*, with a Brief Commentary." In *Realia Dei: Essays in Archaeology and Biblical Interpretation in Honor of Edward F. Campbell, Jr. at His Retirement*, edited by Prescott Williams, 195–214. Scholars Press Homage Series 23. Atlanta: Scholars, 1999.

Moore, Michael. "Two Textual Anomalies in Ruth." *CBQ* 59 (1997) 234–44.

———. "Ruth the Moabite and the Blessing of Foreigners." *CBQ* 60 (1998) 203–18.

Moffat, Donald. *Ezra's Social Drama: Identity Formation, Marriage and Social Conflict in Ezra 9 and 10*. Library of Hebrew Bible/Old Testament Studies 579. London: Bloomsbury T&T Clark, 2013.

Murphy, Roland E. *Wisdom Literature: Job, Proverbs, Ruth, Canticles, Ecclesiastes, and Esther*. FOTL 13. Grand Rapids: Eerdmans, 1981.

Na'aman, Nadav. "The Distribution of Messages in the Kingdom of Judah in Light of the Lachish Ostraca." *VT* 53 (2003) 169–80.

Niditch, Susan. "Legends of the Wise and Heroines." In *The Hebrew Bible and its Modern Interpreters*, edited Douglas Knight et al., 445–63. Chico, CA: Scholars Press, 1985.

———. "Epic and History in the Hebrew Bible: Definitions, 'Ethnic Genres,' and the Challenges of Cultural Identity in the Biblical Book of Judges." In *Epic and History* edited by David Konstan et al., 86–102. Oxford: Blackwell, 2010.

Nieholl, M. "Do Biblical Characters Talk to Themselves? Narrative Modes of Representing Inner Speech in Early Biblical Fiction." *JBL* 111 (1992) 577–92.

Nielsen, Kirsten. *Ruth: A Commentary*. Translated by Edward Broadbridge. OTL. Louisville: Westminster John Knox, 1997.

Nissinen, Martti. "The Dubious Image of Prophecy." In *Prophets, Prophecy, and Prophetic Texts in Second Temple Judaism*, edited by Michael Floyd et al., 26–39. Library of Hebrew Bible/Old Testament Studies 427. London: T&T Clark, 2006.

Noakes John and Hank Johnston. "Frames of Protest: A Road Map to a Perspective." In *Frames of Protest: Social Movements and the Framing Perspective*, edited by Hank Johnston et al., 1–29. New York: Rowman & Littlefield, 2005.

Noll, Kurt. "Did 'Scripturalization Take Place in Second Temple Judaism?" *Scandinavian Journal of the Old Testament* 25 (2011) 201–16.

Notopoulos, James. "Homer and Cretan Heroic Poetry: A Study in Comparative Oral Poetry." *The American Journal of Philology* 73 (1952) 225–50.

Oesterreicher, Wulf. "Types of Orality in Text." In *Written Voices, Spoken Signs: Tradition, Performance, and the Epic Text*, edited by Egbert Bakker et al., 190–214. Cambridge: Harvard University Press, 1997.

Oliver, Pamela and Hank Johnston, "What a Good Idea! Ideologies and Frames in Social Movement Research." In *Frames of Protest: Social Movements and the Framing Perspective*, edited by Hank Johnston et al., 185–203. New York: Rowman & Littlefield, 2005.

Olyan, Saul. "Purity Ideology in Ezra-Nehemiah as a Tool to Reconstitute the Community." *JSJ* 35 (2004) 1–16.

Ong, Walter J. *Orality and Literacy: The Technologizing of the Word*. New York: Methuen, 1982.

Ostriker, Alicia. "The Book of Ruth and the Love of the Land." *Biblical Interpretation* 10 (2002) 343–59.

Paine, Thomas. *Age of Reason*. 1896. Reprinted, Mineola, NY: Dover, 2004.

Pardes, Ilana. *Countertraditions in the Bible: A Feminist Approach*. Cambridge: Harvard University Press, 1992.

Parker, Simon B. "The Marriage Blessing in Israelite and Ugaritic Literature." *JBL* 95 (1976) 23–30.

Person, Raymond. *In Conversation with Jonah: Conversation Analysis, Literary Criticism, and the Book of Jonah*. JSOTSup 220. Sheffield: Sheffield Academic, 1996.

Polak, Frank. "The Oral and the Written: Syntax, Stylistics, and the Development of Biblical Texts." *Journal of the Ancient Near Eastern Society* 26 (1998) 59–105.

———. "On Dialogue and Speaker Status in the Scroll of Ruth." *Beit Mikra* 166 (2001) 196–218.

———. "The Style of the Dialogue in Biblical Prose Narrative." *Journal of the Ancient Near Eastern Society* 28 (2001) 53–95.

———. "On Speaker Status and Dialogue in Biblical Narrative: Part 1." *Beit Mikra* 173 (2003) 98–119.

———. "Style is More Than the Person: Sociolinguistics, Literary Culture and the Distinction between Written and Oral Narrative." In *Biblical Hebrew: Studies in Chronology and Typology*, edited by Ian Young, 38–103. JSOTSup 369. London: T&T Clark, 2003.

———. "Sociolinguistics and the Judean Speech Community in the Achaemenid Empire." In *Judah and the Judeans in the Persian Period*, edited by Oded Lipschits et al., 589–628. Winona Lake, IN: Eisenbrauns, 2006.

———. "Negotiations, Social Drama and Voices of Memory in Some Samuel Tales." In *Performing Memory in Biblical Narrative and Beyond*, edited by Athalya Brenner et al., 46–71. Bible in the Modern World 25. Sheffield: Sheffield Phoenix, 2009.

———. "The Book of Samuel and the Deuteronomist—A Syntactic-Stylistic Analysis." In *Die Samuelbücher und die Deuteronomisten*, edited by Christa Schäfer-Lichtenberger, 34–73. Stuttgart: Kohlhammer, 2010a.

————. "Forms of Talk in Hebrew Biblical Narrative: Negotiations, Interaction, and Sociocultural Context." In *Literary Construction of Identity in the Ancient World*, edited by Hanna Liss et al., 167–98. Winnona Lake, IN: Eisenbrauns, 2010b.

————. "Language Variation, Discourse Typology, and the Sociocultural Background of Biblical Narrative." In *Diachrony in Biblical Hebrew*, edited by Cynthia L. Miller-Naudé et al., 301–38. Winona Lake, IN: Eisenbrauns, 2012.

————. "Orality: Biblical Hebrew." In *Encyclopedia of Hebrew Languages and Linguistics*. Vol. 2, edited by Geoffrey Khan, 930–37. Leiden: Koninklijke Brill, 2013a.

————. "Speaker, Addressee, and Positioning: Dialogue Structure and Pragmatics in Biblical Narrative." In *Interested Readers: Essays on the Hebrew Bible in Honor of David J. A. Clines*, edited by James K. Aitken, Jeremy M. S. Clines et al., 359–72. Atlanta: Society of Biblical Literature, 2013b.

Polen, Nehemia. "Dark Ladies and Redemptive Compassion: Ruth and the Messianic Lineage in Judaism." In *Scrolls of Love: Ruth and the Song of Songs*, edited by Peter Hawkins et al., 59–74. New York: Fordham University Press, 2006.

Pollack, Aharon. "Notes on Megillat Ruth—Chapter 4." *Jewish Bible Quarterly* 24 (1996) 183–85.

Polletta, Francesca. *It Was Like a Fever: Storytelling in Protest and Politics*. Chicago: University of Chicago Press, 2006.

————. et al. "The Sociology of Storytelling." *Annual Review of Sociology* 37 (2011) 109–30.

Porten, Bezalel. "The Scroll of Ruth: A Rhetorical Study." *Gratz College Annual of Jewish Studies* 7 (1978) 23–29.

Pressler, Carolyn. "Sexual Violence and Deuteronomic Law." In *A Feminist Companion to Exodus to Deuteronomy*, edited by Athalya Brenner, 102–12. Sheffield: Sheffield Academic, 1994.

Pretzler, Maria. "Pausanias and Oral Tradition." *Classical Quarterly* 55 (2005) 235–49.

Propp, Vladimir. *Morphology of the Folktale*, edited by L. Wagner. Austin: University of Texas Press, 1968.

Radday, Yehuda T. and Heim Shore, *Genesis: An Authorship Study*. Rome: Biblical Institute Press, 1985.

Rao, Naveen. "The Book of Ruth as a Clandestine Scripture to Sabotage Persian Colonial Agenda: A Paradigm for a Dalit Scripture." *Bangalore Theological Forum* 41 (2009) 114–34.

Rashkow, Ilona. "Ruth: The Discourse of Power and the Power of Discourse." In *A Feminist Companion to Ruth*, edited by Athalya Brenner, 26–41. Sheffield: Sheffield Academic, 1993.

Rauber, D. F. "The Book of Ruth." In *Literary Interpretations of Biblical Narratives*, edited by K. Gros Louis et al., 163–276. Nashville: Abingdon, 1970.

Redford, Donald. "Scribe and Speaker." In *Writings and Speech in Israelite and Ancient Near Eastern Prophecy*, edited by Ehud Ben Zvi et al., 145–218. SBL Symposium Series 10. Atlanta: Society of Biblical Literature, 2000.

Regt, Lénart J. de. *Participants in Old Testament Texts and the Translator: Reference Devices and Their Rhetorical Impact*. Studia Semitica Neerlandica 39. Assen: Van Gorcum, 1999.

Reinhold, Bjorn. "Ruth 3: A New Creation?" *Journal of Asia Adventist Seminary* 9 (2006) 111–17.

Rendsburg, Gary. *Diglossia in Ancient Hebrew*. New Haven: American Oriental Society, 1990.

Rhoads, David. "Biblical Performance Criticism: Performance as Research." *Oral Tradition* 25 (2010) 157–98.

Ro, Johannes Unsok. "Socio-Economic Context of Post-Exilic Community and Literacy." *ZAW* 120 (2008) 597–601.

Rofé, Alexander. "Ruth 4:11 LXX—A Midrashic Dramatization." *Textus* 20 (2000) 129–40.

Rowley, H. H. *The Servant of the Lord and Other Essays on the Old Testament*. Oxford: Oxford University Press, 1965.

Rudolph, Wilhelm. *Das Buch Ruth, Das Hohe Lied, Die Klagellieder*. Kommentar zum Alten Testament 17. Gütersloh: Mohn, 1962.

Rüger, Hans-Peter. "Oral Tradition in the Old Testament." In *Jesus and the Oral Gospel Tradition*, edited by Henry Wansbrough, 107–20. JSNTSup 64. Sheffield: JSOT Press, 1991.

Russo, Joseph. "Oral Theory: It's Development in Homeric Studies and Applicability to Other Literatures." In *Mesopotamian Epic Literature: Oral or Aural?*, edited by Marianne Vogelzang et al., 7–22. Lewiston, NY: Mellen, 1992.

Sacks, Harvey, Emmanuel Schegloff, and Gail Jeffferson, "A Simplest Systematics for the Organization of Turn-Taking in Conversation." *Language* 50 (1974) 696–735.

———. *Lectures on Conversation*. Edited by Gail Jefferson. Oxford: Blackwell, 1992.

Sakenfeld, Katharine Doob. *Ruth*. Interpretation. Louisville: John Knox, 1999.

———. "The Story of Ruth: Economic Survival." In *Realia Dei: Essays in Archaeology and Biblical Interpretation in Honor of Edward F. Campbell, Jr. at His Retirement*, edited by Prescott Williams et al., 215–27. Scholars Press Homage Series 23. Atlanta: Scholars, 1999.

———. "Why Perez? Reflections on David's Genealogy in Biblical Tradition." In *David and Zion: Biblical Studies in Honor of J. J. M. Roberts*, edited by Bernard Batto et al., 405–16. Winona Lake, IN: Eisenbrauns, 2004.

Sancisi-Weerdenburg, H. "Vrouwen in verborgen werelden." In *'t Is kwaad gerucht als zij niet binnenblijft. Vrouwen in oude culturen*, edited by F. van Dijk-Hemmes, 11–35. Utrecht: HES, 1986.

Sandmel, Samuel. *The Enjoyment of Scripture*. New York: Oxford University Press, 1972.

Sasson, Jack. "Ruth." In *The Literary Guide to the Bible*, edited by Robert Alter et al., 320–28. Cambridge: Harvard University Press, 1987.

———. *Ruth: A New Translation with a Philological Commentary and a Formalist-Folklorist Interpretation*. 2nd ed. Biblical Seminar 10. Sheffield: JSOT, 1989.

Savran, George W. *Telling and Retelling: Quotation in Biblical Narrative*. Indiana Studies in Biblical Literature. Bloomington: Indiana University Press, 1988.

Saxegaard, Kristin Moen. "More Than Seven Sons: Ruth as Example of the Good Son." *Scandinavian Journal of the Old Testament* 15 (2001) 257–75.

Schaper, Joachim. "A Theology of Writing: The Oral and the Written, God as Scribe, and the Book of Deuteronomy." In *Anthropology and Biblical Studies: Avenues of Approach*, edited by Louise Lawrence and Mario I. Aguilar, 97–119. Leiden: Deo, 2004.

———. "Exilic and Post-Exilic Prophecy and the Orality/Literacy Problem." *VT* 55 (2005) 324–42.

———. "The Death of the Prophet: The Transition from the Spoken to the Written Word of God in the Book of Ezekiel." In *Prophets, Prophecy, and Prophetic Texts in Second*

Temple Judaism, edited by Michael Floyd et al., 63–79. Library of Hebrew Bible/Old Testament Studies 427. London: T&T Clark, 2006.

———. "The Living Word Engraved in Stone." In *Memory in the Bible and Antiquity*, edited by Stephen C. Barton et al., 9–23. Wissenschaftliche Untersuchungen zum Neuen Testament 212. Tübingen: Mohr Siebeck, 2007.

Schniedewind, William M. "Orality and Literacy in Ancient Israel." *Religious Studies Review* 26 (2000) 327–32.

Shepherd, David. "Violence in the Fields? Translating, Reading and Revising in Ruth 2." *CBQ* 63 (2001) 444–61.

Sherwood, Yvonne. "Prophetic Performance Art." *The Bible and Critical Theory* 2 (2006) 1.1–1.4.

Showalter, Elaine. "Feminist Criticism in the Wilderness." In *The New Feminist Criticism: Essays on Women, Literature and Theory*, edited by Elaine Showalter, 243–70. London: Virago, 1986.

Sidnell, Jack. *Conversation Analysis: An Introduction.* Chichester: Wiley-Blackwell, 2010.

Siquans, Agnethe. "Foreignness and Poverty in the Book of Ruth: A Legal Way for a Poor Foreign Woman to Be Integrated into Israel." *JBL* 128 (2009) 443–52.

———. "Israel braucht starke Frauen und Männer: Rut als Antwort auf Spr 31, 10–31." *Biblische Zeiyschrift* 56 (2012) 20–38.

Smith, Dan. "The Politics of Ezra: Sociological Indicators of Postexilic Judean Society." In *Community, Identity, and Ideology*, edited by Charles E. Carter and Carol L. Meyers, 537–56. Winona Lake, IN: Eisenbrauns, 1996.

Snow, David, and Robert Benford. "Ideology, Frame Resonance and Participant Mobilization." In *From Structure to Action*, 197–218. International Social Movement Research 1. Greenwich CN: JAI, 1988.

———. "Framing Processes, Ideology, and Discursive Fields." In *The Blackwell Companion to Social Movements,* edited by David Snow et al., 380–412. Malden, MA: Blackwell, 2004.

Song, C. S. *In the Beginning Were Stories, Not Texts: Story Theology.* Eugene, OR: Cascade Books, 2011.

Southwood, Katherine. *Ethnicity and the Mixed Marriage Crises in Ezra 9 and 10.* Oxford: Oxford University Press, 2012.

Sternberg, Meir. *The Poetics of Biblical Narrative: Ideological Literature and the Drama of Reading.* Indiana Literary Biblical Studies. Bloomington: Indiana University Press, 1985.

Strouse, Evelyn and Bezalel Porten, "A Reading of Ruth." *Commentary* 67 (1979) 63–67.

Thiem, Annika. "No Gendered Bodies without Queer Desires: Judith Butler and Biblical Gender Trouble." *Old Testament Essays* 20 (2007), 456–70.

Trible, Phyllis. *God and the Rhetoric of Sexuality.* Overtures to Biblical Theology. Philadelphia: Fortress, 1978.

———. "Ruth." In *Women in Scripture*, edited by Carol Meyers, 146–47. Grand Rapids: Eerdmans, 2000.

Turner, Victor. *From Ritual to Theatre: The Human Seriousness of Play.* New York: Performing Arts Journal Publications, 1982.

———. *Schism and Continuity in an African Society: A Study of Ndembu Village Life.* Manchester: Manchester University Press, 1957.

Van Wolde, Ellen. *Ruth en Noomi, twee vreemdgangers.* Barn: Ten Have, 1993.

————. "Texts in Dialogue with Texts: Intertextuality in the Ruth and Tamar Narratives," *Bible Interpretation* 5 (1997) 1–28. Reprinted as "Intertextuality: Ruth in Dialogue with Tamar." In *A Feminist Companion to Reading the Bible*, edited by Athalya Brenner and Carole Fontaine, 426–51. Feminist Companion to the Bible 11. Sheffield: Sheffield Academic, 1997.

Verheij, Arian J. C. *Verbs and Numbers: A Study of the Frequencies of the Hebrew Verbal Tense Forms in the Books of Samuel, Kings and Chronicles.* Studia Semitica Neerlandica 28. Assen: Van Gorcum, 1990.

Washington, H. C. "Israel's Holy Seed and the Foreign Women of Ezra-Nehemiah: A Kristevan Reading." *Biblical Interpretation* 11(2003) 427–37.

Watson, W. G. E. *Classical Hebrew Poetry.* JSOTSup 26. Sheffield: Sheffield Academic, 1986.

Weiss, David. "The Use of קנה in Connection with Marriage." *Harvard Theological Review* 57 (1964) 244–48.

Westby, David. "Strategic Imperative, Ideology, and Frames." In *Frames of Protest: Social Movements and the Framing Perspective*, edited by Hank Johnston et al., 217–35. New York: Rowman & Littlefield, 2005.

Westerman, Claus. *Genesis 12–36: A Commentary.* Translated by John J. Scullion. Continental Commentaries. Minneapolis: Augsburg, 1985.

White, Heyden. "The Value of Narrativity in the Representation of Reality." *Critical Inquiry* 7 (1980) 5–27.

Williams, James. *Women Recounted: Narrative Thinking and the God of Israel.* Bible and Literature Series 6. Sheffield: Almond, 1982.

Wolfe, Lisa. *Ruth, Esther, Song of Songs, and Judith.* Eugene, OR: Cascade, 2011.

Wolfenson, Louis. "The Character, Contents, and Date of Ruth." *American Journal of Semitic Languages and Literature* 27 (1911) 285–300.

Young, I. M. "Israelite Literacy: Interpreting the Evidence," Part 1. *VT* 48 (1998) 239–53.

Young, Ian, Robert Rezetko, and Martin Ehrensvärd. *Linguistic Dating of Biblical Texts: An Introduction to Approaches and Problems.* 2 vols. London: Equinox, 2008.

Younger, K. Lawson. "Two Comparative Notes on the Book of Ruth." *Journal of Ancient Near Eastern Studies* 26 (1998) 121–32.

Zevit, Ziony. "Dating Ruth: Linguistic and Historical Observations." *ZAW* 117 (2006) 574–600.

Author Index

Author Index

Subject Index

Scripture Index